Arthur Gray

The Priory of Saint Radegund, Cambridge

Arthur Gray

The Priory of Saint Radegund, Cambridge

ISBN/EAN: 9783337015749

Printed in Europe, USA, Canada, Australia, Japan

Cover: Foto ©ninafisch / pixelio.de

More available books at **www.hansebooks.com**

Cambridge Antiquarian Society. Octavo Publications. No. XXXI.

THE PRIORY

OF

SAINT RADEGUND

CAMBRIDGE

BY

ARTHUR GRAY, M.A.

FELLOW OF JESUS COLLEGE, CAMBRIDGE.

Cambridge:

PRINTED FOR THE CAMBRIDGE ANTIQUARIAN SOCIETY.

SOLD BY DEIGHTON, BELL & CO.; AND MACMILLAN & BOWES.

LONDON, GEORGE BELL AND SONS.

1898

Price Five Shillings.

THE PRIORY

OF

SAINT RADEGUND

CAMBRIDGE

THE PRIORY

OF

SAINT RADEGUND

CAMBRIDGE

BY

ARTHUR GRAY, M.A.

FELLOW OF JESUS COLLEGE, CAMBRIDGE.

Cambridge:

PRINTED FOR THE CAMBRIDGE ANTIQUARIAN SOCIETY.

SOLD BY DEIGHTON, BELL & CO.; AND MACMILLAN & BOWES.

LONDON, GEORGE BELL AND SONS.

1898

Cambridge:

PRINTED BY J. AND C. F. CLAY,

AT THE UNIVERSITY PRESS.

PREFACE.

WHEN this publication was first projected I had hopes that the portion of it relating to the buildings of the Nunnery would have been, wholly or in part, furnished by my friend, Mr T. D. Atkinson. Though Mr Atkinson's engagements have prevented him from taking so large a part in the work as was originally contemplated, I gratefully acknowledge the assistance he has throughout given me both in exploration of sites and buildings and in placing at my disposal his notes and suggestions.

The extent of my indebtedness to the *Architectural History* is, I hope, apparent in the section dealing with the Nunnery buildings. But my principal obligation to the Registrary is not of the kind that can be acknowledged in a footnote. Without his suggestion this work would never have been written; without the advantage of his counsel and knowledge it would have been much more imperfect than it is.

Among other friends who have given me valuable help are Prof. Maitland, Prof. Skeat, the Rev. J. H. Crosby, Minor Canon of Ely, and the Rev. O. Fisher, Honorary Fellow of Jesus College and Rector of Harlton.

The Catalogue of Charters here printed includes only such as relate to property situated in the town and fields of Cambridge. I have not deemed it worth while to give abstracts of those which are concerned with the scattered holdings of the Nuns in other places. The Catalogue remarkably supplements the very detailed information about medieval Cambridge which is supplied by the Hundred Rolls. Combining what is to be learnt from each source it would be no

difficult task to make a very complete directory of the town in
the last quarter of the 13th century. The witnesses to the
Charters in most cases were the mayor and four bailiffs with
two or three occupants of property adjoining the tenement
in question. I have generally given the name of the first
witness only.

Extracts of some length from the Account Rolls were given
in the First Report of the Historical MSS. Commissioners:
the accounts in full are here printed for the first time. They
furnish some interesting materials for illustrating life in an
English Nunnery at the close of the middle ages. In the
earlier and more prosperous years to which they introduce
us, it is a life wholly untinged by the influences of the
University. The Nuns were drawn from the families of the
better class burgesses and lesser gentry of the county, and
their habits and education were those of their class. The
town and its religious houses still occupied in their outlook
a far larger space than the University. The 'good friendship'
of the Chancellor—in a matter, perhaps, of arbitration with a
College—was appropriately recompensed in the year 1449—
1450 with a present of a crane, value twelve pence; it is
set in quaint juxtaposition with the Christmas box to the
Mayor's waits, who receive the magnificent sum of 2s. 3d. The
proportion of the two sums is possibly an indication of the
relative consequence in the Nuns' thoughts of the academic
and municipal corporations, both of which, it may be observed,
had an origin long subsequent to that of their own establishment.

On the debated subject of the date of the first emergence
of a University at Cambridge the S. Radegund's charters
throw no light. Among the variety of tenants mentioned in
the deeds of the 12th and 13th centuries there is no individual
or corporation whose name or description suggests connection
with an organized community of scholars. The surnames of
the tenants previous to 1300 indicate that they were almost
exclusively from the neighbourhood of Cambridge. Of migrants
from Oxford or scholars from over sea there is no hint; the

Jews were the only strangers to Cambridge with whom the Nuns had acquaintance in those early days. A solitary 'Scolemayster' (Charters 157, 158), who dwelt hard by the site on which Peterhouse afterwards rose, represents the learning of Cambridge in the first years of the 13th century. Possibly he was connected with a monastic school.

Before taking leave of my subject I should not forget to mention two members of my College who have worked in the same field in generations by-gone. John Sherman's History of Jesus College (written about the year 1666) is introduced by a sketch of the History of the Nunnery which he entitles *Reliquiae Sanctae Radegundis sive Fragmenta quaedam Historiae Prioratus.* Sherman had made a faithful study of the Nunnery muniments. He is generally accurate and, as he may have had before him documents which are not now discoverable, it is possible that he is right in some matters about which I have supposed him to be mistaken. But I do not think that since his time there has been any noteworthy subtraction from the Jesus muniments. Well protected from damp, dust and insects, they have probably profited by the neglect in which they have generally lain for 200 years. About the middle of last century their repose was disturbed by the careful hands of Dr Lynford Caryl, who was Master of Jesus, 1758—1780, and Registrary of the University from 1751 to 1758. He arranged and catalogued them in a very exact and methodical manner. Among his merits not the least was that of writing in a very clear and beautiful hand. I have discovered some fifty charters of Nunnery date which escaped his notice, but none of them are of much importance. When the present Treasury was built in 1875 and the documents were transferred to it, some of them were misplaced, and for a time I supposed them to be lost. But gradually all, or nearly all, those mentioned in Dr Caryl's catalogue have found their way back to their places.

ARTHUR GRAY.

JESUS COLLEGE,
October, 1898.

Fig. I. SEAL OF THE PRIORY.

ANNALS OF THE NUNNERY.

§ 1. *Foundation and connection with the See of Ely.*

THE establishment, near Cambridge, of the cell of Benedictine nuns which was later known as the Priory of S. Mary
and S. Radegund seems to date from the earliest years of the
reign of King Stephen.   There is no evidence to fix the precise
year of its institution but it is fairly certain that it falls within
the episcopate of Nigellus, who succeeded the first bishop,
Hervey, in the see of Ely in 1133.

The Priory seems to have had no charter of foundation, nor
is there any extant record of its first endowment.   Such property as it possessed in early days was acquired gradually and
in comparatively small parcels.   Even the endowments which
it derived from royal benefactors such as the Countess Constance and Malcolm of Scotland were not so important as to
entitle the donors to be regarded in any sense as founders or
patrons.

It is true that in the letters patent of Henry VII for the
dissolution of the Nunnery and the erection of the College in
its room it is asserted—evidently on the representation of
Bishop Alcock—that S. Radegund's Priory was 'of the foundation and patronage of the Bishop, as in right of his cathedral
church of Ely.'   This was, I believe, the first and only occasion
on which such a claim was advanced by a bishop of Ely, and,
having regard to the circumstances under which it was made,
I do not think that much importance should be attached to it.
In the charter which the Lady Margaret obtained, a few years

later, from Henry VII for the conversion of S. John's Hospital
into the College of S. John it is similarly stated that the
House or Priory of religious brethren of S. John the Evangelist
in Cambridge was 'of the foundation and patronage of James
(Stanley), Bishop of Ely, as in right of his cathedral church.'
In this latter case the statement is historically inaccurate, for
the founder of the Hospital was unquestionably Henry Frost,
burgess of Cambridge, though Bishop Nigellus had been a
liberal benefactor to it and the Hundred Rolls show that, as
early as the reign of Henry III, Bishop Hugh de Norwold
claimed, as patron, the right of nominating the master. As
regards the Nunnery the full details supplied by the Ely
Episcopal Registers show that in the election of their Prioress
the Nuns exercised a free choice, unfettered by reference to
the wishes of a patron and subject only to the approval of the
Bishop of Ely as diocesan. The motive which prompted the
Bishops to assert their questionable claim to the patronage of
either establishment was perhaps a double one—to make it
clear to the King and to the Pope that no private rights of
patronage were invaded by the dissolution of an ancient
religious house, and to acquire for the Bishops of Ely, as
visitors of the new foundations, a guiding influence in the
development of the University.

Though the Nunnery was not perhaps, in strictness,
founded by a bishop of Ely it is clear that its origin and early
growth was intimately connected with the see and particularly
with Bishop Nigellus (1133–1169). It was he who endowed it
with a portion of the site on which the Nuns' original 'cell'
was raised; of the principal benefactions to the newly established house three were protected by his charters and it seems
likely that they were procured by his influence. Geoffrey
Ridel, who succeeded Nigellus in the bishopric in 1174, appropriated to the Nuns the rectory of All Saints in the Jewry,
Cambridge, and the connection with the see of Ely was maintained by Bishop Eustace (1197–1220), who gave the Nuns
additional lands adjoining the Priory and bestowed on them
the rectory of S. Clement's.

§ 2. Early charters. Grant of Bishop Nigellus.

The earliest in date of the Nuns' charters now extant in the treasury of Jesus College is probably that of Bishop Nigellus, addressed 'to all barons and men of S. Etheldrytha, cleric or lay, French or English,' in which for a rent of twelve pence he grants 'to the Nuns of the cell lately established without the vill of Cantebruge' certain land adjoining land belonging to the same cell (Charters, 1). The position of the land given by the Bishop is not specified in the charter, but it is safe to assume that it adjoined the cell and was identical with the four acres which, according to the statement of the Hundred Rolls (Vol. 2, p. 358), were given to the Nuns by Nigellus and were next the ten acres given them by King Malcolm as a site for their church. It is likely that the rent reserved by the Bishop represented the full letting-value of the land, since for the adjoining ten acres Malcolm stipulated in his first charter for a rent of two shillings. At some later date, Nigellus, like Malcolm, acquitted the Nuns of payment of rent, for the Hundred Rolls state that the Bishop gave them the land in pure and perpetual alms and show that they paid no rent for any of the land which they occupied in the Priory precincts.

There is nothing in this charter of Nigellus which would warrant any definite conclusions as to its date. As the Bishop did not die until 1169 it is of course possible that it is of later date than Malcolm's grant, and that the land mentioned by the Bishop as adjoining that which he gave to the Nuns and as already in their tenure was in fact no other than Malcolm's ten acre plot. The evidence of the Hundred Rolls might be held to countenance this view, for they mention Malcolm's grant before that of Nigellus and in such a way as seems to imply that the jurors supposed the King's grant to be the earlier in date[1]. On the other hand the vagueness of the description of

---

[1] H. R. Vol. II. p. 358. 'Item predicte Priorissa et Moniales tenent quatuor **acras terre** iacentes iuxta terram **predictam** (i.e. the **ten** acres given by King

the Nunnery as a 'cell lately instituted' is more consistent
with the view that the establishment was in an inchoate stage
and had received no distinctive title or dedication. In the
charters in which he confirms the endowments given by
William le Moyne and Stephen de Scalers Nigellus gives the
Nunnery the style, which after Malcolm's gift was the usual
one, of 'the Church and Nuns of S. Mary and S. Radegund.'

§ 3. *Grant of William le Moyne and Confirmation by King Stephen.*

The earliest of the Nuns' charters which can be dated with
any precision is one given them by King Stephen confirming
to 'the Church and Nuns of S. Mary of Cantebr. the grant
made to them by William Monachus, *aurifaber*, of two virgates
of land and six acres of meadow with four cottars (*cotariis*)
with their holding in Shelford, in alms, for the soul of King
Henry and for the faithful in God' (Charters, 2*a*). This
charter is tested by William Martel, the King's *dapifer*, who
played so prominent a part on the King's side in the struggle
with the Empress, and by Reginald de Warenne. It is undated, but the circumstance that it was given 'apud Mapertes
halam in obsidione' enables us pretty definitely to assign it to
the month of January 1138 and brings to light a historical
fact, unnoticed by chroniclers, to which attention was first
drawn by Mr Howlett in his edition of the *Gesta Stephani* for
the Rolls Series (*Chronicles of the Reigns of Stephen* &c. Vol. 3).
Mapertes hala is Meppershall, near Shefford, in Bedfordshire.
King Stephen, as the anonymous writer of the *Gesta Stephani*
records, kept the Christmas feast of 1137 at Dunstable, and
then 'emensis festivis diebus Dominicae festivitatis' attacked

Malcolm) quam quidem terram habent de dono Nigelli Elyensis Episcopi qui
quidem Nigellus dedit eisdem in pura et perpetua elemosina. B. quondam
Prior Elyensis et Conventus Elyensis Ecclesie dictam donacionem eisdem monialibus factam concesserunt et confirmaverunt.' The initial B. is apparently a
mistake: Bentham's list in his *History of Ely*, pp. 215 foll., mentions no Prior
of Ely before the date of the *H. R.* whose name began with B.

Bedford Castle, held by Milo de Beauchamp, who had refused the King's summons to surrender it. Milo's obstinate resistance compelled the King to turn the siege into a blockade, but the castle was surrendered apparently about the middle of January 1138, for by Feb. 2 the King had reached Northumberland, whither he had been called by an invasion of the Scotch. 'The chronicles mention no such event as a siege at Meppershall; but there exists at the present day, close to the church of this small Bedfordshire village, a high mound with a double line of outer ramparts answering in the clearest way to the type of the hastily-built, stockaded "castles" of this reign. Stephen, it thus appears, had to capture this outpost, perhaps during the siege of Bedford in 1138[1].'

The grant of William Monachus which is confirmed by Stephen's charter may have been made a year or two before 1138. King Henry I, whose soul it was designed to benefit, died Dec. 1135. The land to which the charter refers is situated in Great Shelford parish; it is still in the possession of Jesus College and known as 'the Nuns' lands.' The Domesday Survey of Cambridgeshire shows that it formed a portion of a larger estate consisting of three hides and valued at £5 annual rent. In the Confessor's time it had belonged to 'Herald Comes,' afterwards King Harold. After the Conquest it passed into the hands of King William, of whom, at the time of the Domesday Survey, it was held *ad firmam* by Peter de Valongies[2] who was apparently a kinsman of William Monachus, or le Moyne, as his family was otherwise known[3]. From a charter

---

[1] The Meppershall earthworks are marked in the Ordnance Map as 'The Hills.' Mr Seebohm, who gives a small plan of them in *The English Village Community*, p. 426, supposes them to be of Saxon origin, possibly a 'toot-hill.' Mr Howlett compares this charter of King Stephen with another, dated 1138, 'apud Goldintonam in obsidione Bedeford,' Goldington being a village a few miles from Bedford.

[2] This Peter de Valongies, or Valoines, is said to have been a nephew of the Conqueror, and was founder, *circa* 1104, of Binham Priory, Norfolk. A Peter de Selford was Prior of Binham in 1244.

[3] *H. R.* Vol. II. p. 545, 'Dicunt quod dominus Johannes le Moyne, antecessor dicte Agnetis de Walenc' dedit in puram et perpetuam elemosinam

of Nicolas, son of William le Moyne, we gather that the Shelford land came to his father by free gift of King Henry I. Apparently it was bestowed on him in recognition of his services and skill as an *aurifaber,* for he held it by goldsmith's serjeanty, and at the date of the Hundred Rolls Inquisition the lady Agnes de Valence retained a large portion of the same estate by the singular service of making up and repairing the King's crown when required[1].

From the designation of the Nuns' establishment in Stephen's charter as 'Ecclesia et Sanctimoniales Sancte Marie de Cantebr.' it would seem that the original church which was served by the Nunnery during the first twenty years of its existence and either made way for or was incorporated in the building which rose on the site given by King Malcolm was dedicated to S. Mary only. After the foundation of the new church the charters use the fuller style of 'Nuns of S. Mary and S. Radegund.' But the *church* in strictness seems to have kept the older single dedication even after Malcolm's time, for, as late as 1285, a tenement in Radegund (*i.e.* Jesus) Lane is described in a deed as lying ' in the parish of the Blessed Mary of the Priory of S. Radegund.' The Priory apparently took its name from a chapel of S. Radegund which is mentioned in an early undated deed and which seems to have been in the portion of the church reserved to the use of the Nuns. Gradually the original dedication came to be forgotten, and in

Monialibus Sancte Radegundis lx acras terre ad sustinendum j noneam imperpetuum.' *Antecessor* here perhaps means no more than 'predecessor in the title.' At the time of the Hundred Rolls Inquisition another John le Moyne, distinguished by the local agnomen, Atteasse (i.e. at the Ash), was a free tenant of the lady Agnes de Valence at Great Shelford.

[1] *Red Book of the Exchequer* (Rolls Series), Vol. II. p. 530, 'Willelmus Monachus, iij hidas in Selforde per serjanteriam aurifabriae.' *H. R.* Vol. II. p. 545, 'Domina Agnes de Walaunc' tenet j messuagium cum gardino continente iij acras et viij^xx acras terre et de prato vj acras et tenet de domino Rege in capite per sergantiam et non est geldabilis non debet sectam neque auxilium Vicecomiti nichil aliud reddit set erit ultra (?) Coronam domini Regis quando debet confici vel reparari et habebit totidem ij^a ad vadia sua,' &c. Domesday affords several instances of royal grants of land to goldsmiths: see Freeman's *Norman Conquest*, Vol. IV. pp. 41, 85, on the subject.

later times both parish and Nunnery were commonly called
S. Radegund's. Evidence of the earlier dedication is to be
seen in the fact recorded in the Hundred Rolls that King
Stephen granted by charter to the Nuns a fair lasting for two
days, viz. the vigil and the feast of the Assumption of the
Blessed Mary. Fairs, as is well known, originated in most
cases in the gatherings of worshippers or pilgrims about sacred
places, and especially in the neighbourhood of religious houses,
and were held on the feast-day of the saint to whom the church
or shrine was dedicated.

The grant of William Monachus was confirmed to the Nuns
by Nigellus, but as the Bishop's charter (Charters, 2b) desig-
nates the Nunnery as dedicated to S. Mary and S. Radegund
it would seem that it was not given until many years after the
original grant. The long interval is accounted for by the
outbreak of the civil war in 1139. Nigellus, from his active
partizanship in the cause of the Empress, had little time to
attend to the affairs of his diocese, from which he was absent
with only brief intervals until his reconciliation with Stephen
in 1144, and until the accession of Henry II he is said to have
lived in retirement. His charter cannot be of much later date
than 1160, in or about which year died William (of Laventon),
the first archdeacon of Ely, whose name is among the witnesses,
and it can scarcely be so early as 1157, the earliest date to
which it is possible to assign Malcolm's first charter.

All the facts which are ascertainable about William
Monachus show that his relations with the Bishop were of an
intimate kind and point to the probability that the Bishop's
influence contributed to procure his benefaction to the Nuns.
The *Historia Eliensis* [1] reveals him to us as one of a group of
men, lay and cleric, who formed a Bishop's party in opposition
to the Ely monks, who favoured Stephen's side in the war and
had special grounds for complaint against the Bishop for
appropriating the funds of the convent and the treasures of
S. Etheldreda's shrine to defray the expenses entailed by his

[1] This portion of the *Historia Eliensis* is printed (with abridgment) in
Wharton's *Anglia Sacra*, Vol. 1. p. 615 foll.

opposition to the King. Richard of Ely, the writer of this portion of the *Historia Eliensis*, took the monastic side of the quarrel and dwells with particular satisfaction on the exemplary afflictions which overtook the Bishop and his confederates in the spoliation. But William Monachus, we are told, lived to make some amends for the sacrilege which is laid to his charge, and the picture of his end is touched with a kindlier hand. 'With axes, hammers and every implement of masonry he profanely assailed the shrine and with his own hand robbed it of its metal. But he lived to repent it bitterly. He, who had once been extraordinarily rich and had lacked for nothing, was reduced to such an extreme of poverty as not even to have the necessaries of life. At last, when he had lost all and knew not whither to turn himself, by urgent entreaty he prevailed on the Ely brethren to receive him into their order, and there with unceasing lamentation, tears, vigils and prayers deploring his guilt, he ended his days in a sincere penitence.' He was alive in 1153–4 when, along with Nigellus, he witnessed the charter of the Countess Constance.

In the lifetime of William Monachus, and at his request, his son Nicolas re-granted to the Nuns the land given them by his father, which in the deed is stated to consist of 55 acres, together with 1½ acre of meadow and one acre whereon to build barns and cattle-sheds; and he further promised five acres, for which they had petitioned, as soon as he could get them. The Nuns however seem not to have acquired undisputed possession of their property until Henry III, 31, when John le Moyne, in consequence of an assize trial at Cambridge, assigned to them in perpetual alms a portion of the estate consisting of 50 acres. The Hundred Rolls state that the Nuns' estate at Shelford consisted of 60 acres and was given to them by John le Moyne to maintain one nun for ever. In this statement from the facts above given it would appear that there is an error either in the Christian name of the donor or in the number of the acres given. Nor do I know how it is to be reconciled with a deed of Edward I, 29, in which Agnes de Valence, lady of

Offaley and Bailluel[1], renounced the claim to place *two* nuns in the Priory, which she exercised in right of lands held of her by the Nuns in Great Shelford. Beyond ten acres held by annual service to the Bishops of Ely the only land at Shelford in the occupation of the Nuns was that derived originally from William Monachus.

§ 4. *Grant of the Countess Constance.*

The next in order of time of the Nunnery charters is that of the Countess Constance, widow of King Stephen's only son, Eustace of Boulogne. It grants to the Nuns in perpetual alms exemption from hagable and langable for all their lands within and without the Borough, whether already acquired or here-after to be acquired, and also gives them all the fishing right and water belonging to the Borough as freely as they had been held by her husband and herself. The grant of the Countess is for the souls of her husband, Eustace, and Stephen's Queen, Maud, and for the good estate of King Stephen. Queen Maud died in May, 1152, Eustace in August, 1153, King Stephen in October, 1154. The charter therefore belongs to the period between the last two dates. Two undated charters confirm that of the Countess—the first given by King Stephen 'apud Cantebrig,' the other by Bishop Nigellus. In all three charters the Nuns are styled 'Sanctimoniales de Cantebrig,' without dedication.

Independently of their relation to the history of the Nun-nery these charters have a special interest in connection with the subject of the *firma burgi* of Cambridge. Hagable, *i.e.* *huga-gafol*, a payment for a *haw* or messuage in a town, and langable, i.e. *land-gafol*, payment for land occupied by a burgess in the common fields, formed an important part of the customs (*consuetudines*) of the town. At the time of the

---

[1] Philip of Valognes, Chamberlain of Scotland, had a grand-daughter, Lora, who married Henry de Balliol, a cousin of King John Balliol. Offaley is Offley, near Hitchin, a manor which once belonged to the Balliols of Barnard Castle. Bailleul, near Lille, was a fief of the same family.

Domesday Survey the town of Cambridge formed part of the royal demesne and its customs were farmed of the King by the sheriff. It is doubtfully asserted by Cooper[1] that the farm of the borough was granted to the burgesses, as the King's tenants *in capite*, by Henry I, they paying to him the same sum as the sheriff had been accustomed to render. If such a grant was actually made it seems to have terminated with the life of that King, and the concession of immunity from hagable and langable which Constance made to the Nuns clearly implies that in Stephen's reign the fee-farm belonged to her husband and herself. The alienation in perpetuity to the Nuns of a portion of the customs shows that the fee-farm had been granted to the heirs of Eustace and Constance as well as to themselves. There were however no children of the marriage, and in the early years of Henry II the borough was again in the King's possession and farmed by the sheriff. In 1185 it was granted to the burgesses at farm by Henry II and continued to be farmed by them in the reign of Richard I[2]. When the fee-farm of the borough was granted to the burgesses in perpetuity by King John in 1207 the rights acquired by the Nuns from Constance seem to have suffered some curtailment. The immunity from hagable for lands ' hereafter to be acquired ' could hardly extend to property acquired subsequently to the transfer of the hagable rental to the burgesses, and it is therefore not surprising to find from the Great Inquisition of Edward I in 1278 and the Nuns' accounts in 1449–50 and 1481–2 that they were then charged with certain hagable rents. Moreover King John's charter expressly included among the appurtenances of the *Burgus* ' mills, pools and waters[3],' and it is certain that at the date of the Hundred Rolls Inquisition the Nuns had no exclusive rights in the river waters, for the jurors affirmed that the burgesses then had a common *piscaria* in the common waters belonging to the vill of Cambridge. Nevertheless the charter of Constance was not inoperative, for it is rehearsed and confirmed in a charter of

---

[1] Cooper, *Annals*, Vol. I. p. 22.
[2] *Ibid.* pp. 28, 29.   [3] *Ibid.* p. 33.

Edward II, dated in the seventh year of his reign (Charters, 8). The fishing rights claimed by the Nuns seem however to have been limited to a certain portion of the river, beyond the limits of the old borough, which as late as 1505 was known as Nunneslake. A sixteenth century list of the Nuns' muniments describes the charter of Edward II, above mentioned, as 'a grant of y° fishinge alonge by Jesus Greene.' In 1505 it was decided that the fishing in Nunneslake belonged to the town.

It is probable that the fee-farm of Cambridge was held by Constance in right of dower. Cambridge was among the towns usually assigned in dower to the Queens of England and other ladies of the royal family[1]. Queen Catharine, consort of Charles II, was the last English Queen who held the fee-farm of Cambridge. Except in the case of Constance the settlement seems always to have been for life. King Stephen had endeavoured to get his son Eustace crowned in 1152, and, though he failed in this purpose, Constance is said in after times to have borne the title of Queen[2]. The title *Venerabilis* given to her in the charter of Nigellus is probably a quasi-recognition of her claim to be regarded as Queen. It was applied to French kings (v. Ducange, *s.v.*) and more especially (with the variant *Veneranda*) to queens of the Norman period: *e.g.* *Sarum Charters* (Rolls Series) p. 17, 'Adelizae venerandae et illustris Angliae reginae cancellarius.'

§ 5. *First Charter of King Malcolm IV. The Grenecroft site.*

The first charter of King Malcolm IV, which is the next in order of date, is addressed "to all his men cleric and lay of the Honour of Huntedon" and gives to the Nuns of Grantebrige ten acres of land next Grenecroft in alms and to found (*ad fundendam*) thereon their church; it reserves to the King a rent

---

[1] See Cooper's *Annals* under the years 1235, 1353, 1465, 1495.

[2] Stubbs, *Const. Hist.* Vol. I. p. 341.

of two shillings, which his *minister* is directed to offer at the altar of the same church. The charter is dated 'apud Hunted' and still has attached to it in white wax the royal seal bearing on the obverse side the figure of a king enthroned, on the reverse a mounted warrior. The Honour, or earldom, of Huntingdon which included the county of Cambridge was conferred on Malcolm in the latter half of 1157. Among the witnesses is Herbert, Bishop of Glasgow, who died 1164. Sherman in his MS. *Historia Collegii Jesu* (written *temp.* Charles II) states that among the College archives he had seen a charter of Theobald, Archbishop of Canterbury, confirming Malcolm's grant. No such charter is now extant nor is it included in the oldest registers of the Nunnery deeds, though as these early registers (written *temp.* Queen Elizabeth) are by no means complete the fact that it is not contained in them must not be taken as conclusive that it did not then exist. Sherman possibly had in mind an *inspeximus* of Archbishop Stephen Langton (Charters, 4*d*) which confirms charters of Theobald, Becket and Nigellus, though it does not connect them with Malcolm's gift. But as Becket's charter, which is still extant, mentions 'in particular (*nominatim*) the King of Scotland's grant' Sherman was in any case probably right in assuming that Theobald's referred to the same matter. As Theobald died in 1161 the years 1157–1161 mark the limits within which it is possible to date Malcolm's charter.

There is no extant charter of Nigellus confirming Malcolm's benefaction, but the charter of Thomas Becket above referred to is still in the College treasury. It was apparently written in the lifetime of Malcolm, for he is mentioned in it merely as 'Rex Scocie,' without name. Its date therefore falls between 1162, when Becket became archbishop, and 1165, the year of Malcolm's death. It pretty certainly refers to Malcolm's earlier charter for in it the Nuns are described simply as 'Sanctimoniales de Cantebrug[1].'

---

[1] Becket's charter is witnessed by Robert, Archdeacon of Oxford (i.e. Becket's friend, Rob. Foliot, afterwards Bishop of Hereford), Philipp' de Caun (i.e. of Calne, Becket's manciple and *co-exul* in 1165–6), Herbert de Boseham

This charter of Malcolm is the earliest which specifies the position of the Nunnery as being 'next Grenecroft,' though the probability is that it had been established there from the first. Grenecroft, now generally called Midsummer Common, lies wholly within the parish of S. Andrew, Barnwell, and outside the limits of the original borough of Cambridge, whence we find the Nunnery frequently described as being 'near' or 'without' the borough. In part at least it consisted of marsh land and from the earliest historical times it appears to have been the common pasture land of the townsmen of Cambridge. The district which bounded it on its western side, in S. Clement's parish, went by the name of Hulmus, 'the holm,' or island; its eastern extremity towards Barnwell Priory was called Estenhale. On its southern side it was skirted by the higher ground traversed by the road entering Cambridge, from the direction of Bury S. Edmund's, which at different points of its course was known as Barnwell Causey and Rade-gund's or Nuns' Lane. The ground occupied by the Nunnery and its precincts, called Nunnescroft, had for its boundaries the road, the common and the King's Ditch. A portion of it adjoining the angle made by Jesus Lane with Park St. was anciently known as Eldestedecroft, a name which occurs in deeds as late as the 16th century. Though the Nunnery was outside the borough limits it is never described as being in Barnwell. The Nuns were sometimes called 'Nuns of Grene-croft' but there is no direct evidence to show that the sites given by Nigellus and Malcolm had formed a portion of the common land. But there is at least a likelihood that they had been obtained by encroachment on the pasture land of Grene-croft. Both S. John's Hospital and Barnwell Priory were built on common land[1].

(Becket's well-known friend and biographer), and Robert and William, chaplains (probably Becket's chaplains, Robert of Merton and William Fitz-Stephen, who were with him at the time of his murder; the latter wrote a biography of Becket). For references see the indices to the *Materials for the Life of Becket* in the Rolls Series.

[1] The charter of Henry I which granted to Pain Peverel the site of Barnwell Priory describes it as 'locum quemdam in campis Cantebrigie iacentem circa

§ 6. Second Charter of King Malcolm IV. Dedication to S. Radegund.

The second charter of King Malcolm, which re-affirms the former and releases the Nuns from payment of the annual rent of two shillings as well as all secular service, is dated, like the earlier one, 'apud Hunted.' It is tested among others by Engelr[am], the Chancellor, and Nicolas, the Chamberlain. Engelram, who was Chancellor under King David I and continued in the office under Malcolm, succeeded Herbert as Bishop of Glasgow in 1164[1], and Nicolas was Chamberlain from 1160 or 1161 to 1165[2]. As the charter does not give Engelram the title of Bishop we shall probably be right in dating it between the years 1160–1164.

This second charter of Malcolm seems to be the earliest in which the Nunnery has the title 'of S. Mary and S. Radegund.' We may conclude that the building of the church had at this time made such advance that the chapel of S. Radegund already referred to (which was perhaps in the Norman North transept adjoining the dormitory) was completed and had received its dedication. The new ascription to S. Radegund is significant. In 1159 Malcolm with a Scottish army crossed the sea to aid King Henry II in his expedition against Toulouse. At Poitiers he joined the English King and was honourably entertained by him. Poitiers was then, as it still is, the special centre of the cult of S. Radegund, who had there established her celebrated Abbey of the Holy Cross. Malcolm's visit to Poitiers so closely preceding his second charter seems to be connected with the dedication given to the chapel which he had been instrumental in raising[3].

fontes Bernewelle...habendum in sicco et marisco a platea usque in Riveriam de Cantebrigia secundum quod Curia eorum in longum extenditur.' (Barnwell *Liber Memorandorum.*) The jurors at the time of the Hundred Rolls Inquisition were unable to say how King Malcolm acquired the site of the Nuns' church, 'qualiter autem dictus Rex Mancolmus pervenit ad dictam terram nesciunt.' (*H. R.* Vol. II. p. 358.)

[1] Keith's *Scottish Bishops.*   [2] *Exchequer Rolls of Scotland*, Vol. II. p. cxviii.
[3] The parish churches of Scruton (Yorks.) and Grayingham (Lincs.) are

§ 7. *Grant of Stephen de Scalariis and later benefactions.*

Between the two charters of King Malcolm should probably be placed the grant of 80 acres of land 'cum quodam managio' in West Wratting, made by Stephen de Scalariis and his wife, Juliana, on placing their daughter, Sibil, in the Nunnery. This land is stated to be given in perpetual alms, free from all services and customs 'preter Danegild regis solummodo¹.' It formed part of large estates in the neighbourhood of West Wratting which at the date of Domesday were held by Harduin de Scalers². Bishop Nigellus confirmed this grant in a charter which includes S. Radegund in the dedication but cannot be later than 1161, as among the witnesses is William (of Laventon), Archdeacon of Ely, whose death, as before stated, occurred in 1160 or 1161. The West Wratting land is still the property of Jesus College.

It is unnecessary to record in detail the successive benefactions which followed those of Malcolm and Stephen de Scalariis. By far the larger number of the acquisitions evidenced by the Nuns' muniments consisted of houses and lands in the town and fields of Cambridge. Outside the town limits they held property in the county of Cambridge at West Wratting, Weston (Colvile), Little Abington, Littlington, Bassingbourn, Great Shelford, Trumpington, Madingley, Barton, Long Stanton, Hokington, Caxton, Crawden and Ely; in Essex at Little Walden, Steventon, Ashdon, Bartlow, Berden, Little Chetham and Thundersley; in Lincolnshire at Rippingale. Nearly all

---

dedicated to S. Radegund; those of Postling (Kent) and Whitwell (Isle of Wight) to S. Mary and S. Radegund. Bradsole Abbey, near Dover, founded 1191, was dedicated to S. Radegund, as was also the house of Trinitarian Friars at Thelesford, co. Warwick. There was a chapel of S. Radegund in old S. Paul's, London.

¹ 'In 1163 the ancient Danegild disappears from the Pipe Rolls.' Stubbs, *Const. Hist.* Vol. I. p. 582.

² Before the enclosure of the parish of West Wratting in 1808 one of the manors which it contained, of which the Master and Fellows of Peterhouse were lords, was called Escaliers or Charles. The so-called manor belonging to Jesus College was called 'le Great Nuns.'

these grants are of very early date, most of them belonging to the 13th century. Nearly all were of inconsiderable value and many of them had been alienated before the end of the 13th century. A few of the more interesting benefactions deserve more particular mention.

Roger fitz Hugh of Clenewareton in an early undated charter confirms the gift which his father had made to the Nuns of an annual rent of three coombs (*cumbas*) of salt out of a *salina* at Lynn, called Heveckescote. In the time of the Prioress Letitia the Nuns had acquired one half of this *salina*, which they granted for an annual rent of three *octodali*[1] of salt to one Bartholomew fitz Ralf.

One of the principal benefactors to the Nunnery in its early days was Hervey Dunning, generally called Hervey fitz Eustace. His name, either as a benefactor or as a witness to the grants and indentures of others, is of more frequent occurrence than any other in the Nuns' muniments; the deeds in which it occurs belong to the reign of John and the early part of that of Henry III. He belonged to one of the oldest burgher families of Cambridge. A Gilbert son of Dunning is one of the witnesses to Constance's charter, and several generations of the family may be traced in the Hundred Rolls, which attest that Hervey's grandfather, Dunning, derived his title to the large estates which he held in Cambridge 'per anticum successum antecessorum suorum.' The bulk of these estates at the time of the Hundred Rolls had become the property of the Scholars of Merton. The social status of the family is sufficiently indicated by the fact that it enjoyed the then exceptional dignity of occupying a 'stone house,' which is doubtless to be identified with the ancient Norman dwelling-house known as the 'School of Pythagoras.' One of the Nuns' deeds shows that as late as 1342 a tenement in S. Giles' parish was called Dunnyngistede and was then in the possession of Thomas, son of Sir John de Cambridge. Hervey witnesses two deeds in the capacity of

[1] *Octodalus* = a coomb, or half a quarter, in 13th century English called an *eytendele*.

'alderman¹,' and to two others his seal is appended bearing the impression of a mounted knight and the legend SIGILL. HERVEI FILII EVSTACHII. He was a benefactor of Barnwell Priory and of S. John's Hospital, and gave to the latter seven acres in the fields of Chesterton, the Hospital granting him in return 'duo grabata cum pannis ad illa necessaria ad opus infirmorum in domo nostra lapidea².' When the new chapel of the Hospital was built he gave to the Nuns of S. Radegund a rent of 12d. out of land in S. John's parish, Milne St., in part recompense of any loss of parish dues which might be occasioned to their church of All Saints in Jewry (Charters, 180). Hervey had a sister, Roda, who had taken the veil in the Nunnery, and with her he gave to the Nuns many houses and lands scattered in the parishes and fields of Cambridge (Charters, 362). By another deed he granted them 10 acres in Cambridge fields for the soul of his deceased wife, Beatrice (Charters, 330).

Contemporary with Hervey fitz Eustace was Walter de Lindsey, who, with his wife Bertha³, gave to the Nuns the

¹ Doubtless of the Gild Merchant of Cambridge, which was granted to the burgesses by King John in the second year of his reign. The alderman was the chief officer of a gild. (Gross, *The Gild Merchant*, Vol. I. p. 79.) Until the Municipal Corporations Act of 1835, when the Corporation of Cambridge assumed the title of 'The Mayor, Aldermen and Burgesses,' their official style was 'The Mayor, Bailiffs and Burgesses.' In Latin deeds the borough alder. men are always *ballivi*, and in the oldest the mayor is *capitalis* or *major ballivus*. In the Nuns' deeds the earliest mention of a mayor is in 1258, when Robert de S. Edmundo was *major ballivus*.

² Kilner's *School of Pythagoras*, p. 31.

³ Possibly this Bertha de Lindsey may be identified with the Bertha whose coffin-lid on the floor of the south transept of the College Chapel bears the well-known inscription,

Moribus ornata jacet hic bona Berta rosata.

It has been a little too hastily assumed that this good lady was a Nun, but Nuns' graves were generally uninscribed. Sherman has a story about a Nun's gravestone in the College Chapel which is worth repeating, as it is not printed in Halliwell's edition of the *Historia*. In the year 1609 died in his 90th year a fellow of the College, Robert Landesdale, who had dwelt within the College walls as a fellow for no less than 58 years, and had been admitted in the reign of Henry VIII, in 1546. When his grave was being made in the Chapel an 'urna lapidea' was dug up, enclosing the 'ashes' of a Nun. 'So,' says

homage of Ralf le Feutrer and a rent of four shillings paid
by the said Ralf out of a messuage in Trinity parish; also a
messuage at Sarandscroft, opposite the Nunnery. To him and
to his wife, Bertha, the Nuns (Letitia, Prioress) leased a house
newly built and finished, in Cambridge, for the term of their
lives, with the singular stipulation that the rent should be two
shillings until the said Walter should return from his pilgrimage to Jerusalem, but that if he died there it should be
increased to six shillings so long as his wife lived.

Among the benefactors of the Nunnery occur the names of
several members of the family of de Trumpitune. A deed of
Sir Roger de Trumpitune, whose brass in Trumpington church
is dated 1289, releases to the Nuns free entry to certain land
of theirs in Trumpington fields, for which they are to pay him
a rent of 2 lbs. of cumin, and two shillings, as relief, at each
change of Prioress. Another member of the family, Hervey
de Trumpitune, grants to them a rent of two shillings along
with his daughter, Margaret. Another once important Trumpington family was that of Cayli. Ralf de Kailli at a very
early date gave the Nuns 30 acres there, and Simon de Cayli,
for the soul of his wife, who was buried in S. Radegund's
church, gave them an acre at Wyrtones diche.

Sherman, 'the fellows of the College, who living are to this day maintained
by the Nuns' revenues, in death come to be buried in the same tombs with
them.' In the audit accounts for 1608—9 there is an entry, 'Receaved...for a
coffin stone diged out of y⁰ chappell at y⁰ making of M' Landesdales grave,
vjˢ viijᵈ.' Elsewhere Sherman says that an 'urn,' bearing the inscription
'Moribus,' &c., was dug up and desecrated 'by foul and sacrilegious hands'
(i.e. by William Dowsing), in 1644. It contained the skeleton of a Nun, which
'fell to dust and ashes' on being touched. Sherman supposes Bertha to have
been professed in S. Radegund's Nunnery a short time before its dissolution,
but the lettering of the stone is of a 13th century type. The date, 1261, in
Arabic numerals, which the stone now bears, is an addition seemingly of the
17th century. I do not know what evidence there is for fixing Bertha's death
in that particular year. The inscription, it may be noted, is plagiarized from
a similar epitaph, given in Weever's *Funeral Monuments*, p. 242 (ed. 1631), on
Bertha, the Kentish queen, whose marriage with Ethelbert brought Christianity
into England :

> Moribus ornata jacet hic regina beata
> Bertha, &c.

John Porthors[1], a wealthy townsman of Cambridge, *temp.* Edward I, gave, with licence, to the Nuns 7½ acres dispersedly lying in Cambridge fields. He also bestowed on them a yearly rent of 13ᵈ. out of a messuage in All Saints' parish near the Hospital, for the health of his soul and for the souls of his father, John de Berton, and his mother, Agnes, and that his father's soul might not be imperilled by reason of his having retained a yearly rent of two shillings customably due to the Nuns out of a messuage in S. Clement's parish.

About the same period William Sueteye gave the Nuns a messuage in S. Andrew's parish; the moiety of a messuage and croft in S. Radegund's parish to maintain a lamp in the chapel of S. Radegund; a rent of eight shillings out of certain land in the market for a lamp in the Nuns' choir, wheresoever the choir should be; and 32½ acres in Cambridge fields.

John de Trippelowe, *alias* de Dicton, rector of Herdewyk, co. Cambr., was the latest considerable benefactor of the Nuns. He had been appointed in 1325 by the Prioress to the rectory of Reymerston, co. Norfolk, which he exchanged in 1340 for that of Hardwick. A Richard de Dicton was presented by the Nuns to S. Clement's in the latter year. They seem to have been sons of Master Henry de Trippelowe, who figures in some of the Nuns' deeds in connection with them, and who was alderman of the gild of S. Mary in 1321[2]. John de Trippelowe, with licence dated Edw. III, 5, gave the Nuns seven messuages in the parish of S. Radegund, one in the parish of S. Andrew without Barnwell gate, and eight acres in Cambridge and Barnwell fields. Many other grants of property, mainly situated in S. Radegund's parish, were made by him in the reign of Edward III. The last deed in which his name occurs is dated 1349, when he seems to have died, as a new rector

---

[1] The name Porthors = a breviary, *portiforium, portos,* as Chaucer spells it. The names Lominor (the Illuminator) and Parchemeniere, which occur in the Nuns' deeds, are evidence that the trade of book-producing was early established in Cambridge. John Porthors occupied a stone house at the corner opposite to S. Sepulchre's Church, for which he paid a rent of 2½ marks to Barnwell Priory (Barnwell *Liber Memorandorum*).

[2] Master, *History of Corpus Christi College,* p. 9.

2—2

was appointed to Hardwick in June 1349. After the visitation
of the Black Death in that year the Nuns received no considerable accessions of property.

§ 8. *Advowsons of the Nuns. The Parish of S. Radegund.*

The rectories and advowsons in the possession of the
Nunnery were all obtained at an early period of its history.
It will be convenient first to sketch the history of the parish
church of S. Radegund, although its actual appropriation to
the Nuns was not earliest in date. Sherman states that the
rectory of the parish church of S. Radegund was appropriated
to the Nuns about the year 1291, a yearly pension of forty
shillings, to be paid by them, being reserved to the Vicar of
All Saints', and he adds that at the same time the parish of
S. Radegund was united with that of All Saints, from which it
was anciently parted by the King's Ditch[1]. But I can find no
authority for the date given for the appropriation, and Sherman
is clearly mistaken as regards the union of the two parishes.
After 1291 they were never in any sense united so long as the
Nunnery existed. The Nunnery deeds bear witness that, from
the middle of the 13th century to within a very few years of
the dissolution of the Priory, tenements in Radegund Lane on
and adjoining the Nuns' croft were regularly described as being
in the parish of S. Radegund, and after the foundation of the
College and the dedication of the church to the Name of Jesus
tenements are similarly described as being in Jesus parish[2].
Long after the College had taken the place of the Nunnery,
in fact down to the middle of the present century, the Audit
books, in which the receipts from house rental in Cambridge
are classed together according to parishes, though they do not

---

[1] Cole makes a similar statement: 'Anno 1291, ut videtur, ecclesia parochialis in monasterio S. Radegundis Cantabrigiae appropriatur Priorissae et
Conventui et regitur per capellanum. MSS. Wren 242, 8.' Add. MSS. 5820.

[2] The latest mention that I have observed of Jesus parish is in an agreement between Corpus Christi College and Jesus College, dated Edward VI. 6,
i.e. 1552.

make a separate heading for the parish of S. Radegund yet distinguish houses *in venella Jesu* from those *in parochia Omnium Sanctorum*.

Nor was this distinction merely a civil and local one. There is ample evidence that the Nuns' church, and afterwards the chapel of the College in its earlier days, served all the purposes and had all the privileges attaching to a parish church. At the end of the Register of Bishop Gray of Ely (1454—1478) under the heading 'Nomina Patronorum Ecclesiarum et Vicariarum' it is recorded that 'Ecclesia parochialis in monasterio S. Radegundis, Cant., appropriata est eisdem Priorisse et Conventui et regitur per capellanum parochialem.' In the accounts of Agnes Banastre, treasuress in 1450—1451, there is mention of a cover for the font, 'et in factura unius coopertorii pro le font ecclesie Sancte Radegundis, vj^d.' When Bishop Alcock destroyed the western portion of the nave, which served the parishioners as their church, in place of the old west door he made a new door for their use near the south-west corner of the shortened nave[1]. In the Statutes which Bishop Stanley gave to the College in 1514, cap. 19 (de Curato) it is ordained that one of the Fellows shall be annually elected Curate of the parish church of S. Radegund annexed to the College, to have the cure of souls of all dwelling there, to administer sacraments and sacramentals and to receive for his pains as the Master and Fellows may determine. The farmers of the dominical lands adjoining the College retained

---

[1] The authors of the *Architectural History of Cambridge*, Vol. II. p. 173, regard this door as intended for the private use of the Master of the College, on whose garden it now opens. But the statutes of Bishop Stanley, cap. 28, show that in 1512 the ground on the south side of the Master's lodge was not enclosed as a garden, for the Master was thereby empowered either to enclose or to build upon it at his own charges. And in 1592, when Hammond's plan of Cambridge was made, the Master's garden did not extend so far east as the door in question. The eastern portion of the area now comprised in the Master's garden is described in the early Audit accounts as 'the churchyard' or 'garlicke faire close,' and was parted from the original garden of the Lodge by a mud wall, which is mentioned in a lease of 1555. In the Audit accounts for 1558 is a payment for '24 dised nailes for ye churche yard dore xij^d.' Burials in 'Jesus churchyard' are mentioned as late as 1543.

the right of attending the College church so late as the reign
of Queen Mary, for in a lease of the Radegund Manor, dated
1555, it is covenanted that 'bothe the colledge and the vicare
of Alhallows shall suffer hereafter the farmers to come and
frequent the colledge church to hear their divine service,
accordinglie as it is specified in a payre of indentures betweene
the sayde m^r and fellows and the sayde vicare, except it be in
the plaigue tyme.' This covenant is not repeated in later
leases of the Manor, and from the fact that the farmers' privilege
of attending the College church was then protected by covenant
and indenture we may suppose that even in 1555 it was
considered obsolescent.

There is no direct evidence, so far as I am aware, either to
establish or disprove the date, 1291, which Sherman gives for
the appropriation of S. Radegund's rectory to the Nuns. The
Hundred Rolls indeed, though they expressly state that the
churches of All Saints and S. Clement were so appropriated,
say nothing about the appropriation of S. Radegund's, whence
it might be inferred that it had not taken place in 1278. But
the fact that the church was conventual is sufficient to account
for the omission of S. Radegund's from the record of the
spiritual possessions of the Nunnery. Probably it was appropriated to it from its first existence as a parish church.

I have shown that the parish of S. Radegund was un-
doubtedly not united to that of All Saints after the middle
of the 13th century; it may be concluded with almost equal
certainty that S. Radegund's parish had no separate existence
before that time. Tenements near the Nunnery are not described
in the oldest deeds as being situated in S. Radegund's parish,
which is first mentioned in deeds of the time of Milisentia, who
was Prioress in 1246 and was succeeded in the office in or before
1258. Evidence of the late origin of the parish is seen in the
fact that one of its boundaries was the King's Ditch. It is
generally stated that this ditch was made by Henry III in
1268, but there was an earlier enclosure of the town in 1215.
Previous to 1250 the Nuns' croft did not extend so far as to
the King's Ditch, for in that year the Nuns received licence

from Henry III to enclose a certain croft of theirs lying between the Nunnery and the Ditch. It is therefore fairly certain that S. Radegund's parish, which was conterminous with the Nuns' demesne lands, came into existence soon after that year.

Bowtell in his MSS (p. 1011) states, without giving his authority, that the parish of the Holy Sepulchre was severed from that of All Saints in the reign of Henry III. The pension of forty shillings which the Nuns were required to pay to the vicar of All Saints' is tolerably clear proof that S. Radegund's was formed by a similar detachment from the same parish. 'When a chapel was made parochial one of the remaining signs of dependence on the Mother Church was generally some stated pension to the Rector or Vicar of it[1].' Such, no doubt, was the origin of the Nuns' pension to the vicar of All Saints'. The fact that it was paid to the *vicar* is evidence that the parish of S. Radegund was not severed from that of All Saints until after Sturmi's appropriation of the latter church to the Nuns.

The area detached from All Saints' parish to form that of S. Radegund comprised only the demesne lands of the Nunnery, afterwards known as Radegund Manor. At the time of its formation the latter parish can have contained only a very few inhabitants. The Hundred Rolls mention only four messuages in it, all of them paying rent to the Nuns and all of them situated on a croft called Sarandscroft, opposite the Nunnery gates. Later these were subdivided into smaller holdings, and houses began to be built on the south side of the Nuns' croft, next the street and between the Nunnery and the King's Ditch. The occupants of the houses in the parish seem to have been principally the clergy and servants of the Nunnery.

As the whole, or very nearly the whole area of the parish belonged to the Nuns it is natural that the Hundred Rolls referring to one of their tenements describe it as lying in their own parish, 'in sua parochia.' It was probably, like many other

---

[1] Kennett's *Parochial Antiquities*, p. 601, where ample evidence is collected.

parishes whose churches were also **conventual, a** peculiar, *i.e.*
exempt from the jurisdiction and visitation of the archdeacon.
I **do not know** that this is anywhere stated **as a fact, nor do**
I **find any record** of **a** papal bull conferring such exemption.
Nor can reliance be placed on the fact mentioned in one of **the**
Nuns' documents dated 1313 and frequently noticed in **the Ely**
Episcopal Registers (*e.g.* under dates July 24, 1338, and May 9,
1340) that **the** Nuns were discharged from procurations to the
archdeacon ; for this immunity from the charges of visitation
extended evidently **to** All Saints' and S. **Clement's churches**
as well as to S. Radegund's, and was grounded on the **poverty**
of the **Nuns, whose** whole spiritualities **were stated to be of**
less yearly **value** than six marks. In **the absence** of any direct
evidence as to the origin **of** the parish I can only rely on certain
facts which tend to show that S. Radegund's **was not a parish**
of the ordinary kind. Firstly, the *capellanus*, so far as **can be**
gathered from the Ely Registers, was never presented **by the**
Nuns to the Bishop for admission to **the** parish **church.**
Secondly, he appears **to** have been maintained by a stipend,
paid by the Nuns, which in the accounts of 1449—1451 was
£5. **And** thirdly, among the miscellaneous documents contained
in **the Nuns'** treasury there remain a few wills, one of which,
that of Roger Mason of S. Radegund's parish, dated 1392, has
attached to it the *ad causas* seal of **the** Nunnery. The wills
of inhabitants of exempt parishes attached to religious houses,
as is well **known,** were customarily proved before the sacrist or
some **other officer** of the monastery. The parish of the Nunnery
of Carow, **Norwich, was** an example of such an exempt jurisdiction ; **the Nuns'** chaplain proved the wills of parishioners,
and the *ad causas* seal of the convent **was** appended **to them**[1].

§ 9.   *Parish of All Saints.*

The advowson of All Saints' *in Judaismo* or *juxta Hospitale*,
as it was **called to** distinguish it from the church similarly

[1] *Monasticon*, ed. 1846, Vol. 4, p. 68.

dedicated *juxta Castellum*, was given to the Nuns by Sturmi[1] of Cambridge either in or before 1180. His charter recites that the donation is made 'by the wish and with consent of his wife and his heirs, for the welfare of King Henry and his heirs and for the welfare of the faithful departed.' The Nuns are to hold the advowson as freely and quietly as his *antecessores* have held the same. Of Sturmi we know no more than that a person of his name is described as 'frater noster' in a deed of the Prioress Letitia. Geoffrey Ridel, Bishop of Ely, in the presence and with the consent of Sturmi, instituted the Nuns to the rectory, 'jus personatus,' of the same church. His charter is dated on the day after the octave of S. Martin in the year 1180. He appoints one Richard as the Nuns' perpetual vicar in the church and requires him to make to them an annual payment of twenty shillings, and further to perform all customary dues to the Bishop. After the cession or decease of the said Richard the Nuns may make such disposition for their church as they will, saving the episcopal *consuetudines*. At a considerably later date the Convent of Ely (Roger, Prior, *i.e.* Roger de Brigham, Prior from 1215 to 1229) confirmed the Bishop's appropriation to the Nuns. It was also ratified by a bull of Pope Alexander IV (1254—1261) mentioned by Sherman, in whose time it seems to have been extant among the Nuns' evidences.

The Nuns, as already stated, probably when S. Radegund's parish was severed from All Saints, bound themselves to an annual pension of forty shillings to the vicar of the latter parish. As the net result of the cross payments we find the Nuns in 1449-1451 paying the vicar the sum of twenty shillings *per annum*. In the Bursars' Rolls, *temp.* Henry VIII and Edward VI, this payment had been increased to 33s. 4d. Doubtless this was in compensation for the loss of income which the vicar may have sustained owing to the conversion of the Nunnery into a college, for when the Hospital of S. John gave place to S. John's College the vicar complained of the loss which he received from the change, and the College undertook

---

[1] I know no reason for calling him *William* Sturmi, as Sherman does.

to give him an annual pension of five marks in satisfaction of his claims[1]. The Visitors of the University in 1549 decreed that Jesus College should pay the vicar an additional sum of 6s. 8d. by the year, and the pension thus increased to 40s. has continued to be paid up to the present time.

§ 10.   *Parish of S. Clement.*

The advowson of S. Clement's Church was given to the Elemosinary of S. Radegund by Hugh fitz Absolon of Cambridge, acting on the advice of Eustace, late Bishop of Ely. Bishop Eustace died in 1215 and the grant is evidently to be dated very soon after that year, for the Pedes Finium (ed. Rye for the Camb. Antiq. Soc.) mentions among Cambridge pleas *anno* Henry III, 3 (1218) 'Estrilda fil. Scobic *v.* the Prioress of S. Radegund, of the advowson of S. Clement's.' It would seem from this that the Nuns did not acquire pacific possession of the advowson at once, and this is further shown by the fact that Walter fitz William de S. Edmund, in a deed of date seemingly about 1230–1240, released to the Nuns his rights to the advowson and confirmed the grant thereof made by his *antecessor*, Hugh fitz Absolon and his uncle Walter. It would be interesting to know something of the original patrons of Cambridge churches and the circumstances which gave them their right to present to the livings. Unfortunately the Nuns' deeds have very little light to throw on the matter in the case either of All Saints' or of S. Clement's. The only information which I can gather of this Hugh fitz Absolon is obtained from his charters, several of which (two with his seal attached) are to be found among the Nunnery muniments. In one he grants the Nuns a rent of 29½d. out of the land in the Jews' street (*in vico Judeorum*) going down from the highway to All Saints' churchyard. The grant is for the health of the souls of himself and his sister Letitia, and the Nuns are required to celebrate yearly the anniversary of his sister on the eve of the

[1] Cole's MSS. Vol. III. p. 65.

Purification, and on the day of the Purification are to have the whole rent for their *pietancia*. He also gave them a rent of 12*d.* for their Infirmary and six acres in Cambridge and Barnwell fields. His cousin Aldusa, daughter of William Blangernun, who was buried in the convent church, gave them property in the parish of S. Mary the Great.

The Rectory of S. Clement's was appropriated to the Nuns of S. Radegund of Grenecroft by John de Fontibus, Bishop of Ely (1220–1225), saving a competency for a priest to have the cure of souls. The Nuns' muniments include two charters confirming this grant, one of Ely convent, Roger de Brigham, Prior (1215–1229), the other of Geoffrey de Burgh, Bishop of Ely (1225–1229). Other confirmations by Pope Honorius III (1216–1227) and by Hugh Northwold, Bishop of Ely, the latter dated 1238, are mentioned in a volume of 'Old Letters and Extracts' in the College Library, but are not now extant.

The last-named bishop decreed that the vicar of S. Clement's should pay to the Nuns *de bonis altaragii* a yearly pension of five marks. From the Nunnery accounts it appears that this sum was set apart to provide the clothing of the Nuns[1]. The benefice, already denuded of the rectorial tithes, seems from the first to have been ill able to support this heavy additional charge. So early as 1248 we find a lively dispute proceeding between the Nuns and the vicar, Adam, on some pecuniary question, probably connected with this pension. The vicar cited the Nuns before the Dean of S. Paul's, *i.e.* the Court of Arches: the Nuns contested the vicar's right to convene them, on the ground that he was at the time under sentence of excommunication, and when this plea was disallowed by the Dean they appealed to the court of Rome. The Pope, Innocent IV, by bull addressed to the Prior of Linton commissioned him to inquire into the circumstances. Of the Prior's decision we

---

[1] The practice of assigning some part of the income of appropriated churches to the providing of clothing for the religious was not uncommon: examples of it occur at Stodeley, Stamford and Marrick Nunneries. (*Vide* the new *Monasticon.*) The rectory of Harleston was given to Barnwell Priory *ad vesturam* by Geoffrey Peche (Barnwell *Liber Memorandorum*).

are not informed; but the issue between the Nuns and their
vicars remained in an unsettled state for long after. In 1261
Sir Geoffrey, who was then vicar, acknowledges himself to be
indebted to the Nuns for 2½ marks, being part of the pension of
5 marks assigned by Bishop Northwold, and he asks to be
allowed time to pay it. Hugh de Stamford, Commissary
General of the Official of Ely, decrees that he is to pay one
mark on S. Nicolas' Day and 20s. before the Epiphany next
following. A century and a half later, in 1401, Adam de
Walsoken, vicar, takes the opportunity of the metropolitical
visitation of the Archbishop of Canterbury, Thomas Arundel,
to represent to him that he is charged with an annual pension
to the Nuns of five marks, that he has no proper vicarage to
reside in, and that the income of the living is 'tenuis et exilis[1].'
In consequence of the vicar's complaint the Nuns (Isabella de
Sudbury, Prioress) on July 11, 1402, agreed to give up as a
mansum for the then vicar and his successors a house on
the eastern side of the churchyard, next a messuage of the
service of the glorious Virgin Mary, *i.e.* the chantry house of
S. Clement's Church. The deed (Charters, 242) in which they
make this concession bears evidence to the Nuns' extreme
reluctance to accept any responsibility in the matter. The
curiously mixed motives which actuated them are shown in the
reasons given for the concession, viz. that the incomes of
parochial churches are everywhere decreasing, that the results
of actions at law are doubtful, and that it is desirable that the
church, being *baptismalis*, should be served duly and to the
honour of God. The pension of five marks was continuously
exacted by the Nuns up to the time of the dissolution of the
Nunnery, and even survived until late in the reign of Henry
VIII, as shown by the account rolls of the College Bursars[2].

---

[1] The incomes of the parish clergy were seriously affected by the Black
Death and the long financial depression which succeeded it. Compare *Piers
Plowman*, Prologue, 83 (date 1377),

  Persoues and parisch prestes pleyned hem to þe bischop
  þat here parisches were pore sith þe pestilence time.

[2] From the Bursars' accounts of Henry VIII, 26—27, it appears that the

§ 11. *Advowson of Reymerston.*

The advowson of Reymerston Church, co. Norfolk, was conveyed by fine to Letitia, Prioress of S. Radegund's in Henry III, 2, by John de Reymerston. A list of the rectors presented by the Prioress is given in Blomfield's *History of Norfolk*, Vol. 10, pp. 241—2 (ed. Parkyn). The last presented, in 1401, was Mr Robert Braunch, LL.Lic., apparently the same who in 1384 became Master of Trinity Hall.

The names of several of the Nuns, Craneswick, Harling, Cressingham, are taken from villages in the neighbourhood of Reymerston and appear to indicate that the connection with this quarter of Norfolk was maintained after the Nuns parted with the advowson. From the same district probably came John de Pykenham (now Pickenham), whose tombstone, in the

---

vicar of S. Clement's was allowed an annual sum of 6s. 8d. for rent of a dwelling house 'eo quod non est aliqua domus sive mansio dicto vicario pertinens.' A few years later the payment disappears from the Bursars' rolls and the vicar, who was a fellow of the College, is stated to be the tenant of a chamber in College. The Rev. E. G. de Salis Wood, vicar of S. Clement's, informs me that the house traditionally called 'the Vicarage' is that now numbered 8, Portugal Place, which is still the property of Jesus College. Leases of the reign of Elizabeth describe it as abutting on its southern side on 'the backe side of a place sometime called St Clement's hostell.' A deed of Edward III, 47 (1373) shows that it was then leased to Sir Richard Milde, vicar of S. Clement's, jointly with John de Kelesseye, cooper, and Avisia his wife. Another deed of 1377 (Charters, 250 *l*) gives minute details of the rooms which it then contained. In 1616 the southern half of the house was used as a stable by the Master of Jesus College. A letter of the Master, Dr Duport, in that year refers to a dispute between the College and Alderman Ventris with respect to the northern portion of the house, which the latter claimed, asserting that it had anciently been a banqueting house and did not form a part of the College tenement. Ventris also claimed a house called the Chantry-house, situated outside the churchyard on its N.E. side. Dr Duport alleges that this house is not the old Chantry-house, nor on the site of it, but is an encroachment on Jesus College land and has been erected within the last 50 years; in evidence of which he observes that it is built of sound heart of oak which apparently was brought from the steeple of the church, which about the time of the erection of the house was much decayed and vanished quite away.

S.W. angle of the south transept of the Nuns' church, bears the inscription,

Hic jacet frater Johannes de Pykenham magister sacre theologie prior hujus loci cujus anime propicietur Deus.

He was perhaps either *capellanus* or confessor to the Nuns. The office of prior, warden or *magister monialium* is one frequently found in nunneries; *e.g.* at Grimsby, Stanfeld (Lincs.), Stamford, Catesby.

§ 12. *List of Prioresses.*

The following is as complete a list of the Prioresses of S. Radegund as it is possible to make out. Unless otherwise stated the dates given are those of the earliest and latest deeds in which the name occurs. The deeds of the 12th and early 13th century give neither dates nor names of Prioresses.

Letitia was Prioress at the time of Bishop Eustace's composition respecting All Saints' Church and S. John's Hospital, which was not later than 1213: she occurs in Pedes Finium, 1228.

Milisentia is mentioned in Pedes Finium 1246 and 1249.

Dera occurs in 1258.

Agnes Burgeylun, or *Burgeillo*, in 1274 (in the new *Monasticon* wrongly set down *anno* 1301).

Constantia and

Amitia de Driffeld occur in undated deeds *temp.* Edward I, the former in the mayoralty of Roger de Wykes.

Alicia le Chaumberlain was Prioress about 1278; she was daughter of Sir Walter le Chamberlayne, purchaser of the manor of Landbeach. (Clay's *History of Landbeach.*)

Elena occurs in 1284 and in 1299.

Christiana de Braybrok in 1311.

Cecilia de Cressingham, in 1315 and 1316.

Mabilia Martin in 1330 and 1332.

Alicia in 1347.

Eva Wasteneys in 1359; a person of the same name was Prioress of the Benedictine house of Swaffham in 1378.

Margaret Clanyle in 1363: she resigned Feb. 1, 1378 (Ely Registers).

Alice Pilet was elected Feb. 20, 1378; occurs in 1398.

Isabella Sudbury in 1402.

Margaret Harlyng was sub-prioress in 1407; succeeded as Prioress in the same year and occurs in 1408.

Agnes Seyntelowe, or *Senclowe,* first occurs in 1415; she died Sept. 8, 1457.

Joan Lancastre was elected Sept. 27, 1457; last occurs in 1466.

Isabella in 1468.

Elizabeth Walton occurs in 1468 and 1479: she had been succentrix in 1457.

Joan Cambridge was administering the effects of the Nunnery in 1482–3, apparently in a vacancy of the Priorate; she was Prioress in 1483 and died 1487[1].

Joan Fulburn was appointed Oct. 12, 1487; her name occurs for the last time in 1487.

§ 13. *Finances of the Nunnery.*

At the time of the election of Joan Lancastre in 1457 there were eleven nuns who had the *jus eligendi.* There are no data for determining their number at an earlier period, but as most religious houses suffered a decline in numbers during the 15th century it is not unlikely that they had once been more numerous. There seems little reason to doubt that at no time during the existence of the Nunnery were its endowments adequate for the maintenance of its inmates or the repairs of the fabric. As early as 1277 their penury 'haud paucis innotescit'; in 1340 their poverty was pleaded as an excuse for

---

[1] In a fragmentary Computus of Margaret Ratclyff, Prioress of Swaffham, Edw. IV, 22, occurs an entry 'de iiij^s de quatuor busellis (mixtilionis) venditis pr. monial. de Cambrige...de domina Johanna Cambrige cui erat commissa administratio bonorum prioratus predicti.'

exemption from the charges of procuration; and the evidence
of Archbishop Wittlesey's visitor in 1373 shows the Nunnery
in deep embarrassment, its buildings dilapidated, and its services
neglected for want of funds. The flow of benefactions which
was maintained up to the end of Edward I's reign was arrested
about the end of the 13th century, probably because gifts to
pious uses began to be diverted to the various mendicant
orders which had established themselves in Cambridge during
the preceding half century. As already stated, after the great
pestilence in 1349 the Nuns received few fresh endowments,
and those of inconsiderable value. One important source of
endowment entirely dried up about that time, viz. the grants
of lands and rents made by the relations of a nun when she
took the veil. The nuns of the earlier time seem largely to
have been drawn from families of wealth and social standing
in the town and shire. Among those who brought with
them endowments to the Nunnery were Sibil, sister of Fulk
Crocheman, whose family held a considerable amount of
property in and near the Jewry in All Saints' parish temp.
Henry III; Elizabeth and Isabel, daughters of Sir Thomas de
Cambridge, who died 1361; Roda, sister of Hervey Dunning,
already mentioned; Margaret, daughter of Hervey de Trumpitune; Sabina, daughter of Ralf Person of Chesterton, temp.
Henry III; Sibil, daughter of Stephen de Scalariis of Wratting;
and Margaret, sister of Philip de Cestertune, about 1200. The
accounts of the Treasuress, Agnes Banastre, for the two years
1449-50 and 1450-51 probably represent the normal income
and expenditure of the Nunnery in the middle of the 15th
century. They are written on skin in a neat and minute hand,
which is perhaps that of one of the clergy attached to the
house. On the outer surface are written the accounts of the
Grangeress, Joan Lancastre. Also on the outer side of the
earlier roll are copied in a bold but careless handwriting of
late 15th century character three Latin prayers addressed to
S. Etheldreda, to which in another hand have been added two
benedictions of the Name of Jesus. The prayers to S. Etheldreda were clearly intended for use at her shrine at Ely.

These accounts are kept in an exact and orderly way and show that at the time the Nuns were fairly paying their way. In the earlier year the receipts were £77. 8s. 6½d. and the expenditure £72. 6s. 4¾d.; in the later the sums were respectively £74. 2s. 9½d. and £78. 6s. 0d.[1]. The heads of the receipts were in the later year:

	£	s.	d.
Rents in Cambridge . .	32	12	2
Rents agricultural . . .	12	14	7½
Miscellaneous: tolls of fair, receipts from guests, &c. .	8	16	2
Tithes	6	13	4
Pension	3	6	8
Sale of corn, hay, &c. . .	9	19	10
Total	74	2	9½

§ 14. *Incidents in the Annals of the Nunnery.*

There is little in the history of the Nunnery between the time of King Malcolm and that of the dissolution which calls for particular mention. Such facts as are recoverable from the Nuns' own records it is unnecessary here to detail; an outline of them may be found in the Catalogue of Charters. I will set down here only a few particulars which I have gleaned from such external sources of information as the Hare MSS and the Registers of Ely and Canterbury.

Among the Hare MSS (Vol. I. p. 27) is a writ of Henry III tested at Ely, March 30, in the 35th year of his reign (*i.e.* 1250), directed to the bailiffs of the town of Cambridge, requiring them not to distrain the Prioress of S. Radegund and her tenants for an encroachment (*pro preprestura*) and for other matters of which inquisition has

[1] Sherman gives the total of receipts in these two years as £24. 1s. 10½d. and £32. 10s. 2d., figures which correspond to no totals in the rolls. He also refers to a third roll of date Henry VI, 39, in which the receipts are stated as £74. 2s. 4d.; this is no longer extant. He does not mention the roll of Edward IV, 21—22.

been made by William de Axmuth and William Brito at
Cambridge. This writ is clearly connected with the same
King's license to the Nuns, tested at Westminster on April 17
in the same year, to enclose and keep enclosed for ever a croft
belonging to them and lying between their church and the
fossatum of Cambridge. (This license is cited in full in King
Edward II's confirmation, Charters, 8.) From the circumstance that the writ was addressed to the town bailiffs it would
appear that the purpresture of the Nuns consisted of an encroachment on the common lands of the town, *i.e.* on Grenecroft. The writ stays the distraint until the *quindena* of
Easter, by which time, or at least before April 17, an
arrangement seems to have been arrived at by which the
town relinquished its rights in the land annexed. But as
the ownership of the soil of the common land belonged not
to the burgesses but to the King (such at least would be the
King's view) his sanction was necessary to enable the Nuns
to acquire and permanently enclose the croft[1]. The dispute
between the Nuns and the burgesses seems to have been
the outcome of proceedings for encroachment taken by the
King against the burgesses: for by a writ, mentioned by
Cooper[2] and dated March 5 in this year, the King required the sheriff to restore the cattle of the burgesses and
not further to distrain them for a trespass, they having paid
at the royal wardrobe 20 marks. The encroachment for
which the burgesses thus made satisfaction was no doubt
committed on the soil of the *fossatum*. At the time of the
Hundred Rolls it was one of the complaints of the townsmen that the soil of the *fossatum* remained void to their
great loss, and several individuals are reported to have made
encroachments on it by planting trees and otherwise.

---

[1] Pollock and Maitland (*History of English Law*, Vol. i. p. 635), speaking of
the *Firma Burgi*, 'It may be much doubted whether the walls, ditches, streets
and open spaces of the borough were held by the burgesses. They were still
the king's walls, ditches and streets, and he who encroached upon them
committed a purpresture against the king. Nor is it by any means certain
that the king parted with the soil over which the burgesses exercised the right
of pasture.'　　　　[2] *Annals*, Vol. i. p. 46.

The Register of Archbishop Wittlesey (fo. 153), at Lambeth Palace, gives a full and curious account of a visitation of the Nunnery in the year 1373, made by mandate of the Archbishop during a vacancy of the See of Ely. The visitor was Thomas de Wormenhale, who about the same time visited other religious houses in the diocese, viz. Ely, Chatteris, Anglesey, Swaffham, Thorney, Barnwell and the Hospital of S. John, Cambridge. The Nunnery of S. Radegund was visited on the Saturday next following the feast of S. James the Apostle. The Prioress and sisters were separately and privately examined, and the report of the visitor exhibited the following *comperta*.

First, it was alleged that the Prioress made the *officiariae* of the Nunnery discharge payments beyond what was required by the custom of their offices, and without assigning reason for such payments. The Prioress denied this article, but was nevertheless cautioned in future to explain to her officials the reasons for all expenditure required of them.

Item, that the Prioress did not, as she was bound to do, find priests to celebrate for various benefactors of the Nunnery. The Prioress made reply that the means of the Nuns were not sufficient to sustain the said burdens. She was cautioned to discharge the obligations of the Nunnery in this respect as soon as the fortunes of the household would enable her to do so.

Item, that the Prioress suffered the Refectory to remain without cover, so that in rainy weather the sisters were not able to take their meals there in common, as by rule they were bound to do. The Prioress answered that the Nunnery was so burdened with debts, subsidies and contributions in these times that so far she had been unable to carry out repairs, but that she would do so as soon as possible.

Item, that the Prioress did not correct dame Elizabeth de Cambridge for withdrawing herself from divine service, and allowed friars of different orders, as well as scholars, to visit her at inopportune times and to converse with her, to the scandal of religion. The Prioress replied that she had frequently corrected her. She was charged in future strictly to correct and chastise her for the faults alleged..

3—2

Item, that the Prioress was too easily induced to give permission to the Nuns to go outside the cloister. She was cautioned not to do so in future.

Item, that dame Elizabeth de Cambridge provoked discord among the sisters and often murmured against correction, and that she did not trouble to get up (*non curat surgere*) to attend matins, as she was bound to do. She denied the fact, and added that, supposing she had so done, she had been corrected by her Prioress. She was warned to cease from murmuring and provoking discord, and to get up for matins, whenever she could (*cum poterit*), under pain of excommunication.

The Prioress mentioned in this report was Margaret Clanyle. She resigned her office in 1378. Bishop Arundel's Register at Ely (fo. 25) contains the following documents relating to this event.

The Bishop's mandate to his Official, Richard le Scrop, to receive the resignation of *domina* Margaret Clanyle, and to certify to the Bishop what he has done. Downham, Jan. 29, 1378.

Scrop's certification to the Bishop that he has admitted, approved and authorized the resignation. Cambridge, Feb. 1.

The Bishop's license to the sub-prioress, Johanna de Ely, and the convent to elect a successor. Downham, Feb. 6.

Process of election: 'assumptis sibi quibusdam personis secularibus, vidlt. magistris Thoma de Glocestr' et Johanne de Newton, juris peritis, d⁰⁰ Willelmo Rolf, vicario ecclesie Omnium Sanctorum in Judaismo et magistro Roberto de Foxton, notario publico, pro saniori consilio in hac parte habendo,' *domina* Alice Pylet is unanimously elected. Feb. 17.

The election is confirmed by the Bishop, Feb. 20, and publication of it made 'ad januam manerii de Downham et in capella dicti manerii.'

On Dec. 10, 1389, Bishop Fordham of Ely granted indulgence of 40 days to all who should help to repair the Nuns' church and cloister and contribute to their maintenance and relief. (Fordhams' Register, fo. 10.)

In the Register of Archbishop Courtenay (fo. 143), under date 1389, is a letter addressed to the same Bishop of Ely, in which the Archbishop reports that in his recent metropolitical visitation of the diocese of Lincoln he found there 'a sheep wandering from the fold among thorns,' to wit, one Margaret Cailly, a professed nun of S. Radegund's monastery, who had cast off the garb of religion and in secular habit was leading a dissolute life. 'That her blood be not required at our hands' the Archbishop sends her with the bearer of the letter to the Bishop, with an injunction that she should be restored to the Nunnery and kept there in safe custody. The Bishop in a letter to the Prioress (Reg. Fordham, fo. 11) directs that the apostate nun be committed to the *eventus*[1], there to be kept in close confinement until she shows signs of penitence and contrition for her 'excesses,' as the rules of her house and order require. And the Bishop further enjoins that when the said Margaret first enters the chapter-house she shall humbly ask pardon of the Prioress and all her sisters for her offences, and that she shall undergo salutary penances for her excesses, the Bishop having privately absolved her from the penalty of excommunication on the ground of her apostasy.

On Sept. 19, 1401, the Priory was visited by the commissioners of the Archbishop of Canterbury, Thomas Arundel. The sisters were privately and separately questioned but the substance of their answers is not recorded in the Register. (Arundels' Register, fo. 492.)

The Register of Bishop Fordham of Ely (Jan. 26, 1407) contains a license to the sub-prioress, Margery Harlyng, for a private oratory or chapel within the Priory.

On March 18, 1457, Bishop Gray of Ely issued letters, dated from Downham, granting 40 days' indulgence to all who should lend a helping hand ('manus porrexerint adjutrices') for the repair of the bell-tower of the Nuns' conventual church and

---

[1] Possibly this was the conventual prison, which in some monasteries was in the gate-house, in others adjoined the Necessarium. The word is not in Ducange.

for the maintenance of books, vestments and other church
ornaments (Register, fo. 21).

The Ely Registers (Bp. Gray, fo. 140) supply a full account
of the election of a Prioress in 1457 in place of Agnes
Seyntelowe, who died on Sept. 8 in that year. The process of
election was *per formam compromissi*, and the description, in
outline, is as follows. Maud Sudbury, as sub-prioress and
president, informs the Bishop of the vacancy and obtains his
license for the election of a successor. In the Nuns' petition
to the Bishop for leave to elect it is stated that by the canons
a church regular must not be vacant beyond three months ' ue
pro defectu regiminis invadat gregem dominicam lupus rapax.'
On Sept. 23 they elect Joan Lancastre to be sacrist, and then
adjourn to Sept. 27. On that day, after mass *de Sancto
Spiritu*, those who have *jus eligendi* meet and decant the
' ympn,' *Veni Creator*, with versicles and collects. Elizabeth
Walton, succentrix, proclaims notice of the election at the door
of the Priory and at the door of the chapter-house. Master
Roger Ratcliffe, LL.D., Robert Bredon, notary public, Master
Thomas Willis, LL.B., Ds Richard Sampson and Ds Henry
Whitrate, chaplain, are called in as *consiliarii* and *testes*. The
sisters elect as *compromissarii* Joan Lancastre, Eliz. Walton
and Katherine Seyntelowe, cellarer, who retire to the east end
of the chapterhouse with the witnesses aforesaid. E. W. and
K. S. call upon J. L. to nominate; she nominates E. W.;
J. L. and K. S. call upon E. W. to nominate; she nominates
J. L. E. W. and J. L. call upon K. S. to nominate; she
nominates J. L. Without any interval the *compromissarii*
return and call upon the sisters to nominate, beginning with
Maud Sudbury; she nominates J. L., as do Margaret Metham,
Elena Craneswik, Emma Hore and Joan Kay. Emma Denton
is nominated by Agnes Daveys, Katherine Seyntelowe by
Emma Denton, Agnes Daveys by Alice Graunfeld. Eliz.
Walton counts up the votes and declares that Joan Lancastre
is elected. After this all the sisters, devoutly chanting *Te
Deum*, conducted Joan Lancastre, ' renitentem licet ' to the
high altar of the conventual church and there placed her,

prostrate on the ground before the altar. The bell was then rung and proclamation of the election was made to the public in the vulgar tongue before noon. All the sisters then conducted the Prioress elect to the *vestibulum* of the church and let her depart. At a meeting in the chapter-house in the afternoon it was agreed that Eliz. Walton and Katherine Seyntelowe should obtain the assent of Joan Lancastre to the process of election. She at first asked to be allowed to consider the matter; 'tandem vero precibus devicta et post multas excusationes,' she consented to take the oath required of a Prioress. Next follows, Sept. 29, the Bishop's commission to Master Robert Thwait, S. T. P., to confirm the election, with mandate to the Bishop's apparitors to summon all persons objecting or otherwise concerned. In the Bishop's court Master Edmund Kunnesburgh, *decretorum doctor*, appears as the Nuns' counsel and claims that all has been done legally and canonically. Against whom Roger Ratclyffe and others alleged objections to the form of election. Then Master Kunnesburgh on the part of the Nuns 'exhibuit quandam peticionem summariam,' begging the Bishop's official to proceed summarily and confirm the election, which he does, affirming that nothing has been proved affecting the validity of the election.

§ 15. *Decay and Dissolution of the Nunnery.*

Doubts have sometimes been suggested as to the truth of the representations made by Bishop Alcock concerning the lapsed condition, moral and material, of the Priory when he petitioned King Henry VII for license to convert it into a College; and the fact that the royal license to suppress the Hospital of S. John describes the decay of that house in terms which are almost literally repeated from Alcock's account of S. Radegund's Nunnery is perhaps calculated to throw suspicion on the credibility of both accounts. As regards Bishop Alcock's statements there is not the slightest foundation for such a suspicion. The alleged improvidence of the Nuns is established in the clearest manner on their own evidence, and if for the charge of moral shortcomings there is little evidence except the Bishop's it must be allowed that he made the charge in the first instance to them directly and many years before he made up his mind to dissolve their house. All the testimony of his contemporaries and immediate successors gives him the character of an exceptionally single-minded and devout prelate, and he had given pointed proof a few years previously that in dealing with the abuses of a religious house he was disposed to act in a spirit of forbearance and conservatism. In 1480, when he was Bishop of Worcester, he personally visited the Benedictine Priory of Little Malvern, the brethren of which were reported to have dissipated their revenues and to be living ' vagabond ' and like laymen. The Bishop ordered the Prior to be removed and sent to the Abbey of Battle, where he had been first professed, and the four monks, who were all that remained in the house, to be transferred to Gloucester Abbey until their Priory should be reconstituted. Alcock then proceeded to refound the convent; he rebuilt the church, altering its dedication from S. Giles to S. John the Evangelist and S. Giles, repaired the monks' lodging and discharged their debts. In 1482 the brethren were allowed to return and the Priory continued to exist more or less prosperously until the general dissolution, at which time it contained seven brethren besides the Prior. After this reformation of the Priory Bishop Alcock was regarded as its patron and founder; its common seal bore his arms, and his figure was portrayed in the windows of the conventual church.

In the absence of direct testimony an entry in the Register of Bishop Gray of Ely in the year 1461 suggests that symptoms of moral depravation began to show themselves very soon after the election of the Prioress Joan Lancastre. In that year Elizabeth Butlier, aged about 16, not having completed four years in the Nunnery and finding that she cannot serve God there with as much devotion as she wishes, obtains leave from the Bishop to transfer herself to the Nunnery of S. Helen's, London. (Register, fo. 157.)

The first evidence of the financial collapse of the Nuns'
household appears to be the following indenture of the Prioress
Elizabeth Walton, dated March 13, 1478 ; but if we are to
believe the account given by the Prioress the responsibility for
some part of their indebtedness belonged to her predecessors in
office :

'Whereas we and our predecessors, Prioresse and Nunnes of
the saide house at dyvers tymes tofore passed whan we ware
destitute of money for our pore lyffing had flessche of Richerd
Wodecok of Cambrigge, boucher, into the value of the summe
of xxj^{li} of lawful money of Englond, which he for our ease
many day hath forborn, And now he of his special favour and
elmesse for hym and his executours hath granted unto us
license for to paic unto him yeerly xix^s to tyme the said summe
be fully paied and content, as right and conscience requyre, We
therefore considering his benevolence and good wylle anendst
us in this behalve wol and by this our present writyng endented
graunt and have graunted unto the said Richerd Wodecok and
to his executors to have and to receyve of us and our succes-
sours by his awne hands yearly xix^s to be taken of thissues and
profites and ferme of a tenement sett and lyeng in the parissh of
Seynt Andrewe in the Prechour Strete of Cambrygge abuttyng
upon the Kyngs Dyche and of j other tenement lyeng in Seynt
Edwards parisshe of Cambrigge abuttyng upon the Chauncell
of the same chirche, Which tenements the said Richerd
Wodecok hath and holdeth of us to ferme by endenture for the
terme of yeeres as by severall endentures therof by us unto the
same Richerd his executours and assignes made hit appareth
more at large To have and to hold the said proufets issues and
ferme to the value of xix^s yeerly unto the time that the foresaid
Richerd by his awne hands be satisfied and content of the said
xxj^{li},' etc.

This and another indenture of the following year are the
latest of the Nuns' documents which bear the large seal of
the convent figured opposite p. 1. At some time between
1479 and 1485 the matrix of this seal was apparently lost or
sold, for to a deed of the latter year (Joan Cambrygg, Prioress)

is attached the impression of a very small and poorly executed seal, representing S. Radegund crowned and standing with both arms uplifted between two upright palm branches, which in the deed is said to be the common seal of the Nunnery.

More direct evidence of the pecuniary straits to which the convent was reduced in the last quarter of the 15th century is to be found in the accounts of Joan Key, who was treasurer in 1481—2. Her account roll, written on paper, alike in handwriting, arithmetic and Latinity is a performance which contrasts very unfavourably with that of her predecessor, 30 years before. The details moreover which it gives are very scant. But one thing is patent enough, viz. that the income of the Nuns had dropped from £74 odd at the earlier date to something over £31 at the later. It is true that the accounts of Joan Key for some reason extend over three-quarters of the year only, but it is an awkward circumstance that in those nine months her disbursements exceeded her receipts by more than £25. Ominous too is the fact that the sale of farm produce had practically ceased to be a source of income and that the Nuns were driven to purchase barley, oats, malt, etc. A small trifle is obtained from the sale of hay, and there are a few receipts for 'commons' of *perhendinantes*, boarders in the guest-house, two of them being daughters of the Nuns' benevolent creditor, Richard Wodecok. There is one new source of income, the charitable gifts of individuals, cleric and lay.

Bishop Alcock was translated to the see of Ely early in 1486. The death of the Prioress in the following year gave him an opportunity for decisive interference in the affairs of the Nunnery. He has left a record of his proceedings there in his Register (fo. 153) from which the following extracts are translated.

"On the twelfth day of October, A.D. 1487, the Bishop visited the house or monastery of the Nuns of S. Mary and S. Radegund, then destitute of a Prioress and vacant by the death of the late Prioress, Mistress Joan Cambrigge ... and sitting in the chapter-house of the foresaid monastery, on the tribunal, delivered his decree as follows.

"In the name of God Amen. We, John, by divine permission Bishop of Ely, on the 12th day of October, visiting in our right as ordinary (*jure ordinario*) the nunnery of S. Mary and S. Radegund, Cambridge, destitute of the solace of a Prioress, for certain, true, just, notorious and manifest causes find all and singular the Nuns unfit and disqualified to elect their future Prioress and therefore decree that in such manner of election they are justly deprived of voice. Wherefore we take upon ourselves the task of providing from some other like religious place a fit person for the vacancy in the said Nunnery, the right of electing and providing for the same Nunnery having devolved canonically upon us, and having the fear of God before our eyes we thus proceed.

"And you, Mistress Joan Fulborne, duly and lawfully professed of the order of S. Benedict and long time laudably conversant in the same, for your good religion and integrity, sincere virginity and other merits of prudence and holy conversation credibly reported to us we appoint and provide to be Prioress of the same house...

"And consequently, by mandate of the Bishop, the reverend Master William Robynson, bachelor in either law, conducted the same Joan Fulborne to the High Altar, while the Nuns, with others, solemnly chanted *Te Deum*, and assigned to her the stall in the choir and the place in the chapter anciently and of custom appointed to the Prioress, and canonically inducted her into the same with all its rights and appurtenances."

The history of the Nunnery from this year onwards to its dissolution is almost a blank. The accounts of the town treasurer for the year ending the Nativity of the Virgin, 1491, contain an entry, "In reward given the Lady Prioress of S. Radegund of Cambridge for keeping the common bull in the winter time this year, 16^{d1}." The Prioress in question was the Joan Fulborne above-mentioned, whose name occurs in several indentures of the Nunnery, the latest of which is dated

---

[1] Cooper's *Annals*, Vol. I. p. 240.

Aug. 6, 1493. Whether she died or retired from the Priory before the dissolution or was one of the two sisters who were the sole occupants of the Nuns' house at the time of Bishop Alcock's second visit does not appear[1]. It is certain that she was altogether unsuccessful in rehabilitating the character of the household committed to her charge.

The Proctors in their accounts for the year 1496 mention a sum of 16^d expended "for wine given the Bishop of Ely at the Nuns' house." The letters patent of Henry VII. for the foundation of Jesus College, dated June 12 in the eleventh year of his reign, i.e. 1496[2], reveal the condition of affairs reported by the Bishop to the King at the time, it would seem, of this visit. It is therein stated that the King, as well by the report of the Bishop as by public fame, is informed that the House or Priory of S. Radegund of the foundation and patronage of the Bishop, as in right of his church of Ely, together with all its lands, tenements, rents, possessions and buildings, and moreover the properties, goods, jewels and other ecclesiastical ornaments anciently of piety and charity given and granted to the same House or Priory, by the neglect, improvidence, extravagance and incontinence of the Prioresses and women of the said House, by reason of their proximity to the University of Cambridge, have been dilapidated, destroyed, wasted, alienated, diminished and subtracted; in consequence of which the Nuns are reduced

---

[1] Archbishop Parker, in the History of the University which is appended to his *Antiquitates Ecclesiae Britannicae*, states that Bishop Alcock ' Alexandro sexto papae retulit abbatissam sanctimonialium Radegondae, ordinis Sancti Benedicti, haud pie casteque vixisse; eaque decedente abbatiam ad ruinam paratam et a virginibus ordinem deserentibus desolatam fuisse, anno Domini 1496.' Apart from the error in the title of *abbess* Parker's whole account of the Nunnery is so inaccurate that no reliance can be placed on his evidence.

[2] In Rymer's *Foedera* the date is given as 1497; the same date is given in *Documents relating to the University and Town of Cambridge* (where the document is printed in full), in Caley's *Monasticon*, and by Cooper and most modern authorities. But the original in the College Treasury, with royal seal appended, reads beyond question 'anno regni nostri *undecimo*,' i.e. 1495—6. This accords with Sherman's statement that Alcock began to rebuild the fabric, 'instaurare fabricam coepit,' in the eleventh year of Henry VII.

to such want and poverty that they are unable to maintain and support divine services, hospitality and other such works of mercy and piety as by the primary foundation and ordinance of their founders are required; that they are reduced in number to two only, of whom one is elsewhere professed, the other is of ill-fame[1], and that they can in no way provide for their own sustenance and relief, insomuch that they are fain to abandon their House and leave it in a manner desolate.

John Mair, or Major, as his name was Latinized, who was resident at Christ's College for a few months in the early part of the 15th century, when the facts connected with the dissolution were within living recollection, says that the suggestion of converting the Nunnery into a College originated with Dr Stubs. The person indicated was no doubt William Chubbes, S. T. P., the first Master of the College, whose name occurs with a variety of spellings in the earliest deeds of the College.

Sherman, in his Latin History of the College, makes the statement, which has since been copied in other books about Cambridge, that by direction of the Founder the College was dedicated to the Blessed Virgin Mary, S. John the Evangelist and the glorious S. Radegund, and took its popular name of Jesus College from the *conventual* church which was dedicated to the Name of Jesus. For the latter part of this assertion there is not the slightest evidence. The testimony of the Nuns' muniments shows conclusively that the Nunnery, the parish and the lane were as late as the beginning of Henry VII's reign known simply by their old title of S. Radegund's, nor is there any ground for supposing that the church itself received a fresh dedication so long as the Nunnery existed. In the preamble to the Statutes which

---

[1] It is scarcely worth while correcting the many errors in Fuller's account of the Nunnery, but it deserves to be mentioned that his jest, "Tradition saith that of the two [nuns] remaining one was *with child*, the other but a *child*," is based on the misreading of *infamis* in the letters patent as *infans*. Godwin had made the same mistake before Fuller, and *infans* is the reading wrongly given in *Documents relating to the University and Colleges of Cambridge*.

Bishop Stanley of Ely gave to the College in 1514 it is stated that the church of the *College* is consecrated to the Name of Jesus, and that the College is erected and founded in honour of the Blessed Virgin Mary, S. John the Evangelist and S. Radegund, but that it shall be called Jesus College and the Fellows and Scholars shall be called *Scholares Jesu*[1].

A Compotus roll for the year Henry VII, 13—14, *i.e.* 1497—8, apparently the first of the newly founded College, exists in the College Treasury. It throws an interesting light on the financial situation inherited by the College from the Nuns, though unfortunately it gives no information as to the condition of the conventual buildings. The Nunnery indeed is not once alluded to in it, nor is there any express acknowledgement of the fact that the Nuns' property had passed into new hands. The computant has no arrears to account for; in the margin, opposite the heading, 'Collegium Jĥu' occupies the place of 'Prioratus Sēē Radegundis'; otherwise there is no recognition of the changes which had just occurred. The collector is one William Pykerell, who was a Fellow of the College soon after its foundation, but against many of the

---

[1] There seems to have been some uncertainty at first as to the formal title of the College. In the King's letters patent it is described as 'Collegium Beatissime Marie Virginis, Sancti Johannis Evangeliste et Gloriose Virginis Sancte Radegundis.' But in an address of the Master, William Chubbes, and Fellows to the King, of which there is a transcript in the Ely Episcopal Registers (Alcock, fol. 123), belonging apparently to the year 1497, it is called 'Collegium Jesu, Beate Marie Virginis et Sancti Johannis Evangeliste.' Popularly the College seems from the first to have been known only as Jesus College. The name Jesus Lane occurs in the town accounts of 1497: Jesus church and Jesus parish are mentioned in documents of the early years of the 16th century, though, inconsistently enough, there is mention of the parish church of S. Radegund in cap. 19 of Bishop Stanley's Statutes. The original College seal, of which an impression exists in the College Treasury attached to a deed *temp.* Henry VIII., bears the legend, SIGILLVM COLLEGII IHV: MARIE ET IOHIS: EVAG. CANTEBR. In its upper portion are represented under canopies the Virgin and S. John standing on either side of the Saviour, and the base displays a shield bearing the Five Wounds. Archbishop Rotherham's foundation of Jesus College, Rotherham, dates from 1498. Rotherham was Lord Chancellor conjointly with Alcock, and appointed him executor of his will. He was also provost of the collegiate church of Beverley, Alcock's native town.

entries of receipts is set the name or initial of Griggeson, one of the original Fellows, who evidently helped in rent-collecting. Beyond payment of quit-rents, fifteenths, &c. and a few incidental expenses of collection there are no disbursements. There is however mention of certain sums of money, amounting in all to £9. 6s. 8d., paid to Henry Lecheman, who was another of the original Fellows. The purpose of these payments is not stated. They may have been connected with the building of the College, but the absence of fabric charges seems to show that the costs of adapting the conventual buildings to College uses were borne mainly by the Founder or his friends. There are no payments to College officials; neither Griggeson nor Lecheman is described as Fellow, and William Chubbes, who is mentioned, is not styled Master. A sum of £43. 8s. 8d. is advanced to John Ware of Fulburn for farm stock. An indenture of the same year (Henry VII, 14) shows that in consideration of this advance Ware released to the College a farm of 21 acres at Fulburn, of which the College gave him a lease for 8 years. The remaining balance, amounting to £25. 17s. 10¾d., is retained in the hands of Pykerell and Griggeson. The entries under the head of rent receipts show that the College receivers found the Nuns' affairs in a singularly chaotic state which they had not as yet succeeded in reducing to order. There is a long list of tenements whose rent is held over for the time owing to an uncertainty as to the sum, 'eo quod feodum ignoratum est.' Nine tenements in Jesus Lane return no rent, as being vacant. The former occupants seem to have been servants employed by the Nuns.

As late as the year 1511 among the inmates of the Benedictine Nunnery of Davington, Kent, at the time of its visitation by Archbishop Warham, was one Elizabeth Awdeley, who had been professed at Cambridge. As she had been resident at Davington for 20 years she must have been one of the sisters who abandoned S. Radegund's before its dissolution [1].

[1] *Visitation of Archbishop Warham*, by Miss M. Bateson in *English Historical Review*, Vol. vi. p. 27.

§ 16. *Radegund Manor.   Garlick Fair.   Radegund Tithes.*

The name and memory of the Nuns' house were still perpetuated at the beginning of the present century in the manor of S. Radegund and the Radegund tithes, and with the former was still associated another survival of Nunnery days, the fair on the festival of the Assumption. The manor and the fair have long since passed away : the tithe, attenuated into a formal payment of insignificant amount, still exists. All three institutions in their origin were rooted in the beginnings of the Nunnery, and I have thought it on that account worth while to put together here the few noteworthy facts concerning them which I have been able to discover.

The manor of S. Radegund consisted of the old demesne lands of the Nuns, and generally its boundaries coincided with those of S. Radegund parish, but it did not include the dwelling-houses in Jesus Lane. As the Nuns did not let it to tenants it was not styled a manor in their time, nor was there on it any dwelling of the nature of a manor-house. The old manor-house of S. Radegund, which stood nearly on the site of the present All Saints' vicarage, was destroyed in 1831. Its last tenant was the Rev. Isaac Leathes, a former Fellow of the College, who parted with the remainder of his lease of the manor to the College in Dec. 1830. To his descendant, the Rev. Prof. Stanley Leathes, now an Honorary Fellow of Jesus College, I am indebted for the loan of a water-colour sketch of the house, taken from the north, of which the engraving opposite is a reproduction. An aged servant of the College, recently deceased, who well remembered the old manor-house, described it to me as being, just before its demolition, in a dilapidated state, and the garden as a wilderness. Near the end of the grounds where Manor Street has since been built the same authority told me that there was a handsome fountain. The two projecting wings of the house are shown in the sketch to be red brick ; the central portion was apparently stuccoed.

In the first College lease book there is a transcript of a lease of the manor, dated 1555, in which it is stated that the manor-house had then been newly built by Mr Edmund Perpoynte, Master of the College, at his own charge, amounting to £400[1]. It took the place of an older house which recently had been 'utterly burnt by casualtie of fire.' All the dominical lands were included in this lease with these exceptions—the ground enclosed within mud walls, commonly called the churchyard, all woods and underwoods, the inner court, the Master's and Fellows' gardens, and the close at the west side of the school house, *i.e.* the western part of the present Fellows' garden. As the ground occupied by the entrance court of the College was not excepted it is probable that the farm buildings in the Nuns' *curia* were still standing and in use, or others in their place. Except the gatehouse and school adjoining it no College buildings stood there.

The fair on the festival of the Assumption of the Virgin Mary was granted to the Nuns by charter of King Stephen. This charter is not now extant, but the fact is recorded in the Hundred Rolls[2]. The circumstance that the fair was held on the vigil and feast of the Assumption, i.e. August 14 and 15, seems to indicate, as already stated, that the Nunnery church was originally dedicated to S. Mary, but it is to be noted that Aug. 14 was also the day on which S. Radegund was commemorated. A third day was added to the duration of the fair by charter of Henry VI., dated the sixteenth year of his reign (Charters, 9).

The name Garlick Fair, by which it was generally known in its last days, occurs first in an entry in the Bursar's accounts for 1577–8.

---

[1] Bentham, *History of Ely*, Appendix, p. 46, mentions that in a window of the manor-house, in the year 1744, were blazoned the arms of Bishop Goodrich of Ely. Goodrich was Fellow of Jesus in 1510, and Bishop of Ely 1534—1554.

[2] *H. R.* II. p. 359, 'Item predicte Priorissa et Moniales habent quandam feriam ad festum Asumpcionis Beate Marie Virginis duraturam per duos dies, sc. in vigilia Asumpcionis Beate Marie cum die sequenti quam quidem feriam habent ex concessione Stephani quondam Regis Anglie per cartam quam habent de Rege predicto.'

"for ledding ij payns in the sowth wyndowe there (*i.e.* in the chapel) next to the garlicke fayre closse, &c., iijs. vjd."

The close here referred to and otherwise known as 'the churchyard' occupied the position of the eastern portion of what is now the Master's garden, on the southern side of the chapel. It was entered by gates opening on Jesus Lane. In the Nuns' accounts for 1449–50 there is a charge of 12d. for a lock and key for these gates ('pro portis vocatis feyregates'). They stood on the site of the still existing wooden door on the western side of the iron gates through which the new approach from Jesus Lane to the Chapel Court is entered. As late as 1803 this gate was described by the then Bursar as 'Garlic Fair Gate.' The churchyard was enclosed with mud walls dividing it on one side from the Master's garden, on the other from the 'Master's close,' or 'pond yard.' Probably the fair had been held there from the first, but after the inclusion of the site in the Master's garden it seems to have been transferred to the western margin of the College close, adjoining the King's Ditch, where it gave its name to Garlic Fair Lane, now Park Street.

As a trade mart the fair seems never to have had any importance. Though the Nuns and, after them, the College in its earlier days were considerable buyers at both Midsummer and Sturbridge fairs, and on occasions even resorted to S. Audrey's fair at Ely, they seem never to have marketed at the fair which was held in their own grounds. The tolls received by the Nuns in 1449–50 amounted only to 5s. 2d., and in the following year to 5s. In the earlier year the toll collectors received 6d. as wage; a cook hired to help in the kitchen at the fair time also received 3d. In the 16th and earlier part of the 17th century the profits of the fair, including 'waiffs and straythes,' were regularly included in the lease of the manor. After 1635 there appears in the accounts an annual entry of £1 received as profits of the fair, which, with not unfrequent omissions in the later years, continues until 1709, after which it ceases [1]. But until 1838, when the manor-

---

[1] In the College Register, July 16, 1642, occurs an entry, 'Rogerus Har-

house was destroyed and the close thenceforth let on an annual
tenancy, in every lease of the manor there was a covenant that
the College 'shall have liberty to keep a fair within and over
the close, or such part thereof as hath been used for that
purpose, on the feast day of the Assumption of the Blessed
Virgin Mary yearly, or at such other time or times as it may
keep the same.' The fair seems to have been still in existence
at the beginning of the present century, about which time
Bowtell writes (MSS. pp. 205—11), 'On the 14th, 15th and 16th
August this Fair is still constantly observed by the Inhabitants
of Jesus Lane, who claim it as a Privilege belonging peculiarly
to their Situation and invite Strangers to partake of their
Festivity in strong ale and cheerless (*sic*) Frumenty. But
these Meetings are now attended with far less Rejoicings than
they were formerly, when Minstrels and Musicians were
engaged to heighten the celebration,' &c. The New Cambridge
Guide, published in 1809, speaks ambiguously of its existence
at that date. 'There was formerly another festival, called
Garlick Fair, celebrated here; which was granted by Henry VI.
to the Nuns of St Radegund, and held in Jesus Lane, on the
14th of August and two following days; but this is now nearly
abolished.'

The Radegund tithes were commonly leased by the College
to the tenant of the manor. Like the tithes of all the
Cambridge churches they were drawn from the common fields
of the town. These fields, tilled by the possessors on the open
field system, extended on all sides round the town as far as the
borough limits. The fields on the north and west sides of the
town were collectively known as Cambridge fields, and on their
inner side were bounded by a watercourse extending from
Queens' Green to the Bin Brook, and from thence by the Bin
Brook to its junction with the river. The fields on the south
and east sides of the town were anciently known as Barnwell
fields; their inner boundary coincided generally with the
course of the King's Ditch from the point where it leaves the

rison constitutus est Ballivus noster pro Garlicke faire hoc anno 1642.' No
other appointment by the College of a bailiff for the fair is recorded.

river at the King's Mill to the place where it rejoins it at the
angle of Jesus Green.   The Cambridge and the Barnwell
fields were to the last cultivated as distinct, and separate Acts
of Parliament were required for their enclosure, the former
in 1802, the latter in 1807.   Both Acts contained provisions
for making allotments in lieu of tithes, but the great tithes
belonging to Jesus College in the Barnwell fields were specially
retained in the Act of 1807, and, as 'Radegund tithes,' exist
at the present day.   The tithes of Cambridge fields were
known as the tithes of S. Giles and the tithes of S. Radegund, the former apparently including the parishes of S.
Giles, S. Peter and All Saints next the Castle, the churches
of which were appropriated to S. Giles' Priory, Barnwell,
while the latter would represent the tithes of S. Clement's,
which belonged to the almoner of S. Radegund's Priory.   The
tithes of Barnwell fields on the other hand belonged exclusively
to the southern parishes.   The old tithe books show that they
belonged to the churches of S. Andrew the Great, S. Mary next
the Market, S. Mary the Less, S. Bene't and the Holy Trinity,
to the almoner of Barnwell Priory, as impropriator of S. Edward's, S. Sepulchre's, S. John's and S. Botolph's, and to
S. Radegund's Nunnery, in right, no doubt, of All Saints' Church
in Jewry.   In a printed report of an action (Anderson v.
Broadbelt) which took place in 1816, with respect to the right
of Jesus College to the Radegund tithe in Barnwell fields, it is
stated that 'the Inhabitants of All Saints' parish in perambu-
lating their boundaries had uniformly included the fields of
Barnwell in consequence of their right to the Rates on those
Tithes.'

GRAVEYARD
OF THE NUNS

PARISH CHURCH YARD OR FAIRYARD

f
H
e

a
CHAPTER HOUSE
G
b

A C F
D E c d

CLOISTER YARD

REFECTORY with cellars below

CONVENTUAL QUIRE

B O

PARISH CHURCH

P O j N M L K
h
g
J

k
k'
Q

ENTRANCE

R

COURT

"The Chimney"

S

A. Latrina.
B. Well.
C. ? Novices' Dorter on upper floor.
D. 'The Cloister end'.
E. Dark Entry.
F. ? Calefactory.
G. ? Vestry.
H. Sacristan's chamber.
J. Vestibule.

K. Camera of Prioress.
L. 'The Entry'.
M. ? Cheker of Cellaress.
N. 'The Cook's Chamber'.
O. Pincerna.
P. Kitchen.
Q. ? Guest Hall of Prioress.
R. Outer Gates.
S. ? Almonry.

███████ Existing Walls and Foundations.
▢▨▨▢ Hypothetical.

Fig. III. PLAN OF THE NUNNERY BUILDINGS.

To face page 53.

THE BUILDINGS OF THE NUNNERY.

The scope of the *Architectural History* in the chapters dealing with Jesus College, except in the case of the Chapel, does not include any detailed account of the Nunnery buildings. Though such an account was outside the plan adopted by the authors in the case of other colleges it is matter for much regret that Professor Willis left no notes for the treatment of this subject, on which he could have written with the authority of a master.

In the preamble to the Statutes of Nicholas West, Bishop of Ely 1515–1533, the statement is made that the College was ' paene ab ipsis fundamentis noviter aedificatum et constructum ' by the Founder himself. Apparently the construction to be put upon the words ' noviter aedificatum ' is that from the ground-floor upwards Alcock reconstructed the Nuns' buildings in such a way as to give them the appearance of being new ; unless the expression is inaccurate it cannot mean that a new fabric was raised on the old foundations. The former, at least, is the only interpretation which can be reconciled with what is known of Alcock's operations in the case of the Chapel; it corresponds equally with the facts brought to light by recent discoveries connected with the domestic buildings occupying Nunnery sites. It is probable enough, though the fact is not stated in the royal letters patent, that the Nuns left their dwellings in such a state of disrepair as to be scarcely habitable ; that was an incident common to college as well as monastic buildings, and as late as the reign of Edward VI. the Bursars' accounts show that a considerable number of chambers were unoccupied ' per defectum reparacionis.' But the poverty and neglect of a quarter of a century which, no doubt, had made havock of thatched roofs and stud-partitions could have had little effect on the outward walls of

solid clunch, which, under a facing of later brick, still testify
to the durability of the work of the Nunnery builders, and
Alcock had too much practical skill to destroy buildings
which could easily be adapted to the needs of a college, and
harmonized to 15th century fashions in architecture. In the
Refectory, in the whole of the ranges occupying the eastern
and western sides of the cloister, and in their prolongations
northwards into the third or kitchen court the walls of the
Nunnery still rise to their original height. Alcock, or the
builders who succeeded him, cased them with brick, and, as a
third storey was added to the two in which the Nunnery for
the most part was contained, it was necessary to heighten the
whole structure with a few feet of brickwork. A flat roof
having been substituted on the chapel for one of high pitch the
opportunity was taken of bringing the roofs of all the buildings which surround the cloister to a uniform level. In interior
arrangement Alcock worked with a somewhat freer hand, but
with some help from documentary evidence it is not difficult
beneath his alterations and those of later times to trace the
plan of the Nunnery and to locate its principal parts.

The documents which serve this purpose are:

(1) The accounts of the Nunnery Treasuresses, printed on
pp. 145-178.

(2) The statutes of Bishop Stanley (*circa* 1514), which
contain some interesting details as to the chambers assigned to
the various inmates of the College.

(3) The College Bursars' accounts.

The earliest volume of the Bursars' accounts dates from
1557, from which year they are continued in uninterrupted
succession to the present time. The authors of the *Architectural History* have largely availed themselves of the
materials contained in these volumes. They do not appear
to have been acquainted with the existence of a series of
Bursars' Computus rolls, some on vellum, others on paper,
beginning with the year 1534-1535, and continuing thence
to 1548-1549. Unlike the later accounts these rolls are

written in Latin and contain no details of expenditure on repairs and building. But for our purpose they have a special importance in that they contain a complete Rental of the chambers in the College, specifying their locality and mentioning, besides the *camerae* of the Fellows and students, the offices of the College which were not subject to rent. The apartments which they enumerate are those occupying the four sides of the cloister-court, together with those contained in the building which continues the eastern cloister range at the east end of the Hall and into the third court, and the Kitchen range at the west end of the Hall. The chambers allotted to the Master are not stated in detail, and there is no mention of any buildings in the entrance court, except on its eastern side.

It is unfortunate that the Nunnery accounts give us hardly any information which will help us to realise the appearance, or determine the situation, of the various monastic offices. Besides the church the only buildings mentioned in them are the Refectory, the Aula (i.e. the Guest or Cellarer's Hall), the chamber over the outer gates, the Hospicium (a general term for all the buildings external to the cloister—brewing and candle-making were carried on there), the Latrina, the Kitchen, the Cow-house, the Malt-kiln, the Garner (Orreum) and the Barn (Granatorium). The Infirmary and Chapter-house are referred to in several deeds. Of the Dorter, the Parlour, the Warming-house, the Sacristy and the Lodging of the Prioress the Nunnery documents make no mention.

Before proceeding to the buildings grouped about the cloister we may in few words say all that is known of the outer yard or *curia* of the Nunnery. With the authors of the *Architectural History* we may fairly certainly assume that it occupied the position of the entrance court of the College. The accounts for the year 1449–50 mention certain 'magnas portas exteriores' with a building (*domus*) adjoining them, which in that year was thatched with sedge. In the following year's accounts is an item for reeds for the repair of the chamber 'desuper portas exteriores huius monasterii.' As there seems to have been only a single chamber above these gates it would appear that the entrance was not marked by any tower, and resembled the gateways of the older colleges, such as Pembroke and Corpus[1]. The Gatehouse no doubt occupied the position of the present Gate-tower, and was approached from the road by the passage which is now known as 'the Chimney[2].' This passage served also as an approach to the door at the west end of the Nave, which was the entrance to the Church for the parishioners. On its east side was the churchyard.

On the west side of the gate in the earliest College days existed a small building of two storeys (plan, S) which was the grammar-school, founded by the Lady Katherine, widow of Sir Reginald Bray. Sherman states that the school-house was built by the latter; but as the deeds relating to the foundation do not state the fact it must be regarded as to some extent doubtful. Possibly Sir Reginald Bray merely adapted one of the Nunnery buildings, perhaps the Almonry, for the purpose.

On the east side of the Gate Tower is a wing of the Lodge, containing the dining-room on the ground floor (plan, Q). The Statutes of Bishop Stanley show that this wing was occupied by the Master in the first years of the existence of the College. During alterations to the Lodge which were carried out in the course of the year 1886 two window arches were discovered on the inner side of the northern wall of the dining-room (plan, k, k'). They were narrow and lofty, the crown reaching two or three feet above the ceiling. Unfortunately they were covered before any notes or drawings were made of them, but it is sufficiently clear that they must have been blocked early in the 16th century, as three windows of that date have been inserted in the wall. The loftiness of the apartment which they lighted shows that it must have been one of some dignity, and its contiguity to the Lodging of the Prioress suggests that it may have been the Guest Hall of the

---

[1] See *Arch. Hist.* Vol. III. p. 283.

[2] If there were any evidence for the antiquity of the name it might be conjectured that it was descended from the L.-L. *chiminum*, a road; but it does not occur in the Bursars' books before last century.

Prioress. At the N.W. corner of this room is a blocked doorway opening on the passage under the Gate-tower. In the Statutes of Bishop West (chap. 10) it is provided that the Master's servant shall act as *exceptor* or *janitor*. A corresponding arrangement may have existed in the Nunnery: it is at least noteworthy that Jesus is the only Cambridge College in which the Lodge adjoins the Gate.

The Bursars' Rentals already mentioned always begin their enumeration of the College chambers with those which are described as being in 'le North Corner Claustri desuper le Coolehouse.' Next follow those at the east end of the Hall and on the east side of the cloister-court, and then successively those on the south side of the cloister, 'next the west end of the Church,' and those on its west and north sides. There is no mention of staircases, but the rooms are distinguished in the order 'lower,' 'middle' and 'upper.' Each chamber may be readily localized, as there has been practically little alteration of the internal arrangement of this part of the College since the first half of the 16th century.

The 'North Corner' of the cloister mentioned in the Bursars' Rolls is manifestly that portion of the range on the E. side of the cloister which is continued on the N. side of the Hall, and is now known as staircase K. At the extremity of this range, next the modern (1822) building which continues it northwards, there is a low wooden door on the ground-level, which opens on a flight of steps descending about 4 ft. 6 in. below the present ground-surface outside. Descending these steps we find ourselves in what resembles a narrow passage (plan, A), flanked on either side by clunch walls about 4 ft. apart and closed at its further end by the E. wall of the range. The floor of the adjoining rooms on the first floor of staircase K is carried across the passage, so that those rooms are larger than those below them by the space contained between the walls. The wall opposite the door of entrance is pierced by a very small aperture at the height of 12 ft. from the ground on the inner side. From the parallel walls spring the remains of ancient brick arches which have formerly spanned the vault.

In this hardly altered relic of the Nunnery it is easy to recognise the conventual *latrina* mentioned in the accounts of 1450–1451. It continued to be used for the same purpose at least as late as 1567–8. In the accounts of that year it is distinguished as 'the olde privye' from a new 'howse of office' which was then being built in the same quarter of the College[1].

The floor of the *latrina* consists of natural gravel, almost undisturbed. The channel of which it was the bed was conducted from the *fons* often mentioned in the Nuns' accounts. This *fons*, which furnished the water supply of the Nunnery, is still represented by a disused pump on the N. side of the Hall (plan, B), which gave its name to the 'Pump Court,' as the third court of the College was till recently called. From this *fons*, which perhaps was an open trough or cistern, an open channel, called in the accounts of 1572–3 'y° kytching sinke ditche,' or 'the Bog-house ditch' (1650–1), traversed the court in the direction of the *latrina*. In the accounts for 1708–9 are charges for 'covering in y° drayn from y° kitchen and pump.' Beyond the *latrina* the ditch passed into a 'pit' or 'pond.'

As the *latrina* in monasteries adjoined the Dorter it is fairly certain that the latter was contained in the range of which the *latrina* and the N. transept of the Church are the extremities. Like all monastic dormitories it was on the upper floor, and was probably divided in the manner described in the *Rites of Durham* by transverse partitions of wainscote into a double row of chambers, each lighted by a window in the wall adjoining. In the staircase in the N.E. angle of the cloister may be seen a wall recess which appears to mark the position of one of these windows, consisting of a single narrow light (plan, *a*).

---

[1] As there were two distinct sets of shafts descending to the ditch from the closets above, one set in front of the other, like those found in medieval buildings of more than two storeys, it would appear that there were two upper storeys of closets, and that consequently the E. range of the cloister to which these closets formed the termination was, in this part at least, arranged in three storeys. The clunch wall at the N. is carried up to the present roof.

The Dorter seems to have extended over the Chapter-house, but not so far as to the gable-wall of the N. transept. The surmise of the authors of the *Architectural History* that the Nuns had an access from the Dorter to the transept by the circular staircase, or 'vice,' in the N.E. angle of the latter is devoid of foundation. The unaltered wall on the Dorter side of this 'vice' shows no trace of a doorway, and the narrow and dark stair would be a most inconvenient means of entering the church. There is indeed in the N.W. angle of the transept a door, now blocked (plan, *b*), which may very likely have admitted the Nuns from the Dorter without the necessity of passing through the cloister. But, as at first designed, the Dorter clearly did not abut on the transept. The cills of the triplet of Norman windows in this wall are at such a height as to make it clear that there was no building next it on the level of the upper floor. As moreover the 'vice' has a narrow aperture in the same wall, above the first floor level, designed to light the stairs, it can only have had a ground-floor building next it on the N. side. This building (plan, G) probably contained a staircase descending from the Dorter to the transept door[1].

At its N. end the Nuns' Dorter must have been closed by the wall which extends the line of the N. wall of the Hall. This is now the only transverse wall of solid masonry in the range, and unquestionably is of Nunnery date. But it is only on the ground floor that it appears as a continuous wall of clunch. On the upper floors the portion of it nearest the Hall, 10 feet in breadth, is merely a stud-partition with a thin clunch wall on the ground floor below; in the eastern portion the thicker clunch continues to the full height of the Dorter. Here the Nunnery arrangement seems to be practically unaltered. The space next to the E. wall of the

---

[1] The clunch wall of the cloister between the Chapter House and the N. transept was stripped of its plaster in 1894, and was seen to consist of rough materials of all kinds, including a half-worked Norman capital. It bore no trace of either door or window. But there was nothing to show that the exposed face was more than a refacing of post-Nunnery date.

Refectory, having no windows to light it, was perhaps not used
for sleeping chambers, and served as a passage to the *latrina*
and the room next the Dorter on its N. side (plan, C). This
room, if the usual monastic arrangement was followed, may
have been the Dorter of the Novices. Above it, as already
shown, there was a room on the second floor.

The arrangement indicated above remained very little
altered in the 16th century, as is shown by documentary
evidence of that date. I shall not apologise for quoting this
evidence, as in interesting details it illustrates the continuity
of collegiate with monastic life which was, perhaps is, a feature
distinguishing Jesus from other Cambridge colleges.

The existence of a chamber of more than ordinary importance, next to the *latrina*, is indicated by cap. 28 of
Bishop Stanley's Statutes. This statute, which gives particular directions as to the assignment of chambers in the
College, contains the following clause:

"Omnes camerae (exceptis tribus de principalioribus, camera videlicet
ex parte boreali summi Altaris, camera ad occidentalem partem Aulae
quam modo Mr Fitzherbert inhabitat et camera proxima communem
latrinam quam modo Mr Ogle tenet quas volumus pro venerabilioribus
personis ad Collegium nostrum praedictum confluentibus custodiri) nisi
alias magistro placuerit, praefatis sociis, perhendinantibus et scholaribus
per praefatum magistrum distribuantur."

As regards the last of the chambers indicated, that,
namely, which adjoined the *latrina*, the directions of the
statute seem generally to have been observed in the 16th
century. During the years 1544–1550 it was occupied by
a certain Mr Badcocke, who is probably to be identified with
John Badcocke, the last prior of Barnwell, who surrendered
his house to the crown in 1538 and was subsequently incum-
bent of S. Andrew's the Less, Barnwell[1]. In 1572 it was
occupied by Lord Wharton, and in 1576–9 by Bancroft, afterwards Archbishop of Canterbury, who, though distinguished as
a tutor, and, as a continuator of Sherman's *Historia* observes,

[1] Cooper, *Athenae Cantab.*, Vol. I. p. 219.

'potestate plane magistrali pollens,' was never a Fellow of the College. The Bursars' Rentals of 1535–1550 show certain circumstances connected with this guest-chamber which distinguish it from other rooms in the College. As a matter of fact it consisted of two chambers, on the middle and upper floor respectively, and the tenant also sometimes rented the coal-house below them. Each of the chambers is called a 'half-chamber' (*medietas camerae*), but, as the tenant paid for each the same rent as other tenants on the same floors, it would seem that the half-chambers were not inferior in size to ordinary College chambers. The explanation of the designation 'half-chamber' seems to lie in the fact that a portion of the middle and upper floor-space was required for the passage connecting this quarter of the College with the rooms in the upper floors of the eastern cloister-range. This passage, here about 8 feet wide, is still to be distinguished in the gyp-rooms of the four upper chambers at the N. end of the range, which, unlike those on the lower floor, are of substantial masonry. The passage on the second floor was entered from the chamber, now a lumber-room, at the E. end of the Hall through a wooden doorcase, of 16th century design, set in the stud-wall already mentioned as continuing the N. wall of the Hall. This stud-wall apparently did not exist in the Nunnery or early College days, for in the angle next the oriel of the Hall there was formerly, on each of the upper floors a window, the upper one of smaller size, so splayed as to light the dark portion of the passage extending along the E. wall of the Hall[1]. At the end of this passage, on the top floor and over the *latrina*, there is a very small chamber, approached through a stone door-case and lighted from the third court by a diminutive window. Its

---

[1] These windows now exist only as cupboard recesses on the inner side of the wall. But externally they may be recognized by the brick which has been used for blocking them being of a different colour from the rest of the wall. In the highest storey of the building next the W. end of the Hall there is still a passage which leads from the N. wall of the range, over the kitchen as far as the N.W. angle of the cloister-court, and in the N. and S. ends of the gable wall of the Hall there are small windows splayed in the manner above described.

position and dimensions sufficiently prove it to have been a *necessarium*.

Apart from the convenience of a covered approach to the *latrina*, the passage was rendered necessary by the fact that the gate leading from the Nuns' cloister to the third court was always locked at night. The frequent mention in the Bursars' accounts of purchases of keys and repairs to the lock of the "cloisters gate" seems to show that in the earlier College period no egress was permitted at night beyond the cloister-court.

The description in the Bursars' Rolls of this quarter of the College as the 'North Corner Claustri' is an indication of the fact, otherwise established by entries in the Audit books, that a cloister-walk existed here in the 16th century, as, no doubt, had been the case in Nunnery times. The Audit books call this 'the cloister end,' and it adjoined 'the woodyard[1].' It was otherwise described as a 'lane' or 'gallery[2],' both of which words were once used to denote a cloister-walk[3]. This external cloister was an extension of the eastern walk of the cloister-quadrangle, with which it communicated by a passage under the dais of the Hall (i.e. the Refectory), an arrangement common in monasteries. This passage remained in use at least as late as 1648–9, when it was known as the 'Dark Entry[4],' the name which was

---

[1] Accounts 1572–3: 'To Barraker slatinge in the woodyarde over the cloister ende going up to my lord Wharton's chamber...mending the foundations of the cloisters on the outside towards the inner corte and mending the foundation of the wall in the entrie going up to my lord Wharton's chamber,' &c.

[2] Accounts 1567–8: 'Barnes bill for...underpinninge the walles of the lane going to the house of office and for tiling,' &c. Same year: 'Imprimis vij daies before Whitsondaie when Thomas Gallant wrought pulling down the slate of the gallerie and the walle goinge to the walle of the olde howse of office,' &c. In 1576-7 mention occurs of 'y° Layne going down to y° Bocardes.' 'Bocardo,' 'the Bocardes,' a euphemistic Italianization of the vernacular 'bogard,' occurs often in the accounts. Dr Murray's Dictionary does not recognize the word 'Bocardo' except in the more familiar sense of 'prison.' But the last passage quoted *s. v.* in Halliwell and Nare's *Glossary* makes the other meaning plain.

[3] See *Architectural History*, Vol. III. p. 338.

[4] Accounts 1648—9: 'For two latties for y° window in y° dark entry, 6°.'

given at Canterbury to the covered way which led under the
Dorter from the Great Cloister to the Infirmary. It was
entered from the cloister quadrangle through a door-case
which now gives access to the staircase in the N.E. angle
of the court. This staircase is called in the Bursars' accounts
of last century 'the Parlour staircase' from the circumstance
that it then gave access to the Combination Room through a
door, now blocked, on the first floor. It is generally known
in College as 'Cow Lane.' The latter name was given to a
passage next the Porter's lodge in the Old Court of King's
College. Perhaps it was originally applied to the Dark Entry,
which was entered from the cloister through the same doorway as the staircase, 'lane' being, as already stated, one of
the names by which the passage to the 'house of office' was
known. A more modern door under the oriel of the Hall
marks the exit of the Dark Entry on the outer side. The
clunch walls flanking the passage still remain in the Buttery
beneath the Hall, though the central portion of each has been
removed in order to give uninterrupted communication with
the cellar beyond, and the passage has been blocked by recent
walls at either end.

The room on the E. side of the Dark Entry (plan, F), now
a cellar, was entered from it by a door of which traces remain
in the clunch wall. In the early part of the 16th century this
room, as well as the Combination Room and garret above it,
was occupied as an ordinary college-chamber. The present
floor of the cellar is three feet lower than the pavement of the
cloister walk, but its original level was higher, as is shown by
the position in the E. wall of a window, now blocked, and in
the N. wall of a fireplace. The latter has a nearly flat arch
plainly chamfered in the clunch: on its eastern side is a small
locker. We may conjecture that this room was the Nuns'
Common House or Calefactory.

On the inner side of the E. wall of the cloister, directly
facing the northern walk, there may be seen a wide and
plainly chamfered arch of stone (plan, c). Its crown has been
cut away to make the window looking into the cloister. If

the S. wall of the room which we conjecture to have been
the Common House was in line with the S. wall of the
Refectory, there can only have been space between it and
the Chapter House for a passage. It seems probable, therefore, that this archway was the entrance to the passage from
the cloister to the Garden and the Cemetery. The burial-
ground of the Nuns was pretty certainly at the N.E. end of
the Church, that of the parish at the S.E. end; human remains
were dug up on the former site in 1884, and on the latter in
the years 1848–50.

The circumstances which led to the remarkable discovery
in April 1893 of the beautiful arcade which was the cloister-
front of the Chapter House need not here be detailed. Subsequent excavations carried on in July 1894 brought to light
the lower courses of the walls of the eastern portion of the
Chapter House projecting into the Chapel Court. These excavations showed that the Chapter House measured 37 feet
by 25 feet. At the N.E. and S.E. angles there was a pair of
buttresses of slight projection which showed that the building
was of early 13th century date. Running along the eastern
wall on its inner side was a stone bench. The whole of the
west end was occupied by three arches, the middle one forming
a doorway, and those at the sides containing each a window
of two lights with a quatrefoil above. The arches and tracery
spring from rich clusters of detached shafts, most of the capitals of which are carved with foliage, while a few are moulded.
Two capitals in the northernmost pier are remarkable. They
themselves are finished, but their design would seem to have
been suggested by an unfinished carved capital. One of the
annulets which divide the longer shafts broke at some time,
and a continuous shaft was substituted for the two lengths.
It will be noticed that there was no door in the entrance,
and no shutters or glass in the windows. During the excavations at the east end there were found a number of frag-
ments of lancet windows divided by small shafts. These are
of the same period as the other remains of the Chapter House,
and it is probable that they are parts of the eastern window.

They are now preserved on the floor within the entrance. A low stone bench (plan, *d*) extends along the cloister wall from the Chapter House towards the north transept. A tombstone with floriated cross, possibly not in its original position, lies before the entrance; the partial excavation of the site brought to light no tombstones within the Chapter House.

The existing portions of the conventual church have been so fully described by Professor Willis[1] that it is sufficient here to record the few facts which have been discovered since he wrote.

The statute of Bishop Stanley quoted on p. 60 mentions a chamber on the northern side of the High Altar which was set apart for the use of distinguished guests of the College. In the summer of 1894 the foundations of a small building were discovered on the north side of the presbytery (plan, *H*). This building was of the same width as the adjoining choir-aisle and in length extended from the east end of the latter to the east end of the presbytery. Whether it communicated with the aisle or not it is impossible to say, for the old aisle was destroyed by Alcock: but it seems to have been entered from the presbytery by a door now blocked (plan, *e*). The building was clearly of two storeys, for there is a small loop-hole or squint high up in the presbytery wall, which was so directed that the light before the High Altar could be seen from the upper storey (plan, *f*). Probably this upper room was the Sacristan's chamber. It must obviously have blocked up the lower parts of the lancet windows in the north wall of the presbytery[2].

The discovery of a Norman arcade on the western wall of the north transept in the summer of 1882 is briefly alluded to in the Appendix to the second volume of the *Architectural History* and is more fully detailed in a communication to the Antiquarian Society by Mr W. M. Fawcett, M.A.[3]

[1] *Architectural History*, II. pp. 122—141.

[2] It may here be mentioned that previously to 1828 only *four* lancet windows were open on the north side of the presbytery, corresponding to the four in the opposite wall. The fifth lancet on the north side, and the blind half-arch next it, were discovered in that year by the Rev. C. Green, M.A., Dean.

[3] *Communications*, XXV. p. lxxxvi.

There is good reason for believing that the choir of the
Nuns' church extended into the nave, and even that the
present west wall of the Chapel stands in the position, if it be
not the actual structure, of the wall which divided the conventual from the parochial part of the church. An early deed
(Charters, 220 c) grants a rent of eight shillings 'for maintenance of a lamp in the choir of the nuns, wheresoever their
choir shall be,' words which imply that the ritual choir was not
limited to the chancel. Alcock's screen, on the other hand, if
we may judge from the mention in the Audit accounts for
1560—1 of a 'barre at the chansell dore,' would seem to have
occupied the position of the present one. The view that the
Nuns' choir-screen was near the western end of the Chapel
perhaps derives some support from the fact that in digging for
the supports of the new organ gallery in 1888 a large earthen-
ware vessel, 13 inches in height, was discovered a few inches
below the pavement. It was empty and may have served as a
'resonator,' such as in the middle ages were sometimes placed
under organs and stalls, e.g. at Fountains Abbey.

The hope expressed by the authors of the *Architectural
History* (vol. II, p. 128) that a fine western door might at some
time be discovered in the western wall of the old nave received
a fulfilment, unfortunately only partial, in the year 1886, when
the lower portion of the northern jamb of this door was discovered during alterations to the Master's Lodge. The remains
disclosed showed that the jambs had been filled with clusters
of detached shafts of the 13th century, like those in the
entrance to the Chapter House. At the same time remains of
some of the northern piers of the nave were found embedded
in a wall of Alcock's work[1].

Inspection of the plan will show that the westernmost
pier (plan, *g*) of the northern arcade of the nave is not, like the
corresponding one on the opposite side, placed against the
western wall of the church, but slightly advanced to the east.

[1] Mr J. W. Clark has kindly furnished me with a plan (made in 1886)
showing these discoveries and the arrangement of the west end of the church.
This I have employed in drawing the plan opposite p. 53.

Between this pier (g) and the western wall there seems to have been a doorway. Previous to the alterations which took place in this part of the Master's Lodge in 1886 the wall at the N.W. angle of the old nave was pierced on the ground-floor by a door which opened on a rectangular area (plan, J) containing a staircase which ascended to the first-floor rooms. The walls enclosing this area were of solid character and were carried to the full height of the building. That on its north side is a prolongation of the north aisle wall; that on the west is similarly an extension of the exterior wall of the western cloister-range and is parallel in direction with the western front of the church. Now the buildings which surround the cloister are all disposed in an exactly rectangular fashion; but the angle which the west cloister range makes with the south range of the entrance-court is not a right angle. It seems not improbable that the Nuns' gate-house was originally detached from the cloister-range. The hypothesis that the range connecting them was erected at a later date accounts for the unsymmetrical plan of the dining-room of the Lodge (plan, Q) the east and west walls of which are not parallel. The east wall of the dining-room was, on this supposition, once the external wall of a small tower-like structure projecting from the church at its N.W. angle. Loggan's view of the S. front shows just such a projection from the wing which contained the old nave. Like that wing it contained three storeys, whereas the wing between it and the gateway has only two. Further proof of the original connection of this quasi-tower with the church is seen in the fact that the battlements over the present nave and the part of the old nave now converted into domestic buildings, as shown by Loggan, are continued round the south and west sides of this projection. These battlements, we know, were the work of Sir John Rysley, who died in 1511[1]. Between 1718 and 1720 the wing of the Lodge next the gate was heightened by the addition of another storey,

---

[1] Commemoration Book: "Sir John Rysley covered the Cloisters with timber and lead and completed the Roof and Battlements at the West End of the Church."

whereby the turret was completely smothered in external appearance, and, no doubt, at the same time the battlement above it was removed.

The ground floor of the structure above described (plan, J) obviously served as a vestibule to the church, to which the Prioress had access from her lodging in the western cloister-range by the entrance at the N.W. angle of the nave. From the account of the ceremonies attending the installation of a Prioress, given on pp. 38-9, we learn that after the publication of the election 'coram populo congregato,' i.e. probably in the parochial part of the nave, 'omnes sorores predictam Joannam electam duxerunt ad vestibulum ejusdem ecclesie ibidemque dimiserunt,' i.e. they conducted her to this vestibule and left her at the door of the lodging which she was to occupy as Prioress. The door was probably the still existing one (plan, h) by which the Hall of the Lodge is entered. On the first floor immediately above this door, and communicating with the room above this Hall, is another ancient door which, no doubt, was reached by a staircase ascending from the vestibule.

A common arrangement in monasteries of which the Head did not reside in a detached building was to place the Lodge of the Prior in the west side of the cloister next the Church. On the ground floor was placed his *camera,* or private chamber, above it his solar with an oratory adjoining. At Jesus the rooms in this quarter of the College, as shown by the Bursars' Rentals, were allotted from a very early period to the Master, and they lend themselves so exactly to the uses above-mentioned that it is highly probable that Alcock assigned to the Master of the College the dwelling which had formerly belonged to the Prioress. The large room on the ground floor next the vestibule (plan, K) is called in the Bursars' Rentals the *camera Magistri.* Since the publication of the *Architectural History* it has been restored very much to the dimensions and appearance which belonged to it in Alcock's time. The wooden partitions which divided it before the alterations of 1886 have been removed, the ceiling taken down and the joists of the floor above it exposed. These joists are coloured with ver-

milion and adorned with repetitions of the monogram IHS.
On its north side this room is bounded by the passage (plan, L)
which until last century was the approach from the entrance
court to the cloister[1]. In the Bursars' Rentals this passage is
simply called 'le Entre.' The handsome wainscoted room above
the Master's chamber goes by various names in the Audit
Books—the Conference Chamber, the Audit Room, the *coena-
culum Magistri* and the Founder's Chamber. Probably the
last name indicates that Alcock designed it for the use of
himself and his successors in the see of Ely. It was probably
the Solar or Guest Chamber of the Prioress. Next to it on the
north side is a narrow chamber contained within the walls
which flank the 'Entry' below, and approached by a door at
the east end of the Conference Chamber. Though it is only
eight feet in width this room is lighted by a large eastern
window of three lights. This was clearly the Oratory of the
Prioress. Sherman tells us in his *Historia* that Dr Reston,
who was Master 1546—1549, converted this chamber into his
private Oratory, and it continued to be used as the Master's
Oratory as late as 1635[2]. In another passage Sherman informs
us that the 'insignia' (?arms painted on glass) of Sir Reginald
Bray (d. 1503) were in his time still to be seen in this
Oratory.

The rest of the ground-floor of the western cloister-range
is stated in the Bursars' Rentals to be occupied by two chambers
let to students of the College, and a room beyond them to the
north which was occupied by the Cook. The purposes which
the two former chambers served in the Nunnery it is not easy
to determine. One of them may perhaps have been the Parlour
(*Locutorium*) where the Nuns were allowed to converse with
visitors, or with servants and tradesmen on the business of the
Nunnery; the other was not improbably the Cheker, or office
of the Cellaress. The room in which the College Cook lived
(plan, N) from the fact that there was no chamber over it—
the space being occupied, as it still is, by the Library staircase—

---

[1] See *Architectural History*, II. p. 122.
[2] See the extract quoted in *Architectural History*, II. p. 169, *note*.

is easily identified with the passage by which at the present day the cloister is entered from the first court.

An interesting feature in this chamber is a low aperture (plan, *j*) in its north wall, opening into the room marked *O* in the plan and now serving as the Kitchen Office, but in early College days used as the *pincerna* or Buttery. This aperture is 16 in. wide and its apex is not more than 4 feet above the pavement of the passage, but the floor of the Buttery cellar on which it opens is 2 ft. lower than this pavement, though formerly, no doubt, level with it. On the side next the passage it is widely splayed, and a single hinge exists on which a shutter seems to have been hung. It is quite evident that this opening was not a window looking into an external court, for the walls of the old Buttery are of massive clunch and evidently Nuns' work of an early date. Moreover on the side of the cellar the aperture is flush with the wall surface, and shows no kind of recess nor any window jambs. West of the opening on this cellar side the wall has been plugged with lead as though for fixing some object of wood or iron.

In this singular opening we may recognise a contrivance like the *Rota* or *Turn*, which is thus described in Prof. Willis' *History of the Monastery of Christ Church, Canterbury,* (p. 39, *note*).

"The Turn or Rota is a contrivance employed in Nunneries, Foundling Hospitals, and elsewhere, and consists of an upright cylindrical box turning on an upright axis, and having an opening on one side only. It is fixed within or in front of an opening in a partition wall, so that a person on one side placing an object in the Turn can, by twisting the box half round, bring the object within the grasp of a second person on the other side, without either party seeing the other."

Prof. Willis gives a description of a cellar wall-hole of this kind at Christ Church Monastery, which, with a few differences, might be applied to that in the Cook's Chamber. The Cellarer, he says,

"was lodged at the end of the Refectory buildings, and in contact with the court of the Guesten-hall....Two doors in the western alley [of the cloister] lead to his territory, the one at the north end, opposite to the northern alley, the other near the south end. The first is remarkable for having at the left side a singular octagonal opening of sixteen inches diameter through the thickness of the wall, in the form of a horizontal spout, the middle of which is about four feet from the ground. It pierces the wall, narrowing to a circular form a foot in diameter at the back, where it appears to have opened into one of the Cellarer's offices.

"Milner, describing the remains of the conventual buildings at Winchester, mentions a small ornamented arch in a wall, which communicated with the buttery and the cellarage, and remarks, 'It is not improbable that here was what is called a Turn, by which the brethren who were exhausted with fatigue and thirst, might, with the leave of their superior, at certain times call for a cup of beer of the cellarer.' Our spout may have been a contrivance to carry out this indulgence. The opening from the cellarage at the back being contrived at right angles with the present opening, it is plain that the cup would be placed by the Cellarer's man within reach of the applicant and returned without mutual recognition. But at present there are no traces of the form of its termination inwards," &c.

The room called in the Bursars' Rentals the 'pincerna' (plan, O) served as the Buttery until the year 1579–1580 when a 'new buttrye' was constructed, apparently under the Hall. The accounts of 1563–1564 mention 'a doore betwene ye butleres chamber and ye kechine.'

In the upper floors of the part of the western cloister-range which extends from the Oratory to the wall between the Cook's chamber and the *pincerna* there are no partitions of solid masonry. The whole of the highest floor is now occupied by the Library. In its upper portion this room is probably Alcock's work, as seems to be shown by the use of brick in its lateral walls. But there is reason to believe that in this quarter of the Nunnery there was a large room occupying on the first floor the space which the Library now occupies on the floor above it. The usual monastic arrangement would place here the Guest House, or Lodging of the Cellaress.

In the Nuns' accounts for 1449–50 reference is made in the same item to repairs in the Aula (i.e. Hall of the Cellaress) and in the Kitchen, and for practical reasons there can be little doubt that these two departments were in close communication. The Aula then most likely occupied the space above the Nuns' Buttery. In its N. wall is contained the flue of the Kitchen range and in its N.W. corner, where the clunch of this wall ends and a wooden party wall closes the room, there was most likely a wooden staircase descending inside the Kitchen. The Kitchen, which, except for alterations by Alcock in the door and windows, is substantially the Kitchen of the Nuns, has always occupied the height of two storeys.

The means of access from the entrance-court to the Hall and Lodging of the Cellaress have now to be considered. The Nunnery accounts for the year 1450–1451 mention a 'Poorche' or 'Portecus prope Aulam.' The only side of the Aula detached from other buildings was the west: on the other sides there could not have been any door requiring the shelter of a porch. If the Lodging of the Cellaress reached, as we must suppose, to the N. wall of the present cloister entry, its door must have opened directly into the Guest Hall without any interposed staircase and landing. The staircase to the Guest Hall was therefore external to the building. We note that the same workman was engaged in 1450–1451 in mending with tiles and 'sclate' the 'Porch' and the cloister. Probably the so-called Porch was of the nature of a pentise, ascending by a covered stair to the first floor. The splendid Norman staircase of the New Hall at Canterbury is a familiar example of such an arrangement.

The chamber at the west end of the Hall, occupying the position of the old Guest Hall, it may be remembered, was one of the three principal chambers which by the statutes of Bishop Stanley were allotted to distinguished visitors to the College.

The passage from the cloister to the Kitchen was, in the Nunnery, as now, under the vestibule of the Refectory or Hall. The Kitchen door (*hostium coquine*) must have stood where Alcock's door now stands, and was nearly opposite a newel staircase which opened above on the platform outside the screen[1]. Above the entrance from the cloister was the small room which until 1875 was the College muniment room and in the Bursars' Rentals is called the Treasury (*occupatur cum*

---

[1] A plan of the west end of the Hall, previous to the alterations of 1875, which includes this staircase, is given in the *Architectural History*, II. p. 163.

Thesauro Ecclesie). It may have served the same purpose in the Nunnery.

The Bursars' Rentals mention two rooms under the Hall. The first had one door opening S. into the cloister and another N. next to the well. It was used for the storage of fuel (*focalia*). The other had a door opening E. in the 'entre' (*i.e.* the Dark Entry) and was 'le Storehowse.' The word *staurus* was more particularly applied to salted or dry fish. After the rooms under the Hall were converted into the 'new buttrye' we hear of a 'new fish-house,' which was in the Kitchen. It was placed over the 'leads,' *i.e.* the kitchen coppers, and hence was called 'ye house in ye leads.' It was between the outer wall of clunch on the N. side of the Kitchen and an inner parallel one of brick, the enclosed space being about six feet wide. The fish was piled on layers of sedge in a high stack, and to get at it there was a door in the brick wall now visible only on the side interior to the two walls. This door is at about the first floor level, and was reached from the Kitchen by 'a new ladder for ye fish house' (1584–1585). The Nuns appear to have stacked their fish in a similar fashion, if we may judge from the fact that several of them travelled by water to Lynn in 1450–1451 in order to buy salt fish and at the same time purchased a 'piece of timber called "a Maste" required for making a ladder.'

The Founder's skilful treatment of the Nuns' Refectory has given the Hall completely the appearance of a late 15th century building; but in no part of the College is it clearer that he left the fabric of the Nuns' building entire, inserting only new windows, heightening the walls and constructing a new roof. The extent to which he raised the walls is best seen in the garret over the Combination Room, where the clunch of the Refectory gable is surmounted by a brick addition four or five feet high at its middle part. The entrance to the Hall from the cloister was until 1875 through a door-arch of Alcock's time which opened into the space between the west gable of the Hall and the screen[1]. A flight of steps led thence to the vestibule of the Hall.

---

[1] *Architectural History*, II. p. 162.

CHARTERS OF THE PRIORY.

ROYAL AND EPISCOPAL CHARTERS.

1   Charter of Nigellus, second bishop of Ely (1133—1169).

    N. Dei gratia Eliensis Ecclesie Episcopus universis baroni-
bus et hominibus Sancte Etheldrythe tam clericis quam
laicis tam Francis quam Anglis salutem.   Notum sit
vobis omnibus tam presentibus quam futuris me concessisse et dedisse et carta mea confirmasse quandam terram
sanctimonialibus cellule extra villam Cantebruge noviter
institute prope terram eiusdem cellule iacentem quietam
et liberam absque omni consuetudine reddendo per
singulos annos xij^d.   Presentibus testibus istis Rad. Olaf,
Petro clerico, Gileberto capellano de Hornungesheia.
Valete.

2 a Charter of King Stephen confirming a grant of William
Monachus or le Moyne.

    S. Rex Anglie Episcopo de Eli et Justiciariis et Vice-
comitibus et Baronibus et Administris et omnibus
fidelibus suis de Cantebr. scira salutem.   Sciatis me
confirmasse et concessisse Ecclesie et Sanctimonialibus
Sancte Marie de Cantebrugia donacionem illam quam
Wills Monachus aurifaber eis fecit de ij virgatis terre
et de vj acris de prato et de iiij cotariis cum teneura
sua in Schelforda in elemosina pro anima Regis Henrici
et pro Dei fidelibus.   Quare volo et precipio quod
Ecclesia illa et Sanctimoniales terram predictam et
pratum et cotarios cum teneura sua bene et in pace et
libere et quiete et in elemosina teneant solutam et

quietam omni seculari exactione et servicio sicut idem
Wills illam eis dedit et concessit. T., W. Martell et
Rain. de Warenna. Apud Mapertes halam in obsidione.

b Charter of Bishop Nigellus confirming the same grant.

Witnessed by 'Willō Archid., Ric. de Sancto Paulo, Ric. de
Pontecardon, Ric. filio Ilberti, Magistro Ernulfo, Johē de Sancto
Albano, Gileberto clerico, Radulfo Dapifero, Alexandro Pincerna,
Henrico Peregrino.'

3 *a* Charter of the Countess Constance.

Constantia Comitissa N. Eliensi Episcopo et omni clero
et omnibus Baronibus Cantebrigscir et Burgensibus de
Cantebrig tam futuris quam presentibus salutem. Sciatis
me dedisse et concessisse Sanctimonialibus de Cantebrig
totam terram earum infra Burgum et extra tam possi-
dendam quam possessam quietam de hagabulo et de
langabulo et totam piscaturam et aquam que Burgo
pertinet ita libere et quiete et honorifice sicut maritus
meus Eustacius et ego liberius et honorificentius ha-
buimus pro anima mariti mei Comitis Eustacii et pro
anima Matilde Regine et Antecessorum meorum necnon
pro salute Regis Stephani in perpetuam elemosinam.
His testibus: N. Eliensi Episcopo [   ] cum
Rodberto fratre suo, Radulfo Vicecomite, Alexandro
pincerna, Eustacio de Bans, Will. Monaco de Selford,
Rodberto Grim, Gisleberto filio Dunning, Hereberto,
Herveo filio Warin.

An ancient exemplification of the above charter of Nunnery
date gives the names of the missing witnesses, viz G. de Waltervill,
Rogero le Equaham. The copy is endorsed ' Haygabil.'

b Confirmation of the above charter by King Stephen.

Stephanus Rex Anglie Episcopo de Eli et Justiciariis et
Vicecomitibus et Baronibus et Ministris et omnibus
fidelibus suis de Cantebrigscir salutem. Sciatis me
concessisse et confirmasse donacionem illam quam
Comitissa Constantia uxor Comitis Eustachii filii mei
fecit Sanctimonialibus de Cantebrig in elemosinam de

tota piscatura et aqua que Burgo Cantcbr. pertinet et de
quietancia totius terre sue. Quare volo et precipio quod
Sanctimoniales ille totam terram suam et piscaturam et
aquam bene et in pace et libere et quiete teneant solutam
et quietam ab omni seculari exactione et servicio sicut
predicta Comitissa Constantia illis dedit et concessit et
carta sua confirmavit. T., Fulc. de Oilli et Rob. fil. Unfr.,
et Ric. de Badu, et Henr. de Novo Mercato. Apud Cantebrug.

c Confirmation of the same charter by Bishop Nigellus.

4 a First charter of King Malcolm IV. of Scotland, Earl of
Huntingdon.

M. Rex Scotic omnibus hominibus suis tam clericis quam
laicis de honore Hunted. salutem. Sciatis me concessisse
et dedisse Deo et monialibus de Grantebrige x acres (sic)
terre iuxta Grenecroft in elemosinam et ad fundendam
(sic) ecclesiam suam in ea per duos solidos reddendos et
precipio quod minister meus cum eos receperit (sic) ad
altare ciusdem ecclesie offerat eos. T., Herberto Episcopo de Glasgu, Walt. Cancellario, Hugone de Morevill,
Fulc. de Lusures, Dd. Olifat, Walt. de Lind. Apud
Hunted.

Royal seal appended ; see p. 12.

b Second charter of King Malcolm.

M. Rex Scott. omnibus probis hominibus suis et amicis de
honore Huntendunie et Cantebrugie salutem. Sciant
clerici et laici presentes et posteri me in perpetuam
elemosinam dedisse et concessisse et hac mea carta confirmasse Deo et Ecclesie Sancte Marie et Sancte Radegundis de Cantebrug. et Sanctimonialibus ibidem Deo
servientibus decem acras terre iuxta Grenecroft. Quare
volo et firmiter precipio ut predicte Sanctimoniales illas
decem acras habeant et possideant liberas et quietas ab
omni servicio et consuetudine et ab omni redditu et ab
omni seculari exactione et nominatim eas precipio fore
quietas de illis duobus solidis quos predicte Sanctimoni-

ales inde mihi annuatim reddere solebant. T., Engelr.
Cancellario, Nicol. Camerario, Willō. Burdet, Hug. Ridel.
Apud Huntend.

c Confirmation of King Malcolm's grant by Archbishop
Becket.

Thom. Dei gratia Cant. Ecclesie minister humilis omnibus
Sancte Matris Ecclesie filiis salutem. Noverit universitas
vestra nos sigilli nostri atestatione corroborasse et confirmasse Sanctimonialibus de Cantebrug. ibi Deo servientibus omnes terras et tenuras suas eis rationabiliter
datas et cartis donatorum confirmatas et nominatim
decem acras terre in Cantebr. quas Rex Scocie eisdem
Sanctimonialibus dedit et carta sua confirmavit. Qua-
propter volumus et firmiter precipimus quatenus memorate Sanctimoniales omnes terras et tenuras suas cum
pertinenciis suis in liberam elemosinam teneant et possideant sicut carte donatorum eis testantur. Teste Rob.
Archid. Oxineford, Magistro Philippo de Caun, Magistro
Herberto de Boseham, Rob. capell. et Willmō capell. et
Willō de Leigrecest.

d Confirmation by Stephen Langton, Archbishop of Canterbury, of previous charters of Archbishops Theobald and
Becket and of Bishop Nigellus.

5 Confirmation by Bishop Nigellus of a grant of 80 acres of
land in Wratting made to the Nuns by Stephen and
Juliana de Scalariis, along with their daughter, Sibil.

Witnessed by Will., archdeacon of Ely, Augustus, Adam and
Walter, monks, Roger, chaplain, John and Paian, clerks, Martin,
Ralf and Ric., deacons, Ralf, dapifer, Alex., pincerna, Stephen and
Geoffrey de Scalariis, &c.

6 Bull of Pope Innocent IV. directed to the Prior of Linton
respecting a dispute between the Nuns and the Vicar of
St Clement's.

For the subject see p. 27.
Dated 'Lugdun., 18 Kal. Maii nostri [*blank space*] anno sexto,'
i.e. 1248-9. *Bulla* appended.

7 a Charter of John de Fontibus, Bp of Ely (1220—1225).

Confirms a charter of Bp E[ustace] of Ely, granting to the Nuns all the land which Bp E. had between the monastery and Grenecroft. No date.

b **Charter of Hugh** Northwold, Bp of Ely (1229—1254).

Confirms the charters of Bishops Eustace and John de Fontibus. No date.

8 *Insperimus* charter of Edward II.

Dated 'apud Westm. quintodecimo die Octobr. Anno regni nostri septimo. Per ipsum regem. Examinatum per A[dam] de Brom.' Seal attached. It recites and confirms the charters of King Stephen, 2 (*a*) and 3 (*b*); also the following charter of Henry III. 'Henricus Dei gratia, &c. Sciatis quod concessimus pro nobis et heredibus nostris priorisse et monialibus Sancte Radegundis quod claudere possint et clausam tenere imperpetuum quamdam croftam suam quae iacet inter ecclesiam ipsarum priorisse et monialium et fossatum de Cantebr. ex parte occidentali salvo nobis in omnibus et per omnia fossato nostro. In cuius rei testimonium has literas nostras fieri fecimus patentes. Teste me ipso apud Westm. decimo septimo die April. anno regni nostri tricesimo quinto.' It also confirms the charter of the Countess Constance, 3 (*a*), various grants of land principally at West Wratting, and a confirmation by Ely convent of the first charter of Bp Nigellus.

9 Charter of King Henry VI.

Dated ' Apud Dertford quintodecimo die Marcii Anno regni nostri sextodecimo.' Seal attached. Grants to the Nuns 'quod ipse et successores sue imperpetuum habeant singulis annis unam feriam in villa predicta per tres dies duraturam videlt. in vigilia in die et in crastino Assumptionis Beate Marie cum omnibus libertatibus et liberis consuetudinibus ad huiusmodi feriam pertinentibus.' It also grants the Nuns exemption from tenths or other quotas on their spiritual and ecclesiastical possessions.

10 License of Mortmain of Henry VI.

Dated Westminster, Dec. 5, in 27th regnal year. Seal attached. Generally empowers the Nuns to acquire lands, &c., to the value of £5 ; also exempts them from the requisitions of *provisores, emptores* and *captores victualium* for the King and Queen and their successors and others their Magnates.

INDULGENCES. BRIEFS.

(These are printed in full in the *Architectural History*, vol. ii,
pp. 183—186.)

11 Walter de Suffield, Bp of Norwich, grants relaxation of
penance for 25 days to persons contributing to the aid of
the Nuns. Dated Cantebrig., Ides of August, 1254.

12 Letter from Ric. de Gravesend, Bp of Lincoln, to the Arch-
deacons of Northampton and Huntingdon ordering
collections to be made in the churches of their Archidia-
conates in behalf of the Nuns. Dated Huntingdon, 12
Kal. Junii, 10th year of pontificate (1268).

13 Letter of Roger de Skerning, Bp of Norwich, ordering
collections to be made in his diocese for the repair of the
Church of S. Rad., injured by the fall of the Bell-tower.
Dated Hoxne, 5 Kal. Maii, 1277.

14 Letter of the Official of the Archdeacon of Ely to the
parochial clergy of the diocese recommending the Nuns
to them as objects of charity, having lost their house and
all their substance by fire. Dated Herdwyk, 4 Kal.
Sept. 1313.

15 John de Ketene, Bp of Ely, confirms certain grants of indulgence made by his brother Bps in favour of persons
contributing to the relief of the Nuns and the rebuilding
of their house destroyed by fire. Dated Hatfeld, 4 Kal.
July, 1314.

16 Thomas Arundel, Bp of Ely, grants indulgence of 40 days
to all who contribute to the relief of the Nuns on the
occasion of the destruction of their dwellings by fire.
Dated Dodyngton, 2 April, 1376.

17 William Courtenay, Archbp of Canterbury, grants indulgence of 40 days to persons contributing to the relief of
the Nuns whose buildings have been ruined by violent
storms. Dated Croydon, 6 April, 1390.

MISCELLANEOUS DEEDS AND DOCUMENTS.

18 Ric. Wastinel grants to Nuns a rent of 2 pence (*nummos*) of the service of Everad de Batford.

19 Will. fitz Rob. fitz Walter gives to Nuns a rent of half a mark. Witn. Seher de Quinci, Gilbert fitz Dunning &c.

20 Acquittance of Simon Blakeboane, sergeant at arms, to the Prioress, Agnes Scyntclowe, and Ric. Broune, vicar of All Saints'. Henry V. 7.

21 Acquittance of the Nuns to Ric. Pyghttesley for a year's rent of Tylydhostelle, viz. 2ˢ 3ᵈ. 1437.

Arch. Hist. II., 426.

22 Walter fitz Walter de Scalariis confirms his father's grant of 20ˢ *per ann.* for the maintenance of three lamps in the ch. of S. Rad. Witn. Will. de Abington, *miles.*

23 Simon de Turre gives to Nuns one acre of meadow land in Hunimade and ½ an acre in Chabligwelle. Witn., Roger de Caudecote.

24 Simon, Camerarius of E[ustace], Bp of Ely, gives to Nuns a rent of 2ˢ paid by Hervey fitz Eustace of Cantebrige. Witn. Hugh de Bodegesham, official.

25 Ric. de Histon, capellanus, holds of the Nuns (Pr. Letitia) a portion of their land in Tornechroft; rent two shillings and two capons. Witn. Hervey fitz Eustace.

26 Walt. fitz Segar, capellanus, holds of the Nuns (Pr. Letitia) land formerly held by his father: rent 14ᵈ and two capons.

27 *a* Bond of Will. Spaldyng for £10. Jan. 6, Henry VI. 10.

'The condycion of this obligacion is yᵗ mastyr William Spaldyng, clerk, of Cambrigge, with inne wretyn shall not entre in hese owyn persone the several crofts and closures of the Prioresse and yᵉ convent of seint Radegundis in yᵉ toune of Cambrigge adiugnant to yᵉ said Priorie ne destroye ne soyle corne gresse arboris ne closures of yᵉ seyd Prioresse and convent growyng or beyng upon the seyd closures with outyn licens of yᵉ seyde Prioresse yᵉ same time beyng.'

b The Master and Brethren of St John's Hospital grant to King Henry VI. a close lying within the *fossatum* of the Nuns to the W. of the Nunnery, now in the tenure of Will. Spaldyng, clerk. Thos. Clerk, mayor. Henry VI. 26.

c The King gives the same to Nuns. Dated Westminster, Henry VI. 26.

28 The. Nuns are discharged from payment of procurations to the Archdeacon. Date 1313. Document imperfect.

29 Will of Roger Mason of S. Rad. parish. July 5, 1392. (In Latin.)

Body to be buried among Friars Minor; to said Friars 10ˢ; to high altar of S. Rad. 5ˢ for wax; cottage in S. Rad. lane to be sold to discharge debts. Residue to wife Felice; she to make disposal for his soul.

Seal attached (seemingly *ad causas* seal of Nunnery): S. Rad. crowned and veiled, standing in a niche, in right hand a wand: under trefoiled arch below a nun kneeling prays with upraised hands: a small crescent L. of the praying figure. Traces of legend, STE RADEGVNDIS CONV.

30 Will of John Grenelane: dated Feb. 1, 1431, proved in the Gild Hall, Cambridge, before the Mayor, Thos. Jacob, and bailiffs, Monday next before S. Barnabas day. Hen. VI. 10.

Among the items: to the high altar of S. Andrew's ch. where his body is to be buried before the cross, 10ˢ; for his burial there 20ˢ: for new bells to the same ch. 100ˢ; for new leading the bell tower 20ˢ: to each priest assisting at his funeral 12ᵈ, and to every clerk helping such payment as executors deem fit: the executors to find an honest chaplain to celebrate for him in said ch. for 10 years after his decease, preference being given to Dˢ Brian Ffisshewyk: to each convent of mendicant friars in Cambridge 10ˢ: for making a roodloft in Haddenham ch. 20ˢ: for the fabric of Rampton ch. 20ˢ.

TRIPPELOWE'S BENEFACTION, CAMBRIDGE AND BARNWELL.

31 *a* Luke fitz Walter of St Edmund's to Joh. fitz Paulinus of Camb.: ½ acre at the Claypittes in Camb. field, betw.

Nuns' land and Hadestoc Weye, ab. at one head on
Pushwelle Weye; rent 1ᵈ and ⅓ mark *pre manibus.*
Witn. Joh. Martyn. Edw. I. 16. .

b Cecilia, sister of above-named Luke, confirms same and adds
land in Swinescroft. Witn. Barth. Goggyng. Edw. I. 18.

c John fitz Paulinus to Walter the Butcher: same land.
Joh. Morice, mayor. Edw. II. 9.

d Walter the Butcher to Joh. de Trippelowe, Rector of Reymerston, dioc. Norwich: same land. Henry de Toft,
mayor. Edw. III. 3.

32*a* Rob. de Cumberton of Camb. to Reginald fitz Ralf Ledbeter
and wife Joan: one selion in Swinescroft, ab. on Hady-
stock Way. Symon de Refham, mayor. Edw. II. 15.

b Joh. Cullingg of Camb. and wife Joan to Reginald Ledbeter
de Ely of Camb. and wife Joan: 3 selions in Swinecroft.
Symon de Refham, mayor. Edw. II. 15.

c Reginald le Ledbeter and wife Joan to Joh. de Tr., Rector
of Reymerston, and Joh. de Bodekesham, clerk; the
above 4 selions in Swinecroft. Eudo de Helpryngham,
mayor. Edw. III. 2.

d Stephen Morice of Camb., clerk, to Joh. de Tr., Rector of
Reymerston: 2 selions in Swynecroft. Eudo de Helpringham, mayor. Edw. III. 2.

e Joh. de Tr., Rector of Herdewyk, co. Camb., with license,
to the Nuns: land in Swynecroft. Barth. Morice, mayor.
Edw. III. 17.

33*a* Same, with license, to same: 6⅓ acres in Camb. and
Barnw. fields. Philip Cayly, mayor. Edw. III. 16.

b General release of Joh. de Tr. for last-mentioned lands
to Nuns. Barth. Morice, mayor. Edw. III. 17.

34*a* Joh. de Tr. and Will. Lavenham assign 3 mess. in par.
of S. Andr., S. Mary and S. Edw. to Margt., widow of
Will. de Tr., in lieu of dower. Edw. III. 16. (In
French.)

b Will. de Lavenham to Joh. de Tr. and others: reversion
of said 3 mess., expectant on death of said Margt.
Edw. III. 22. (In Latin.)

c Confirmation of last deed. Rob. de Brygham, mayor. Edw. III. 22. (In French.)

d Joh. de Tr. to Nic. de Wyght and others: all the lands, tenements, &c., which he bought of Will de Lavenham. Witn. Joh. de Toft. Edw. III. 23.

35 License from Rob. Dunning to Joh. de Tr. to convey to Nuns 5 acres in Barnw. fields, with reservation to R. D. as over-lord of rent of 4ˢ. Joh. Pitcok, mayor. Edw. III. 10.

36*a* Thos. Engayne and wife Kath. to Joh. de Tr., Rector of Herdwyk, and Ric. de Dytton, vicar of S. Clement's: ½ acre in Barnw. fields ab. on Meldych and on Horspath. Ric. Tuylett, mayor. Edw. III. 19.

b Release from Dytton to Tr. of above ½ acre. Edw. III. 19.

37*a* Joh. Cadam of Long Stanton and wife Joan to Joh. de Tr. and Joh. de Bodekysham, clerks: 8 acres in Camb. and Barnw. fields. Eudo de Helpringham, mayor. Edw. II. 19.

b Release of above land from Joan, wid. of Joh. de Cam (*sic*) of Long Stanton to Tr. and Bodekysham. Edw. III. 1.

38 *a* Roger, chaplain, fitz John Wodeward of Wode Weston to Adam de Clifford, dwelling in Barnw.: 5 selions in Barnw. Crofts ab. on Grenecroft. Witn. Symon Bernard. Edw. II. 18.

b Executors of Ad. de Clifford to Joh. de Tr.: 2 selions in Barnw. fields, one next land of Prior of S. Edmund's chapel in Camb. and ab. on Horspath, the other next land of Nuns and ab. on Hynton Way. Witn. Joh. Pyttok. Edw. III. 19.

c Joh. de Tr., with license, to Nuns: same 2 selions. Witn. Ric. Tuyllet, mayor. Edw. III. 19.

39 Ric. de Dytton to Joh. de Tr.: land in Barnw. Myddylfeld. Barth. Morice, mayor. Edw. III. 17.

40 Barth. Moriz and wife Margt to Joh. de Tr.: 3 acres in Barnw. fields. Witn. Gilbert de London. Edw. III. 5.

41 Joh. de Tr. to Nuns: 18 selions (= 8 acres) in Barnw. Myddylfeld. Barth. Moris, mayor. Edw. III. 17.

42 Joh. de Hilburghworth and wife Elena, wid. of Henry de Tr., quitclaim dower in lands of her late husband. Joh. Pyttok, mayor. Edw. III. 8.

43a Joh. de Tr., with license, to Nuns: mess. bought by him from Joh. Friday, sit. in S. Rad. St., betw. ten^t of Joh. de Lincoln and ten^t of Robert Gome, clerk, ab. on highway and on Nuns' croft called Eldestedcroft. Ric. Tuyllet, mayor. Edw. III. 19.

  b Same parties and ten^t: Prioress, Alicia: Joh. Friday, cutler. Rob. de Brygham, mayor. Edw. III. 21.

44a Hen. de Tr. to Joh. de Tr.: land and houses in S. Rad. par. betw. ten^t of Nuns and ten^t late of Thos. de Tendring on one side and ten^t late of Alice de Bernewell and a croft of Nuns called Sarantescroft and ten^t late of Rog. de Haford on the other, ab. on Radegund St. and Wales St. Eudo de Helpringham, mayor. Edw. III. 2.

  b Joh. de Tr., by license, to Nuns (**Pr.** Mabilla **Martini**): mess. bought of Hen. de Tr. betw. mess. of Nuns called Gregorieshostell and mess. late of Alice de Bernewell, ab. on highway and on Drosemer. John Pittok, mayor. Ed. III. 6.

45 Agnes, wid. of Milo de Trumpington to Joh. de Tr.: mess. in Rad. St. betw. mess. of Joh. de Tr. and mess. late of Stephen le Terteyner, ab. on highway and Sarentescroft. Eudo de Elpringham, mayor. **Edw.** III. 2.

46 Dionysia, wid. of Hen., *scriptor*, to her bro. Joh. de **Tr.**: mess. in Rad. St. betw. mess. of Roger le Redere and mess. of Ralf, *bercarius*, ab. on street and S. Rad. croft. Eudo de Elpringham, mayor. **1319.**

47a Joh. de Tr. to Joh. de Berneye, burgess and *cissor*: ten^t in Rad. St. betw. ten^t of Joh. de Tr. and one of Joh. de Lincoln, ab. on highway and Nuns' croft called Eldested croft. Philip Cayly, mayor. Edw. III. 21.

  b Berneye reconveys same to **Tr.** Rob. de Brygham, mayor. Edw. III. 21.

48 Joh. de Tr. to Joh. Purry of Wyvelyngham : tenᵗ in Rad. St. betw. tenᵗ of Nuns and tenᵗ of Lyna le Gome, ab. on highway.   Barth. Moriz, mayor.   Edw. III. 16.

49 a License of mortmain to Joh. de Tr. to grant to Nuns 8 mess. and 8 acres of land to find a chaplain to celebrate daily in S. Rad. ch.   At Bermundeseye, 9 Apr.   Edw. III. 5.

 b Under above license Joh. de Tr. conveys to Nuns (Pr. Mabilia Martyn) 7 mess. in S. Rad. par. and one in par. of S. Andr. without Barnw. gates, and 8 acres in Camb. and Barnw. fields : Nuns to celebrate in their monastery 30 masses in each year for donor and his parents, and his anniversary as is done in the case of a nun deceased. 7 Apr.   John Pilet, mayor.   Edw. III. 5.

PARISH OF S. RADEGUND.

50 Reginald de Argenton to the Nuns: all the land which he bought of Hugh Pilate in Grenecroft except a piece in Walter Pilate's garden (*erberio*): the Nuns to pay 2ˢ yearly to S. Giles' ch. in Barnwell.   Witn. Mr Geoffrey, official.

51 a Walter de Lindsey, with consent of his wife Berta, to Nuns: mess. held by him of Nic. Sarant, betw. land of said Nic. and land of Aunger le Feleper: rent to said Nic. so long as he lives 2ˢ.   Witn. Hervey fitz Eustace.

 b Nuns (Pr. Letitia) regrant same mess. to de Lindsey and his wife for their lives.   Witn. Hervey fitz Eustace.

52 Nic. Sarant to Walter de Lindsey: mess. in S. Rad. par. betw. land of Godman de Bernewelle and land of Nic. Sarant: rent 2ˢ, and *gersuma* 4ˢ.   Witn. Ric. de Winepol.

53 a Nuns (Pr. Letitia) to Martin fitz Hugh de Swaffham : land formerly held of Nic. Sarant by Elias, chaplain, which is opposite the Nunnery gate : rent 2ˢ.

 b Joh. fitz Baldwin de Swaffham releases to Nuns his rights in a mess. late of Margt., mother of Peter, late chaplain of S. Rad., lying opposite the gate of S. Rad. and betw.

a mess. of Ysabel Gibet and one of Wymer, clerk; rent 3ˢ.
Witn. Joh. de Escalariis.

c Joh. fitz Joh. Baudewin de Swaffham Prioris de Ely releases
to Nuns land formerly held by above-named **Martin**,
which lies betw. highway and Nuns' land, ab. on a croft
of Prior of Barnw. and a mess. of Maud ad portam, Nuns
acquitting said Joh. of 2ˢ arrears of rent. Witn. Joh.
Portehors.

54 Agnes de Norfolchia, *mulier*, to Geoff. fitz Hubert: mess.
formerly of Nic. Sarant, in suburbs of Camb., betw. mess.
of Reginald, *cementarius*, and one of Will. Carpenter of
Wimondham; rent 8ˢ and a half-penny, *gersuma* 12
marks. Witn. Thos. Toylet.

55 Maud, dau. of Michael de Wyttlesford, to Hen. Martyn,
clerk, dwelling in Camb. and to his wife Alice le Longe
Locci: land &c. in S. Rad. par. in suburbs of Camb.,
betw. land of Ric. Mareschal, W., and land of Warin le
latymer, E., which land was formerly held by Clement
fitz Joseph Cuttyng of Edywethorp (i.e. Edingthorp) from
Agnes de Norfolk: rent 2ˢ, and *gersuma* 40ˢ. Joh. Wath,
mayor. 1285.

56 Nuns (Pr. Letitia) to Wymer, clerk; a piece of their croft,
late belonging to Nic. Sarant, behind Wimer's yard:
rent 6ˢ, *gersuma* 3ˢ. Witn. Rob. Saman.

57a Will. Sueteye to Nuns: moiety of mess. in S. Rad. par.
betw. mess. of Geoff. Cook and mess. of Rob. de Cogges-
hale with moiety of croft extending from said mess. to
Drusemere: to provide a lamp in chapel of S. Rad. and ½
mark *ad pitanciam* on his anniversary. Witn. Will. Tuylet.

b Nuns (Pr. Milisentia) to Geoffrey Cook: mess. in S. Rad.
par. betw. mess. of Will. Sueteye and mess. of Hugh
Ragenhill on one side, mess. of Alan Dalles de Bernewell
on the other: rent 3ˢ. Witn. Roger de Habitun, seneschal
of Bp of Ely.

c Nuus (Pr. Milisentia) to above Alan: mess. in S. Rad. par.
betw. mess. of Walter Porter and mess. of Geoffrey, cook:
rent 4ˢ. Same witnesses.

d Nuns (Pr. Milisentia) to Maud, dau. of Alan: mess. betw.
mess. of Wimer, clerk, and mess. of Joh. Gibet: rent 5ˢ.

58 Nuns (Pr. Mabilia) to Joh. Friday, *cotelerius*: portion of
their croft called Sarandescroft enclosed with walls and
lying at the end of S. Rad. St. betw. tenᵗ of Joh. de
Trippelowe, Rector of Reymerston, and their own croft:
rent 6ᵈ. Joh. Pilat, mayor. 1330.

59*a* Nuns (Pr. Eva Wasteneys) to Thos. de Revede, serjeant at
arms, his wife Alice and children: tenᵗ in Radegundes-
lane, betw. a tenᵗ of Nuns, E., and garden of Minor Friars
and a mess. of Nuns, W., ab. on garden of Minor Friars
and a mess. of Nuns, S., and on lane, N.: rent 6ˢ 8ᵈ.
Stephen fitz Barth. Moriz, mayor. Edw. III. 33.

b Counterpart of above with seal of Thos. de Revede.

c Alicia, wid. of Thos. Revede, and Joh., her son, quitclaim same
tenᵗ to Joh. Pilat. Joh. Giboun, mayor. Edw. III. 44.

d Joh. Pilet of Ely releases same tenᵗ to Nuns. Ric. II. 5.

60 Nuns (Pr. Agnes) lease for 50 years to Ric. Sexteyn, senʳ, of
Camb., butcher, a croft called Sarantescroft with buildings
thereon, ab. on croft of Barnw. Priory, E., on tenᵗ of Nuns,
W.: also an enclosure with dovehouse, betw. house of
Minor Friars and said croft: also mess. with garden next
close of Minor Friars and ab. on Nunneslane and said
enclosure: rent 17ˢ with reservation to sacrist of S. Rad.
ch. of tithes on said tenements. May 2, Hen. VI. 14.

61 Decision of the arbitrators, Rob. Coope of Camb. and Joh.
Musgrave of Barnw., in a dispute betw. the Nunnery (Pr.
Joan Lancastre) and Barnw. Priory (Pr. John) respecting
a wall extending from Nunneslane on N. to Walleslane
on S., betw. a croft of Barnw. Priory, E., and a croft of
Nuns, W. The wall is declared to belong wholly to the
Nuns who are to repair and maintain it. 10 June,
Edw. IV. 2.

62 Rob. fitz. Will. de Nonacurt quitclaims to Nuns land
without the Ditch at Camb. betw. land of Nuns and
land held by Joh. Aclard of the Nuns of Ikilinton.
Witn. Hervey fitz Eustace.

63 Ric. fitz Laurence de Litleberi gives to Nuns a croft with
ten' in front towards street in exchange for $2\frac{1}{2}$ acres in
Camb. fields. Witn. Rob. Saman. Endorsed 'Paroch. Sc̄e.
Rad.'

> In the *H. R.* (II. p. 371) Ric. Laurence is said to hold a meadow
> next the *curia* of S. Rad. which he bought from Joh. Adelbard,
> clerk, and for which he pays a rent of 12ᵈ to the Nuns of Iclitone.

64 Nuns (Pr. Milisentia) to Eustace Carter: land in suburbs
of Camb. at Eldestede betw. land of Roger Garlek and
land of Nuns: rent 3ᵈ and King's service. Witn. Will.
Toilet.

65 Nuns (Pr. Helena) to Roger le Redere, of Camb.: land in
Rad. St. betw. Nuns' croft and land of Henry Scrivener
(*scriptor*) ab. on highway and Nuns' land: rent 4ᵈ. Rob.
Tuylet, mayor.

66 Hubert le Redere of Rydelingfeld releases to his bro. Roger
a mess. in suburbs of Camb. towards the Nuns' house,
which was granted to him by Will. fitz Adam Carpenter.
John But, mayor. 1291.

67 Nuns (Pr. Milisentia) to Adam fitz Hubert Carpenter: land
in suburbs of Camb. betw. land of Maud, dau. of Helewis,
and Nuns' land: rent 3ᵈ, and *gers.* $\frac{1}{2}$ mark. Witn. Rob.
de S. Edmund.

68 Nuns (Pr. Elena) to Roger and Juliana, his wife: mess.
with houses in S. Rad. par.: rent 10ᵈ. John But, mayor.
Edw. I. 20.

69*a* Ralf de Wendeye, vicar of S. Clement's, Camb., to Roysia,
his niece, dau. of Letitia de Wendeye: mess. with houses
in S. Rad. St. betw. mess. of Stephen le Tyrtener and
mess. of Will. le Gom: failing heirs of Roysia to the heirs
of her mother. Eudo, clerk, mayor. Edw. II. 13.

 b Said Roysia, with consent of her husband, Joh. Styward de
Trippelowe, grants same mess. to Will. le Gom. Joh.
Pyttok, mayor. 15 Feb., Edw. III. 8.

70 Hen. Custance de Lolleworthe, *capellanus*, to Joh. de
Lincoln, *portitor*, of Camb.: mess. *cum duabus haiis vivis*
in S. Rad. par. betw. land late of Hen. Scrivener (*scriptor*)

and land of Custance, ab. on highway and Nuns' land.
Henry de Thofts, mayor. Edw. III. 3.

71 Hen. fitz John Kocs of Camb., *scissor*, to Joh. de Toucestre,
of Camb., tournour: mess. with quickset hedge in S. Rad.
par. betw. Nuns' land and mess. of Joh. Locoks, ab. on
highway and Eldestedcroft. Stephen fitz John Morice,
mayor. Edw. III. 27.

72 Nuns (Pr. Margt. Clanyle) to Thos. de Badburnham, cordwainer: mess. with five cottages and curtilage in S. Rad.
par. betw. mess. of Will. Mason and the King's ditch, ab.
on highway and Nuns' croft. Joh. Morice, mayor. Edw.
III. 37.

73a Matt. Wesenham of Camb. and wife Juliana to Roger de
Barwe: mess. in Rad. lane. Joh. Gÿbon, mayor. Edw.
III. 49.

 b Roger de Barwe grants to Will. Rolf of Ixning and others
the above mess. Ric. Masterman, mayor. Ric. II. 13.

74 Arbitration betw. Nuns and S. Michael's College: decision
of the arbitrator, Marmaduke Lumley, LL.B., Chancellor
of the University.

> The dispute was connected with certain houses in Nuns' Lane
> then occupied by Joh. Cranwell, senr, and Ric. Cranwell, junr.
> The College maintained that the occupants of these houses were of
> the par. of S. Michael, the Nuns that they belonged to S. Rad. par.
> The arbitrator decides that they belong to S. Rad. par. but that to
> satisfy any claims on the part of the College the Nuns shall pay to
> it 4ᵈ annually. (This acquittance is still, 1898, paid by Jesus
> Coll. to Trinity Coll.) Decision given *in quadam bassa camera* in
> Clare Hall, 9th June, 1425. Signed &c., Rob. Wright, priest,
> notary of the dioc. of York: attorney for Nuns, Will. Spencer ; for
> College, Will. Pentecost. Three seals attached : the first two
> seemingly of the College and Nunnery ; the third has impression of
> a head emerging from a font-like vessel supported on 5 legs, and
> legend CANCELLAR. UNIVERSITATIS CANTEBRIG.

75 Nuns (Pr. Agnes) to Edm. Lavenham and wife Marion:
garden &c. enclosed with clay walls in S. Rad. par. betw.
tenᵗ of Joh. Plumpton, W., tenᵗ of Nuns occupied by Joh.
Eversdon, E., ab. on Nunneslane, S., and Nuns' croft, N.,

near the King's ditch: for 80 years, rent 6ˢ 8ᵈ. Henry
VI. 22.

76 Nuns (Pr. Elizabeth) to Joh. Wyghton and wife Agnes:
ground in Nunnescroft ab. on King's ditch: lease for
lives, rent 6ᵈ. **Edw. IV. 11.**

77 Nuns (Pr. Eliz. Walton) to Will. Wareyn: tenᵗ &c. in
S. Rad. par. betw. garden of Nuns in tenure of Will.
Warde, W., and garden of Corp. Chr. College, E.: for 60
years, rent 5ˢ. Aug. 12, Edw. IV. 18.

78 Nuns (Pr. Joan Fulburn) to Joh. Marchall and Laur.
Elverede: garden and dovehouse in S. Rad. par. betw.
house of Minor Friars, W. and tenᵗ of Nuns, E., ab.
on highway, N. and on S. partly on a stone wall of
Minor Friars 21½ yards long, partly on Nuns' close in
tenure of Will. Pechard: for 30 years, rent 10ˢ. Joh.
Hesewell, mayor. Henry VII. 6.

PARISH OF ALL SAINTS IN JEWRY.

79a Grant of the advowson of A. S. ch. to the Nuns by Sturmi
de Cantebrig.

Notum sit omnibus quod ego Sturmi de Cantebrig. concessi
et dedi et hac carta mea confirmavi in elemosinam deo et
ecclesie beate dei genetricis Marie et Sͨͤ Radegundis de
Grenecroft et monialibus ibidem deo servientibus advocationem ecclesie Omnium Sanctorum infra burgum de
Cantebr. Hanc autem donationem feci voluntate et
consensu uxoris mee et heredum meorum pro salute
Dͫͥ Regis Henrici et heredum suorum et pro salute
fidelium defunctorum. Quare volo ut predicte moniales
prefatam advocationem habeant et teneant ita libere et
quiete sicut ego vel aliquis antecessorum meorum melius
et liberius eam tenuit. Hiis testibus: Rogero decano,
Rodberto de Sͨͦ Clemente &c.

b The Bishop of Ely (Geoffry Ridel, 1174—1189) institutes
the Nuns in the rectory.

Universis sc̄e matris ecclesie filiis Gaufr. dei gratia Elieñ.
Eps̄. salutem. Universitati vestre notum fieri volumus
nos instituisse scīmoniales de Grenecroft et eis ius
personatus concessisse in ecclesia Omnium Scōrum de
Cantebrug perpetuo habenda in perpetuam liberam et
quietam elemosinam cum omnibus pertinentiis et libertatibus suis presente et consentiente Sturmi qui ius
advocationis habebat in eadem ecclesia prius quod eis
concesserat et carta sua confirmaverat Constituentes eis
communi assensu perpetuum vicarium in prenominata
ecclesia scil. Ric. capellanum soluturum eisdem annuatim nomine memorate ecclesie xx sol. ad duos terminos
scil. x sol. ad Pascha x sol. ad festum Scī Michaelis et
praeterea facientem omnes consuetudines episcopales. Et
per predistinctam pensionem prenominatus R. capellan.
habebit prefatam ecclesiam perpetuo libere et quiete
cum omnibus pertinentiis et libertatibus suis. Et post
recessum vel decessum predicti R. capellani possidebunt
prefate scīmoniales sepedictam ecclesiam plenarie et
integre et ei pro voluntate sua disponent salvis semper
consuetudinibus episcopalibus. Facta est autem hec
institutio et vicarie concessio anno ab incarnacione
verbi MCLXXX feria vero infra octav. Scī Martini. Et
est primus terminus solutionis proximo venturum Pascha.
Testibus Roberto priore et Will̄o canonico de Bernewell, &c.

c The convent of Ely (Prior, Roger de Brigham, *circa* 1215—
1229) confirm the Bishop's institution. Witn. Thos. de
Heyden, Vincentius, Official of the Archdeacon of Ely, &c.

80 Ordinance of Bishop Eustace of Ely respecting the Hospital
of S. John and the church of A. S.

This is a modern copy of the original document said to exist in
the treasury of S. John's College : though I have not been able to
discover this original there exists there a confirmation of the
Bishop's ordinance by the Nuns (Leticia, prioress) in almost
identical terms. The Bishop's ordinance is printed in full in Le
Keux's *Memorials*, vol. II. (Parish of A. S. p. 11). Charters 180,
181 deal with the same matter.

81 Maud Grim to Will. Sausintune, her servant: moiety of her
land &c. in the Jewry, betw. land of Warin le Cachepol
and land formerly of Symon le Talur: rent 5*, and *gers.* 4*,
he to be ready to do her service when summoned. Witn.
Rob. Saman.

82 Christiana, dau. of Godard Carter, to Nuns: lands &c. in
A. S. par. betw. land of Reginald de Fordham and land of
Symon Black: also lands &c. betw. land of Fulk Crocheman and land of Ric. Bullokprest: also land held by her
from Rob. de Bruiera with service of Adam Weaver
(*textor*): also land in Felterestreet betw. land of Holy
Trinity and land of [   ] Doy, with service of Hugh
Ruffus for land next ch. of Holy Trinity. Witn. Hervey
fitz Eustace.

83 Fulk Crocheman gives Nuns, along with his sist. Sibil, land
in Jewry formerly held of him by Brito, the Jew. Witn.
Baldewin Blangernun.

84 Absalon Ampe to Reg. de Fordham: land in A. S. par.
betw. land formerly of Ralf Swane and lane leading from
street to river bank: also said lane: rent 4*, *gers.* 2 marks.
Witn. Andrew de Winepol.

85 Hen. fitz Geoffrey, with consent of his wife Edusa, to Reg.
de Fordham: land in A. S. par. next highway, &c.: rent
3*. Witn. Michael fitz Ordgar.

86 Simon le Blund releases to Nuns a mess. held by him of
them in A. S. par. betw. land of Andrew de Winepol and
land of Barth. le Talur: *pre manibus* 4 marks. Witn.
Hervey fitz Eustace.

87 Thos. fitz Rob. de la Bruere, with consent of his mother
Helen, to Nuns: land in par. of A. S. next the Jewry,
held of him by Ralf Prudfot, betw. land of Ralf Ballard
and land of Walter Pie: rent 6^d, and 6^d to Hosp. of S.
John the Ev., the brethren giving him 2 marks towards
the charges of his pilgrimage. Witn. Hervy fitz Eustace.

88 Hugh fitz Absalon of Cambr. to Nuns for health of souls of
himself and his sister Letitia: a rent of 29$\frac{1}{2}$^{d} paid to him
by Fulk Crocheman out of a ten^t *in vico Judeorum qui*

descendit a via usque ad cimiterium Omnium Sanctorum :
possession of said ten[t] reserved to donor during life : Nuns
to celebrate anniversary of his sist. Letitia on eve and day
of the Purification, when Nuns are to have the whole rent
for their *pitancia.* Witn. Baldwin Blangernun.

Vicus Judeorum otherwise Pilate's Lane.

89 Stephen de Elvenegard in Eswell and wife Emma to Nicol
de Well, rector of S. Etheldred's ch., Histon : mess. in
Jewry, Camb. next land of Joh. de Coteham, extending
from highway to King's ditch : rent a pair of gloves,
price $\frac{1}{2}$d, hagable 1d and *gers.* 8 marks. Witn. Hervey
fitz Eustace.

Seal : flower of eight petals : legend EMME DELAMORE
(Delamore, i.q. de la Bruere *supra*).

90 Azo Coleman to Rob. Seman : land in A. S. par. on bank
called Blancwyneshithe, next land of Walter son of Scolas-
tica : rent 8d, *gers.* $\frac{1}{2}$ mark. Witn. Baldwin Blangernun.

91 Nuns (Pr. Letitia) to Will. Pilate : land in A. S. par. next
land of Ailitha, widow, formerly held by Maud de cimi-
terio : rent 8d and 2 capons. Witn. Rob. Seman.

92 Nuns (Pr. Letitia) to Will. Athelard : mess. &c. in A. S.
par. betw. land of Hosp. of S. John and land of Will. Pye :
rent 4ˢ 6d. Witn. Adam fitz Eustace.

93 Nuns (Pr. Letitia) to Barth. le Noble : mess. in A. S. par. in
which Symon le Blund dwelt, betw. land of said Barth.
and land of Andr. de Wynepol, extending from highway
to land of Bernard Grim and land of Ric. Bullok : rent 2ˢ,
gers. 5$\frac{1}{2}$ marks. Witn. Hervey fitz Eustace.

94 Nuns (Pr. Letitia) to Eustace fitz Will. Barun de Newenham : land &c. in A. S. par. in Jewry betw. land of
Michael Malherb on one side and the burial ground of
the ch. and land of Barth. le Noble on the other : rent 2ˢ
and four gallons (*lagenae*) of oil to maintain a lamp at the
altar of the blessed Mary in our ch. of S. Rad. for the
anniversary for souls of Will. Holdgord and others. Witn.
Thos. Tuylet.

95 Nuns (Pr. Milsentia) to **Ernisius**, merchant, of Camb.: **mess.**
   in A. S. par. betw. land of Cate Crocheman **and land**
   formerly of Ric. Bulloc, ab. on highway and land **formerly**
   in tenure of Durout le **Lung**: rent 4ˢ besides *gersuma.*
   Witn. Thos. Tuylet.

96 Nuns (Pr. Elena) to Ric. Crocheman: mess. in **A. S. par. in**
   Jewry betw. land of R. C. and land formerly in tenure of
   Joh. le Seenz, **ab.** as the last-mentioned mess.: rent 4ˢ.
   Joh. But, mayor. Edw. I. 13.

97 Joh. Porthors of Camb. to **Nuns**: rent of 13ᵈ out **of a mess.**
   in A. S. par. held of him by Joh. Waubert, **near the**
   Hospital, betw. a mess. formerly of Walter **Pilat and the**
   King's lane. **Joh. But, mayor.**

> The grant is for the souls of his father, Joh. de Berton, and
> his mother Agnes 'pro eo quod anima Johis predicti patris mei
> dampnum seu periculum habere non debet occasione retencionis
> duorum sol. argenti annui redditus quos predicte sc̄imoniales de
> capitali messuagio Johis patris mei in parochia ecclesie Sc̄i Cle-
> mentis ad terminos predictos percipere consueverunt.'

98 Nuns (Pr. Amitia de Driffeld) to **Ric.** fitz **Walter Croche-**
   man: tenᵗ in A. S. par. in **Jewry betw.** Pilateslane **and**
   land of said R. C., ab. **on highway and** land of Thos. de
   Luchefeld: **rent 6ᵈ and a mark** *pre manibus.* **Barth.**
   Goggyng, mayor.

99 Ric. Plowwryghte, carpenter, of Trumpitone bound **in sum**
   of £20 to erect for Joh. Pilate and complete satisfactorily
   before festival next following **of S. Peter ad Vincula eight**
   annexas **in a** void place in A. S. par. at end of Nunneslane,
   ab. on highway: 'sparre' **used to be of value not less**
   than 2ᵈ: Plowwryghte to receive for timber **and labour**
   £5. 2s. 6d. in three **instalments.** Witn. Joh. **Stokton.**
   Edw. III. 41.

TRINITY PARISH.

100*a* Geoff. Grim gives to Alan fitz Edward, in marriage with his niece Maud, land betw. land formerly of Ralf the Deaf (*Surdus*) and land of Hen. de Bertham, in H. T. par. next Garvin cross. Witn. Rob. Seman.

  b Maud, relict of Alan Edward of Camb., to Roger de Herdwic, servant of the Nuns: an annual rent of 4ˢ out of a tenᵗ in H. T. par. held of her by Fulk le Haneper, outside the ditch and near Garewycscruche; rent a pound of cummin, *gersuma* 25ˢ 4ᵈ. Witn. Anger le Rus.

  c The afore-mentioned Maud releases to Nuns (Pr. Constance) same land, Nuns paying her one bisant. Witn. Walter of Hauckestone, *capellanus*.

  The besant in the Boldon Buke is rated at 2s.

101*a* Walter de Lindsey to Ralf fitz Reiner: all his land in H. T. par. betw. land of Benedict Feutrer and land of said Ralf: rent 4ˢ, *gersuma* 5ˢ. Witn. Will. fitz Edward.

  b The same Walter, with consent of his wife Berta, in alms to Nuns: homage of Ralf le Feutrer and rent of 4ˢ paid by said Ralf: hagable ½ᵈ. Witn. Hervey fitz Eustace.

102 Hugh fitz William to Gudman, merchant: mess. betw. H. T. ch. and house of Isabel Sephare: rent 16ᵈ.

103 Nuns (Pr. Mabilia) to Ric. fitz Rob. de Fulburne, baker, and wife, Alice: tenᵗ in H. T. par. betw. land of Minor Friars and land formerly of Anger le Rus: rent 12ˢ. Witn. Ric. fitz Laurence.

104*a* Nuns (Pr. Custancia) to Rob. fitz Ralf le Chapeler: mess. formerly held of them by his father, Ralf, in H. T. par. outside the ditch betw. land formerly of Will. Filtrarius and land of Prior of Barnw., extending from highway to Nuns' croft: not to alienate to Jews: rent 12ᵈ. Witn. Will. de Hauckeston.

  b Ralf fitz Ralf Filtarius to his bro. Rob.: mess. in suburb of Camb. in Felterestrete betw. land of Prior of Barnw., land formerly of Will. Filtarius and Sarandescroft: rent pair of gloves, price $\frac{1}{2}^{d}$, and to Nuns 4ˢ. Witn. Magr. Martin de S. Radegund.

Felter St. = Wales Lane or King St.

105 Hen. de Berton to Will. de Henxcham: $\frac{1}{2}$ acre opposite the house of Ralf le Feuterier: rent 3ˢ, and *gersuma* 8ˢ. Witn. Ervey fitz Martin.

106 Will. Rolff, vicar of All Saints' next the Hospital, and others to Joh. Impyton of Camb., smith; a tenᵗ in H. T. par. betw. land of Laur. de Talworth and tenᵗ of Rob. Martyn ab. on tenᵗ of R. Martyn and on Conditstrete: rent 12 silver pennies to Nuns. Joh. Moris, mayor. Edw. III. 40.

107 Nuns (Pr. Margt. Clanile) to Simon Wyntleflete of Camb., cutler, and wife Isabel: mess. in Walyslane, betw. mess. of Joh. Norton, cordwainer, and mess. of Joh. de Refham, ab. on highway and on garden of Joh. Blaunpayn: for their lives: rent 5ˢ. Edw. III. 46.

108 Nuns give license to Geoff. Castro and wife Margt. for an eavesdropping from their house in Wales lane upon Sarant's croft for the breadth *unius pedis Sancti Pauli*. Edw. III. 48.

Pes Pauli. v. Arch. Hist. glossary.

109 Nuns (Pr. Alice Pilet) to Rob. Foxton and wife Alice: a portion of Sarent's croft to enlarge the house and garden which R. F. holds of the mayor and commons of Camb.: rent 6ᵈ. 1383.

110 Nuns (Pr. Alicia Pylet) to Alice, wid. of Geoffrey Castre: 3 shops &c. in Wales lane betw. a tenᵗ of Minor Friars and a tenᵗ lately of Joh. Baude, ab. on a croft of the Nuns late in tenure of Edw. de Ovyngton: for her life, rent 6ˢ. Ric. II. 20.

111 Nuns (Pr. Margery Herlyng) to Joh. Bylneye: mess. &c. in Walyslane in H. T. par. betw. land of Joh. Asschewell decd. and King's ditch, ab. on a stone wall of Minor Friars and on a tenᵗ of Asschewell: for 60 years, rent 2ˢ. Joh. Gaynysford, mayor. Henry IV. 10.

112 Nuns (Pr. Margery Herlyng) to Joh. Essex, saddler : ten^t in
Walyslane betw. house of Minor Friars and a ten^t of
Essex, ab. on highway and Sarantiscroft: for 60 years,
rent 5^s. Henry IV. 10.

113a Alice, wid. of Rob. Foxton, notary, releases to Nuns (Pr.
Agnes Seyntlowe) a corner ten^t in H. T. par. ab. on highway opposite the chain bridge towards W., on lane going
towards Barnw. opposite wall of Minor Friars towards N.,
on land of said Alice, E., and on a ten^t of Barnw. Priory
occupied by Thos. Goode, S.: the ten^t having been leased
to her husband by the Nuns. Henry VI. 22.

  b Thos. Goode of Camb., chandler, and his son Thos. release
the above ten^t to the Nuns. Ric. Wryghte, mayor.
Henry VI. 24.

  c Nuns lease same ten^t for 12 years to John Elys of Camb.:
rent 13^s 4^d. Nuns undertake to find timber, straw, clay,
splentys, boards &c. for doors, windows, plaunchyng and
all nails necessary : tenant to repair. Henry VI. 24.

114 Nuns (Pr. Agnes) to Rob. Coope of Camb. and wife Agnes:
two ten^{ts} in H. T. par. in lane leading from Waleslane
brigge towards Barnw. betw. ten^t of Joh. Heyward, W.
and ten^t of Edw. Hyderston, E., ab. on lane, S. and on
Nuns' croft N.: for lives, rent 8^s. Joh. Belton, mayor.
Henry VI. 35.

115 Nuns (Pr. Agnes Senclowe) to Joh. Stowe of Camb. and
wife Elena: farm &c. with buildings lately erected in
H. T. par. betw. le comen diche, E. and ten^t of Nuns, W.,
ab. on Waleslane N. and on garden of Rob. Coope, late
of Rob. Browne, S.: for 80 years, rent 2^s. Joh. Belton,
mayor. Henry VI. 35.

116 Nuns (Pr. Joan) to Joh. Chapman of Camb., brewer: void
place in H. T. par. in Wales lane betw. wall of Minor
Friars, W. and a ten^t of Nuns in tenure of Thos. Thorne,
E., said lane, S., and garden of the Nuns occupied by
Joh. Hayward, N.: for 26 years, rent 2^s. Tenant to
build and maintain a house on said place and let it to the
Nuns. Rob. Coope, mayor. Edw. IV. 6.

117 Nuns (Pr. Eliz. Walton) to Ric. Thorn, cordwainer: ten[t] &c. in H. T. par. in lane leading from Wallyslane brigge towards Barnw. betw. a ten[t] of Joh. Heyward, E. and a ten[t] of the Nuns in occupation of Joh. Chapman, W., ab. on said lane and on land of the Nuns in occupation of Joh. Heyward: for 40 years, rent 4[s]. Edw. IV. 12.

118 Nuns (Pr. Joan Cambridge) to Agnes Hungyrford, wid. of Rob. H.: ten[t] &c. in Wallyslane betw. ten[t] belonging to the Pascal of H. T. ch. and a ten[t] of Thos. Rede, M.D., ab. on lane and on a garden of Thos. Rede: for 20 years, rent 6[s] 8[d]. 1483.

119 Nuns (Pr. Joan) to Joh. Dale: mess. in H. T. par. in street leading from Cope's cross to Barnw. betw. a mess. of Nuns late in tenure of Ric. Thorne, W. and mess. of Dale, E., ab. on Wales lane, S. and mess. of Dale, N.: rent 2[s] and 2 capons, value 4[d]. Nich. Hylton, mayor. 1485.

120 Nuns (Pr. Joan Cambrigge) to Joh. Dale of Camb.: garden in Wales lane in H. T. par. betw. a mess. of Nuns in tenure of Ric. Thorne, S., croft of Nuns in tenure of Will. Pechard, N., ab. on a barn of Dale, late of Joh. Heyward, E., and wall of Minor Friars, W.: for 30 years, rent 8[d]. Henry VII. 1.

S. ANDREW'S PARISH.

121a Humphy fitz Bernard le Herde to Peter de Rising, clerk: one acre in S[t] A. par. outside Barnwell gates, betw. land of Nuns and land of Tho. Wolward with buildings thereon and all rights except his mother's dowry so long as she lives: rent ½[d], and 2 marks *gersuma*. Witn. John le Rus.

  b Peter de Rising, clerk, to Geoff. fitz Tho. de Littlebery: the same acre &c., excepting a third part which Sabina, wid. of Bernard Pastor, holds as dowry: rent &c. as above, and to Nuns 2[s] 6[d] and two capons. Witn. Tho. Tuillet.

  c Above Geoff., clerk, quitclaims same acre to Nuns in consideration of their releasing him from the aforesaid rent

of 2ˢ 6ᵈ and from a rent of 4ˢ due to the Nuns from a
piece of land in the suburbs of Camb., betw. highway
and land of Will. Sveteye and betw. the great street and
land of Tho. de Dittone, clerk.   Witn. Nich. Childman.

122a Nich. fitz Mich. Malherbe of Camb. to Will. de Bestun,
clerk: a rent of 3ˢ out of a mess. in Sᵗ A. par. held by
Will. de Mordun, betw. land of Joh. Parleben and land of
Mʳ Martin de S. Radegund: rent a root of ginger, and 20ˢ
gersuma.   Witn. Rob. de S. Edmundo, *capitalis ballivus*.

 b The same to the same: a rent of 5ˢ out of a mess. in Sᵗ A.
par. held by Will., the smith, betw. land of Hen. de
Mordun and land of Hugh Newecumen: rent a root of
ginger, and 40ˢ *gersuma*.   Witn. as above.

 c Will. de Bestone, clerk, to Nuns (Pr. Custance): a rent of
8ˢ out of two mess. in Sᵗ A. par. outside Barnwell gates:
gersuma 5 marks.   Witn. Ric. fitz Laurence, *capitalis
ballivus*.

123 Nuns (Pr. Custancia) to Andr. fitz Ralf Knapere de S.
Edmundo and his wife Alice, dau. of Rob. ad fontem de
Hyntone: mess. formerly of Rob. de Trumpitone, in
Sᵗ A. par. betw. land of Jas. le Wauter, land of Elena
Alshope and land of Pet. de Wilburham, ab. on highway
and land of Alan de Teversham: rent 5ˢ 6ᵈ.   Witn.
Will. Elyot.

124 Ysabel, dau. of Alan de Teversham, widow, to Pet., nephew
of Pet., late vicar of H. T. church, Camb.: mess. in Sᵗ A.
par. betw. land of Mabilia Golofer, the highway, land of
Marg. de Abiton and Rokislane: 4 marks *gersuma*, rent
to Nuns 7ˢ 4ᵈ and lights for the altar of the B.V. in
Sᵗ A. church.   Barth. Goggyng, mayor.

   Rokislane, otherwise Rogues', Hangman's or Hinton Lane, now
Christ's Lane.

125 Crestiana, dau. of Godard, to Hugh fitz Will.: land in Sᵗ A.
par. betw. land of Barnwell Priory and land of Ric. de
Bernewell, behind the chapel of the H. T.: rent 12ᵈ, and
2ˢ 6ᵈ *gersuma*.   Witn. Gregory fitz Hugh.

126a Rob. de Tychewell, *cissor*, of Camb. to Alan de Badburham
of Camb. and his wife Marg.: mess. in St A. par. in
Rokeslane. Eudo de Helpringham, mayor.

  b Stephen fitz Adam Godesone quitclaims same mess. to same
Rob. Symon de Refham, mayor. Ed. II. 16.

127 Ralf de Derham and wife Maud, dau. of Adam, *pictor*, to
Will., parson of Morpad: land in St A. par. Witn.
Baldwin Blangernun.

128a Nich. fitz Alexander, Almoner of Ely, to Everard fitz
Philip: land in St A. par. betw. land of Rob. de Taxstede
and of Will. Duzedeners: rent 4^s, and 2^s *gersuma*.
Witn. Baldwin Blangernun.

  b Same Everard to Joh. fitz Joh., smith; same land: rent to
Ely Almoner 4^s, and 6^s *gersuma* to Everard. Witn.
Hervey fitz Eustace.

129 Alan de Hynton, *piscator*, of Camb. to Joh. Paulin and his
son Joh.: land in St A. par. Joh. Buth, mayor. Edw.
I. 19.

130 Oldeburga, dau. of Ric. Gulafre, to Hen. de Berton: land
in St A. par., betw. lane to Hinton and land of her bro.
Ric.: rent 8^d, and 30^s *gersuma*. Witn. Hervey Grim.

131a Tho. fitz Tho., mercer, to his sister Cecilia: mess. in S^t A.
par. betw. Hinton lane and Mabel Gulafre: rent 8^d.
Witn. Rob. Seman.

  b The same Tho. to the Nuns: mess. in S^t A par., butted as
the last. Witn. Hervey fitz Eustace.

132 Ric. Gulafre to Hen. Leverton: land in S^t. A. par., betw.
land of same Ric., land of Absalon fitz Segar and lane
leading to Hintone: rent 8^d, and 3^s *gersuma*. Witn.
Hervey Grim.

133a Marg., dau. of Stephen, to Rob. de S. Edmundo: a rent of
6^d out of a mess. formerly belonging to her father in
St A. par. Witn. Rob. Saman.

  b Joh. Aelard to the Nuns for their Infirmary: the rent of
6^d which he bought from Rob. de S. Edmundo proceeding out of the above-mentioned mess., formerly of Stephen
fitz Adelin in Willeghes. Witn. Rob. Saman.

134 Nuns (Pr. Elena) to Joh. de Biccleswade of Camb.: land in
St A. par. in Deus Deners lane, next highway and land
of Benet Godesone, ab. on land of the chapel of S. Edmund
and land of the Hosp. of S. John: rent 2^s 6^d. Witn.
Joh. Martin.

135 Joh. Pawe of Camb. and dau. Katerina to Nich. Pawe of
Camb.: a garden &c. in St A. par. in Preachers' St. betw.
a garden of the Prior of S. Edmund's chapel and a mess.
of the Hosp. of S. John, ab. on common lane and a garden
of Mr Tho. de Suthwerke: the said garden &c. being held
by him of the Nuns: rent 2^s 6^d. Eudo de Helpringham,
mayor. Edw. II. 18.

136a Marg., dau. of Emma, to Nuns for their Infirmary: mess.
in lane leading from St A. ch. towards Hintune, betw. land
of Hen. Elyot and land of Nuns. Witn. Tho. Toilet.

  b Ric. fitz Walter de Pynchebek of Camb. and his wife
Muriel to Joh. Edward: the mess. above described.
Symon de Refham, mayor.

137 Cecilia Sagar to Mr Martin de S. Radegund: land in the
great street outside Barnwell gate, betw. land of Will.,
smith, and land of Ric. Marscal: rent to Nuns 7^d. Witn.
Simon Godeloth.

138 Nuns to Hen. de Mordon: cortillage and house formerly of
Mr Martin in St A. par.: rent half a mark. Witn. Will·
de Newenham.

139a Roger de Capella to Will. de Barlham, clerk: burgage &c.
outside Barnw. gate, occupied by Walter Seger: rent to
Nuns 18^d and a hen, to heirs of Nich. Doy 4^d, hagable
1^d. Witn. Ric. fitz Laurence.

  b The above Will. de B. to Will. fitz Roger de Norwyc: the
same burgage: 30 marks gersuma, rent to Nuns 18^d,
hagable 1$^{3d}_{4}$. Witn. Joh. Porthors.

140 Nuns to Tho. Engayne of Camb., his wife Katherine and
son Tho.: a garden in St A. par. at south end of town,
betw. a tenement of Reg. de Trumpyton and land of the
Nuns, ab. on Nuns' land and highway: rent 4^s. Edw.
III. 17.

141 Nuns (Pr. Margaret) to Joh. Berlee of Camb.: a tenement
in S¹ A. par. betw. a tenement of Corp. Chr. Coll., a
tenement of Joh. de Toft and a tenement of Rob. de
Parys, ab. on highway, the King's ditch and Pouches
croft: for 40 years, rent 18ˢ. Tenant to repair buildings
on the tenement, viz., a hall with solar and two cellars
under the solar, a chamber to W. of the hall, three
chambers in front of the tenement and a dovehouse.
Joh. Morice, mayor. Edw. III. 43.

142 Nuns (Pr. Margery Harlyng) to Rob. Pynnington: a tenement in S¹ A. par. betw. a tenement of Corp. Chr. Coll.,
a tenement of Joh. Huntyngdon, (late of Joh. Cotton)
and a garden which Joh. Weston holds of the Nuns, ab.
on the highway, King's Ditch and Pouches croft (which
belongs to the Prior and Canons of S. Edmund's chapel):
for 80 years, rent 17ˢ. The Nuns to supply tenant after
wheat harvest with one acre of wheat-straw, and tenant
to be allowed to cut down trees to repair premises, planting others in their place. Joh. Gaynesford, mayor.
Henry IV. 9.

143 Ric. Busshe and others to Will. Mast, baker, and others: a
mess. in S¹ A. par. in Prechourstrete, betw. a tenement
of Corp. Chr. Coll. and a tenement of Adam Peyntour,
ab. on highway and a garden of Joh. Baldok. Joh.
Biluey, mayor. Henry V. 3.

144a Will of Will. Mast, dated Dec. 3, 1432.

   Among the legacies are : to the high altar of All Saints' church
(where he is to be buried) 20ˢ: to his brother in law, Andr.
Sharp, his tenement in Preacherstrete for life: to each order of
mendicant friars in Camb. 20ˢ: to the Nuns of S. Rad. 20ˢ, the
Prioress to have as much as two nuns : to the Nuns of Swafham
10ˢ: executors to find 5 priests to celebrate for his soul.

   b Probate of above will. Dec. 16, 1432.
   c The executors of the same will convey to Andr. Sharp the
tenement in Preacherstrete. Henry VI. 12.
   d Sharp's release to Mast's executors. Henry VI. 13.

145 *a* Marg., wid. of Will. Mast, to Rob. Koker and others: a mess. in Preacherstrete. Witn. Tho. Heyrman, mayor. Hen. VI. 29.

b Letter of attorney from Marg. Mast to Tho. Porter to deliver seisin of last named mess. Henry VI. 29.

c Rob. Coker to Nuns (Pr. Elizabeth): the same mess., described as betw. a tenement of Corp. Chr. Coll., S., a tenement of Joh. Coloffe, N., a garden of Geoff. Newell, W.: for 99 years, rent 16^d to Corp. Chr. Coll., as quit rent of a tenement in S. Mary's par. *juxta forum*, betw. a tenement of Rob. Coker, S., and Cutlerrowe, N., which he holds of the Nuns   Rob. Cooper, mayor. Dec. 10, 1468.

d Rob. Coker releases to Nuns (Pr. Elizabeth) same mess., reserving power to distrain in case the Nuns fail to pay to Corp. Chr. Coll. the above mentioned quit rent.   Rob. Cooper, mayor.   Feb. 25, Edw. IV. 8.

146 *a* Mariota, wid. of Joh. Quenburgh of Horningsey, to Joh. Foster: mess. in Preacher Strete, betw. a tenement of Corp. Chr. Coll. and a tenement of Adam Peyntour, ab. on the street and a garden of Joh. Baldok.   Ric. II. 13.

b Joh. Foster of Bodekesham to Rob. Brigham of Camb.: the same mess.   Ric. II. 21.

147 Joh. Baynard of Stapleford to Simon de Sleford and others; a shop with solar above it in St A. par., bounded by highway, land of said Simon, and a tenement of Walter Hervy.   Witn. Joh. de Essex.   Edw. III. 32.

148 Simon Sleford to Joh. Asschwell, tailor, of Camb.: a tenement betw. Rokeslane and a tenement late of Walter Hervy, ab. on a tenement of Joh. de Badburgham and highway.   Witn. Ric. Fowke, mayor.   Edw. III. 42.

149 Andr. Beauchamp of Stowe to Walt. Pannfold, goldsmith, of Camb.: a barn and garden in St A. par. betw. land of Ely Sacrist and Hangmanueslane, ab. on garden of same Andr. and land of Joh. de Badburgham.   Joh. Gybon, mayor.   Edw. III. 45.

150 *a* Same Andr. to Joh. de Wauton: mess. in St A. par. betw. a mess. of the Prior of Ely and Hangmauneslane, ab. on

Preachoure Streete, which mess. said **Andr.** bought of
Joh. de Asschewelle, tailor. Joh. Gybon, mayor. **Edw.**
III. 46.

b **Joh.** de **Wauton** to **Will.** de Wykmer, University bedel:
mess. above described. **Joh.** Gybon, mayor. **Edw.** III.
46.

151 **Margery**, wid. of above Will., to the Nuns: a tenement in
St A. par. next the lane leading to Hynkton. **Hen. V. 8.**

152 **Nuns** (Pr. **Agnes** Seynctlowe) to Ely Priory (Prior, Edmund
Walsyngham): a void place in St A. par. lately held by
Will. Wygmer, University bedel, of the Nuns for a rent
of 8^s, betw. a void plot of Ely Sacrist, S., and lane leading
to Hynton, N., ab. on a tenement of the Nuns leased to
Joh. Grenelane, E., and on highway, W.: rent 4^s. **Ely,**
Hen. V. 9.

Seal of Ely Convent.

153 **Nuns** (Pr. **Agnes** Senclow) to Rob. Gotobedde: mess. in
Waleslane in St A. par. betw. a tenement late of **Joh.**
Refham and a tenement late of **Joh.** de **Norton**, ab. on
highway and a toft late of **Joh.** de **Blancpayn**: lease for
60 years, rent 4^s. The tenant to build a new barn and a
new house for two tenants on said mess. **Joh.** Grenelane,
mayor. Feb. 18, 1422.

154 **Indenture**, in English, betw. the Nuns (Pr. **Elizabeth**) and
Ric. Wodecok, butcher.

For the matter, see p. 41.

155 **Nuns** (Pr. **Eliz.** Walton) release to **Joh.** Ely a rent of 6^s
proceeding out of a void place in St A. par. called the
Swerd on the Hope, betw. land of the Nuns leased to
Joh. Baldewyn, glover, S., and a tenement of **Hen. Paris,**
gentleman, N., ab. on a farm of the Nuns occupied by
Joh. Ely, E.: tenant to pay instead a rent of 1^s 8^d. **Joh.**
Wyghton, mayor. **Edw. IV. 19.**

S. Peter's Parish extra Trumpington Gate.

(The old church of S. Peter fell down soon after 1325: before 1349 the new church dedicated to S. Mary was completed. The deeds in the list below are all of the 13th century.)

156a Ralf Sigan, priest, to the Nuns: land without Trump. gate next land of Hen. Meso and land of which his son Coleman has the reversion after his death. Witn. Maurice, *capellanus*.

  b The same to the same: land in same place. Same witnesses.

  c Hugh fitz Algar Brest releases to the Nuns (Pr. Leticia) land given to them by Ralf Sigan. Witn. Hervey fitz Eustace.

157 Nuns (Pr. Letitia) to Ric. Burs, butcher, land in St P. par. without Trump. gate, betw. land of Ric. Sincreles and land of Hen. Scolemaister: rent 12^d, two capons, and half a mark as *gersuma*. Witn. Sir Drogo, *capellanus*.

158 Nuns to Mabel Blangernun for her life: a mess. in Trump. street formerly held of them by Hen. Scolemayster, betw. a mess. of Ric. Burs, butcher, and a mess. of Ric. Cau: rent 5^s. Witn. Joh. Ruffus.

159 Nuns (Pr. Custancia) to Pet. de Wilburham and wife Sabina: a mess. in St P. par. without Trump. gate, lately held of Nuns by Mabel Blangernun, betw. land of said Sabina and land of Tho. de Cotenham: rent 3^s. Joh. Leacon, mayor.

160 Nuns (Pr. Elena) to Joh. de Eylesham and wife Sabina: plot of ground in St P. par. without Trump. gate, betw. his land and land of Mr Hugh de Hulmo, ab. in front on the highway: rent 6^d. Joh. Martin, mayor.

  This plot was included in the site of Peterhouse: see *Arch. Hist.* I., p. 3, and Hundr. Rolls II., p. 371.

161 Marg., wid. of Ralf, to Rob. fitz Maud: land in St P. par. *extra portam Cantebr.* betw. land of St P. church and land

of Absalon fitz Wymund, next the chapel of S. Edmund:
rent 4ᵈ, two capons, and 2ˢ *gersuma*. Witn. Walt., son
of Mr Geoffrey.

S. Botolph's Parish.

162 Ric. Bateman of Camb. to the Nuns (Pr. Agnes Burgeillo)
in exchange for a mess. late of Will. Nonacurt: a rent of
12ᵈ out of a mess. near the King's Ditch next Trump.
gate, and another of 8ᵈ out of three shops in Pirones
lane, betw. a mess. of Tho. le Moner and a mess. of Alice
de Bradelee. Witn. Barth. Goggyng.

Pirones lane, see *Arch. Hist.* I. p. 335.

163 Alice, dau. of Ric. Gibelot, to Nuns: a mess. next the
cemetery of Sᵗ B. and ab. on highway and land of Sᵗ B.
Witn. Will. Morice.

164 Nuns (Pr. Mabilia) to Hen. de Cotes: a mess. in Sᵗ B. par.
in Melnestrate, given to them by Symon Godelote, betw.
land late of Pet. de Well and land of Ric. fitz Laurence:
rent 20ᵈ besides a rent charge to S. John's Hospital.
Witn. Humfrey Brithnod.

165 Nuns (Pr. Letitia) to Martin Brictnot: land &c. in Sᵗ B.
par. betw. his land and land of Will. Mildes: rent 16ᵈ
and 16ˢ *gersuma*. Witn. Hervey, clerk.

166 Nuns (Pr. Elena) to Joh. Martin and wife Avice: a mess.
in Sᵗ B. par. betw. his land and a mess. of Joh. Hardy:
rent 2ˢ. Rob. Tuyllet, mayor.

167 Nuns (Pr. Elena) to Ralf fitz Joh. Roger de Cumbertone:
plot of ground in Sᵗ B. par. betw. a mess. of Hen. Hardi
and a mess. of Will. Martin, ab. on highway: rent 3ˢ.
Witn. Joh. Porthors. 1299.

168 Will., vicar of All Saints' ch., and others to Joh. Cheseman
and wife Joan for their lives: a mess. in Sᵗ B. par.: rent
18ᵈ. Roger de Harleston, mayor. Ed. III. 31.

S. Benet's Parish.

169*a* Walter son of Master Geoff. of Camb. to Peter fitz Bur-
chard : land in St B. par. which Filurun held of his
father : rent 2^s, two capons and two hens and 20^s *gersuma*.
Witn. Bartholomew, chaplain.

b Will. de St Edmund to Nuns : the above mess., described as
in the great street towards Trump. gate ; rent as above,
the Nuns releasing to him an acre of land in Camb. fields
which they hold of the same Walter, son of Geoff. Witn.
Maurice Ruffus.

c Alice, wife of above Will. de St Edmund and dau. of Master
Geoff., confirms the above grant. Witn. as above.

d Walter, son of above Will. and Alice, confirms the same
grant. Witn. as above.

170*a* Alice, dau. of Ric. fitz Peter to Nuns : land in St B. par.
betw. land of John Smith and land of Hugh Ruffus,
reaching from highway to land of Greg. Salter : also land
in same par. betw. land late in tenure of Godlomb and
land of Nich. Kyp : also a shop in S. Edward's par. betw.
a shop of Alan Macston and a shop late of Reg. fitz
Osbon : Nuns to pay all services, viz. 32^d to the Hosp.
of St John, 30^d to Almoner of Ely and 2^s, two capons
and two hens to heirs of Master Walter fitz Geoff.
Witn. Hervey fitz Eustace.

b Ivetta, widow of Peter, quitclaims dower in the second of
the above premises. Witn. as in the last.

171*a* Cecilia de Wynepol to Nuns : an annual rent of 6^s 7^d,
viz. 4^s out of a mess. held of her by Serlo le Waunter in
St B. par. betw. land of Joh. Goggyng and land of Alan
Weaver, and 2^s 7^d out of a mess. held of her by Joh.
Goggyng in same par. next the former mess. and towards
Trump. gate. Nuns to pay yearly to St B. ch. 4^d and a
wax candle and 2^d for hagable. Witn. Thos. Toylet.

b The same Cecilia releases same mess. to Nuns subject to
above mentioned charges. Same witnesses.

172a Walter Scissart to Nuns: land in S' B. par. which he
    bought of Rob. fitz Ormar, and land in S' John's par.
    which he bought of Hildebrand Gabyt: Nuns to pay rent
    of 6ᵈ to heirs of Rob. fitz Ormar for the first-named and
    2ᵈ to the King for the other. Witn. Fabianus, priest.

  b Alice, wife of Bernard fitz Edricius, releases above lands
    to Nuns. Witn. Dominus B., official of the archdeacon
    of Ely.

  c Bernard fitz Edricius releases the same. Witnesses as
    in last.

  d Symon fitz Reginald ad portam releases the same. Wit-
    nesses as before.

173 Thos. le Mercer to Nuns: an annual rent of 16ᵈ out of
    land in S' B. par. held of him by Will. Scurri. Witn.
    Hervey fitz Eustace.

174a Nuns (Pr. Letitia) to Margaret, widow of Thos. Merchant:
    a mess. in S' B. par. betw. land formerly of Walter, son
    of Master Geoff., and land of Margaret Suneman: also a
    mess. in Milne St. in S' John's par. betw. land of the
    Nuns in tenure of Nicolas, *capellanus*, and land of Alan
    Wiclof: rent 7ˢ and two capons with three marks
    gersuma. Witn. Hervey fitz Eustace.

  b The above Margaret grants the mess. in S' John's par. to
    her son Walter: rent to Nuns 4ˢ and two capons.
    Witn. Rob. Seman.

175 Nuns (Pr. Letitia) to Thos. Baker: a mess. in S' B. par.
    betw. land of Peter le Huute and land formerly of
    Godlomb: rent 3ˢ and two capons, with one mark *ger-*
    suma. Witn. Thomas, parson of S' Benet's.

176 Nuns (Pr. Letitia) to Peter le Hunte: land with buildings
    thereon in S' B. par. betw. land of Nich. Kyep and land
    of Nuns in tenure of Ivetta, widow of Peter Butcher (*sic*):
    rent 3ˢ, and two marks *gersuma*. Witn. Hervey fitz
    Eustace.

PARISH OF S. JOHN THE BAPTIST IN MILNE STREET.

177 Apsolon fitz Roger confirms to John fitz Azo the grant
made to him by Walter Cros of a mess. in M. St. betw.
land of Peter fitz Yvo and land of said Apsolon : rent 4ˢ
to Walt. Cros. Witn. Rob. Seman.

178a Aspelon fitz Roger to his dau. Ysabel: a mess. in Sᵗ J.
par. betw. a mess. lately occupied by his bro. Hugh and a
mess. of his dau. Margaret: rent half a pound of cumin
and 1ᵈ hagable. Witn. Geoff. Potekin.

 b The same Apsolon repeats to the same Ysabel the above
grant and adds a piece of land formerly belonging to the
mess. of his bro. Hugh : rent and witnesses as in the last.

179 The same Absolon fitz Roger, priest, to Martin Wolward : a
part of the land held by him of Hervey fitz Eustace, next
land of Reginald fitz Alfred, in the little lane leading to
Sᵗ John's ch., together with a house on the same land :
rent 20ᵈ. Witn. Hervey Grim.

180 Hervey fitz Eustace to the Nuns: a rent of 12ᵈ to be paid
by Absolon, priest's son, out of land in Sᵗ J. par. next
the lane leading from Sᵗ Edward's ch. to Sᵗ John's ch., to
recompense them for any loss which may result to All
Saints' ch. out of the common land on which the Hosp.
of Sᵗ John is situated, and that the same Hosp. may
have right to bury where they will, *salva eidem hospitali
libera cantaria sua in perpetuum.* Witnesses Dominus
E[ustace], Eliens. Eps̄., R. Barre, Archidiac. Eliens.,
Will., Prior of Barnwell, Fulk son of Teobald &c.

181 Maurice Ruffus in the same terms grants to the Nuns a
rent of 12ᵈ out of land in Sᵗ J. par. in the tenure of
Symon fitz Reginald, next land of Goding de Cestertun.
Witnesses as in the last.

182a Geremias Banastre of Elteslee to Ysabel, sister of his wife
Margaret : land in M. St., par. of Sᵗ J., being part of the
land given to him by Aspelon fitz Roger in marriage with

his dau. Margaret: rent 6ᵈ, and 40ˢ *gersuma*. Witn.
Hervey fitz Eustace.

b Margaret, widow of Jeremias Banastre, to the Nuns: the
above mentioned land: rent 6ᵈ, and two marks *gersuma*.
Witn. Rob. de Sᵗ Edmund.

183 The same Margaret, widow of German (*sic*) Banastre to her
dau. Lecia: a rent of 3ˢ payable by Simon ad aquam,
and one of 12ᵈ payable by the Nuns: Lecia to pay yearly
a silver farthing. Witn. Rob. Banastre &c.

184 Amycia, dau. of John Banastre of Eltisle, to Sir John de
Triplawe, Rector of Reymerston, dioc. Norwich: a rent of
12ᵈ payable by the Nuns out of a mess. in M. St., par. of
Sᵗ J., formerly of Roger de Costyshey and Rob. de
Wynebotisham: no rent. John Pylat, mayor. Edw. III. 5.

185*a* Aspelon fitz Roger confirms to Nuns a rent of 4ˢ out of
land in tenure of John fitz Acius, betw. the land given
by said Aspelon to his dau. Margaret and land of Yvo
fitz [*blank*], which rent his son Reginald gave to the
Nuns for one lamp in their church. Witn. Hervey fitz
Eustace.

  b The Nuns (Pr. Letitia) to John fitz Acius: a mess. in
M. St., betw. land of Peter fitz Yvo and land of Jeremias
of Eltislee, which mess. was bequeathed to them by
Reg. fitz Absolon for a lamp before the altar of the B.V.
and confirmed to them by said Absolon: rent 4ˢ, and
4ˢ *gersuma*. Witn. Hervey fitz Eustace.

186 The Nuns (Pr. Leticia) to Alan Whitlof and his wife
Alice: a mess. in M. St. given to them by Walter Gyffard:
rent 18ᵈ. Witn. Rob. Saman.

187 The Nuns (Pr. Milisentia) to Symon de Wynebodesham
and wife Margaret: land and buildings thereon in M. St.,
par. of Sᵗ J., betw. land of Thos. Wolward and land of
Jeremias de Elteslee, extending 220 ft. from the great
street to the river (*fossatum*) and at the river end 102 ft.
betw. land of Alice Belbar and land of John fitz Azo:
rent one mark, and half a mark *gersuma*. Witn. Thos.
Tuyllet.

188 Agreement betw. the Nuns (Pr. Agnes Shenkelowe) and
Joh. Bridbrok, clerk, before Joh. Bilneye, mayor, respecting the rent of 4ˢ arising from the mess. given by Reg.
fitz Absolon to Letitia, late Prioress. The position and
bounds of the said mess. being unknown to any living
person the said J. B. agrees that the said rent shall
in future be paid out of a mess. of his in M. St. betw.
a mess. once of Will. Wynde, afterwards of Nich. Hethe,
now of Joh. Ascheman and a tenement of Clara Hall,
called Hospicium Wallicorum, ab. on M. St. The Nuns
to pray for him as one of their benefactors. Henry VI. 5.

189 Mariota, widow of Ric. de Berton, to Maud, her dau.; a
mess. in M. St., par. of Sᵗ J., opposite the church, betw. a
tenement of Alberis de Saltrega and a tenement of Will.
Pitcock (held *de feodo* Hospitalis Sc̄i Johannis de Jerusalem) on N., and a shop and yard and Pyrones lane
on S., ab. E. on a tenement of Maud de Walda and a
tenement of Derota la Parchiminere, and W. on the
street and yard of said shop: rent a silver penny as
hagable, and one penny to said Mariota. John But,
mayor. Ed. I. 20.

The Hospital mentioned is not that of St John, Cambridge, but
that of St John of Jerusalem, in England, which possessed property
in the par. of St J. See Hundr. Rolls, II., p. 360.

190 Nuns (Pr. Elena) to Joh. le Lominor, his wife Mabel and
heirs: a mess. in Melne strete in the par. of S. John
Baptist, betw. Pyron lane and a mess. of said Joh. le L.,
ab. on Melne strete and a mess. of the same John:
rent 3ˢ. Rob. Tuylet, mayor.

191 Nuns (Pr. Margaret Clanille) to Will. Stote and his son
Thos.: a rent proceeding out of ground in the par. of
Sᵗ J., betw. a mess. of Marg. le Clerk of Chesterton and a
mess. of the said Will., ab. on a void place of Damalis de
Felstede and highway: they to pay annually 12ᵈ, and for
the first seven years 7ˢ in advance. Joh. London, mayor.
Edw. III. 38.

S. EDWARD'S PARISH.

192 Stephen de Schalariis grants to Absalon fitz Roger of Camb. three shops *in stallis Cantebr.* rented respectively at 5ˢ, 4ˢ and 3ˢ, receiving from him 100 shillings *pre manibus* 'ad magnum negocium meum perficiendum.' Witn. Geoff. Potekin.

193 Adam Sellarius grants to Hen. Hubert in marriage with his sister Edusa a shop in Sᵗ E. par. betw. land of Baldewin Blangernun and land lately in tenure of Barth. Taillur: rent 3ˢ. Witn. Geoff. Potekin.

194*a* The Nuns (Pr. Letitia) to Henry Huberd: a shop in Sᵗ E. par. betw. land of the Nuns and land formerly of Peter, capellanus de Neweham : rent 3ˢ. Witn. Geoff. Potekin.

 b Henry Hubert grants to Thos. Pertehaye in marriage with his dau. Eva the shop mentioned in the last : rent 3ˢ to the Nuns. Witn. Thos. Thuilhet.

195 The Nuns (Pr. Letitia) to Ric. Morin : a shop betw. a shop of Hen. Hubert and a shop of Nigel le Seller, both held of the Nuns: rent 5ˢ, and 4ˢ *gersuma*. Witn. Rob. Seman.

196 The Nuns (Pr. Letitia) to Ralf fitz Hervey : three mess. *in circuitu cimiterii Sci Edwardi*, one next a mess. of the Nuns occupied by Maud Dun, the others on either side of a mess. of Ivo de Bramton : rent 4ˢ and four capons, with 20ˢ *gersuma*. Witn. Hervey fitz Eustace.

197 The Nuns (Pr. Milesentia) to Will. Tuylet : land *in stallagio* formerly held of them by Hen. Hubert : rent 2ˢ. Witn. Thos. Tuylet.

198 Robert fitz Anger le Rus to the Nuns (Pr. Custancia) : a quit rent of 3ˢ out of a mess. formerly of Hen. Spileman in the Cornmarket, betw. land of John ad portam and land of Nicholas ultra forum : in return the Nuns release to John de Sausitone a rent of 3ˢ due to them from Ralf de Bancis for a virgate of land in Pampesworth. Ric. fitz Laurence, mayor.

199 Maud Pinniger binds herself to pay to the Nuns a rent of
7ˢ for a shop in the Butchery, between the stalls given
to them by Ric. ad portam, the said shop having been
formerly held of the Nuns by Eustace Selede. Witn.
Dominus Walter de Havekestone, *capellanus*.

200 John de Branketre (or ? Brankstre) and his son Thos. to
Richard de Sᶜᵒ Neoto of Camb. butcher: a mess. in
Tripereslane betw. a tenement of Andrew Wolleward
and a tenement of Geoff. le Feror: rent to the Almoner
of Ely 2ˢ, to the Nuns 6ᵈ and 6 capons (or 12ᵈ), and 18ˢ
to the said John. Edw. I. 34.

201 William Flemyng of Camb., butcher, releases to the Nuns
a shop which has escheated to them, *in Bocheria* in Sᵗ E.
par. Symon de Refham, mayor. Edw. II. 5.

202 Thomas de Maddyngle quitclaims to Dˢ William, chaplain,
son of Thos. de Wynepol, scrivener, a mess. formerly of
Joan Casteleyn in Sᵗ E. par. at the end of the Bucherie
betw. a tenement of Walter fitz Thomas, butcher, and
the Oatmarket and ab. at either end on the street. Rob.
Dunnyng, mayor. Edw. II. 10.

203 William de Ixnyng, vicar of All Saints', and others lease to
Ste. Moriz a mess. containing two shops in the Bocherie,
betw. a shop belonging to Sᵗ John's House and a shop of
Sᵗ Rad. House, for 53 years: rent to the Prior of Barnwell
4ˢ 4ᵈ, to Sᵗ John's House 4ˢ, to the Prioress of Swaffham
4ˢ 6ᵈ, to the Prioress of Sᵗ Rad. 4ˢ 2ᵈ and to the said
William 12ᵈ. John de London, mayor. Edw. III. 40.

204 Ely Convent (John, Prior) leases to John Frenge, his
wife Agnes and son John, two mess. in Camb., the one
in Sᵗ E. par. ab. on a mess. of the Almoner of Ely,
occupied by the said J. F., and on a mess. of the Nuns,
and extending along the lane next the churchyard of
Sᵗ E.; the other with hithe appertaining called Cholles-
hithe in the parish of Sᵗ John, in the lane called Water-
lane, betw. a mess. of Edm. Lyster and the said lane, ab.
on the river bank and a mess. of Will. Wynde: for the
term of their lives: rent 18ˢ. Dated Ely. Edw. III. 40.

205*a* The Nuns (Pr. Alicia Pilet) lease to Rich. Hynton, butcher, and his wife Alice a shop in the Bocherie, betw. a shop late of Will. de Lavenham and a shop late of John Baldwyn, ab. on the street and St E. churchyard: for the term of their lives: rent 14^s. John Blannpayn, mayor. Rich. II. 2.

  b The Nuns (Pr. Alicia Pilet) lease the above mentioned shop to John Baldwyn, butcher, his wife Joan and dau. Isabel for the term of their lives: rent 14^s. Witn. Will. Cumburton. Rich. II. 22.

206 John de Lincoln to John Roiston of Camb.: a mess. in St E. par. betw. a mess. of Adam Lolleworth and a mess. of John Oreford, ab. on the Cornmarket and on a garden of Angleseye Priory. Ric. Maisterman, mayor. Rich. II. 12.

207 Acquittance of the Nuns (Pr. Agnes) to John Chance for 10^s, being two years rent of a mess. in St E. par. in the Bochere Rowe, betw. the Otemarket and a shop late of John Broun, butcher, and ab. on the street and a mess. late of John Sexteyn. Henry VI. 10.

208 The Nuns (Pr. Eliz. Walton) lease to Richard Woodcok, butcher, and his wife Joan, a mess in St E. par. betw. a mess. of John Roys, S., a mess. of Thos. Reede, N., ab. on the Bocherie, E., and on St E. churchyard, W., for 99 years: rent 15^s. Edw. IV. 14.

209 The Nuns (Pr. Joan Fulburn) lease to Mr Rob. Goodknape, clerk, a mess. in St E. par. betw. a mess. of the Coll. of St Clare, S., a mess. of Simon Bentybowe, late of Will. Barford, N., ab. on a mess. of the Solfham Nuns, W., and on St E. churchyard, E., for 40 years: rent 4^s. Aug. 6, 1493.

PARISH OF S. MARY JUXTA FORUM.

210 Maud Corde, widow, to Nuns: a rent of 3^s 1^d and 2 capons out of a mess. in St M. par. betw. land of Marg^t de Abiton and land late of Hugh Alderman, reaching from highway

to land of Cecilia Pernes: also a rent of 3ˢ out of a mess. next a mess. formerly of Laur. Fitien in par. of S. Peter *versus castrum*, next the street leading towards Hulmus and ab. on a mess. formerly of Margᵗ Fitien and on the highway. John Martin, mayor.

211*a* John fitz William for welfare of souls of himself and his lord, Hugh, gives with his body to the Almoner of S. Rad. the northern half of a mess., late of Ruold, in Sᵗ M. par., granted to him by said Hugh: rent to the *dominus feodi* 6ᵈ: the Nuns to find a lamp before the altar of the B.V. Witn. Rob. Seman.

b Hugh fitz Apsolon to his kinswoman Aldusa: the southern half of the above mess., which he bought of his uncle Ruald, reaching from the highway before S. Mary's ch. to the street leading to S. John's ch.: rent 6ᵈ, and one mark *gersuma*. Witn. Thos., dean of Sanford.

c Aldusa, dau. of Will. Blancgernun for welfare of souls of herself and Hugh fitz Apsalon gives with her body to the Nuns the above land, formerly of Ruald Cari: rent 6ᵈ to said Hugh. Witn. Hervey fitz Eustace.

212*a* Hugh fitz Apsolon to his kinswoman Aldusa: mess. held of him by Mabilia Harre: rent 12ᵈ, and 16ˢ *gersuma*. Witn. Thos., dean of Sanford.

b Hugh fitz Apsolon grants to Nuns the above rent of 12ᵈ to find a lamp for the Nuns' Infirmary: service of the King 1ᵈ. Witn. Fabian, *capellanus*.

213*a* The same Aldusa gives with her body to the Nuns her land and buildings in Sᵗ M. par. betw. land of Stephen Corduaner and land of Ric. Pernes. Witn. Hervey fitz Eustace.

b The Nuns (Pr. Leticia) to Andrew fitz Galien: the above land and buildings: rent 8ˢ. Witn. John and Richard, 'our chaplains.'

214 Henry fitz Hugh to Symon fitz Henry: a shop in Camb. market betw. a shop of same Symon and a shop of William fitz Henry: rent to John de Bertun 2ˢ, and 3 marks *gersuma*. Witn. Dˢ John Fitz Hugh.

215 Henry de Bertun, with consent of his wife Alice, to Henry
     fitz Alan: a shop near the shop which Henry fitz Hugh
     holds of him: rent 2ˢ, and 2ˢ *gersuma*.   Witn. Mr Henry
     Pilat.

216 Maurice fitz Albric to John, the smith, fitz Philip: 17 feet
     of land in Sᵗ M. par. next land of Warin Anketin reaching
     in longum vie ubi fabri manent, and from the same way
     to land of Ric. de Ingham: rent 5ˢ, and 10ˢ *gersuma.*
     Witn. Gilbert, the goldsmith.

217*a* Cristina, relict of Warin fitz Anketil, leases to John, the
     smith, fitz Philip a shop in the market betw. land of
     Maurice Ruffus and land of Gilbert Blancgernun for 20
     years: rent 2ˢ.   Witn. Rob. Seman.

  b Godfrey fitz Warin fitz Anketil to John, the smith, fitz
     John, the smith: the above shop: rent 5ˢ, and 10ˢ *gersuma.*
     Witn. Hervey fitz Eustace.

218 Gilbert fitz Arnulf, le Plumer, to John fitz John, the smith:
     shop in the market betw. land of Thos. le Ferriman and
     land of Ric. le Feleperer: rent 12ᵈ and a pair of gloves
     worth ½ᵈ, and a mark *gersuma.*   Witn. Maurice Ruffus.

219*a* Leonius fitz Adam to Bartholomew le Noble: a shop in
     the market at the corner of Potteres rowe, betw. land of
     same Barth., W., and land of William, the miller, S.:
     rent 6ᵈ, and one mark *gersuma.*   Witn. Thos. Tuyllet.

  b Bartholomew le Noble to his son Hugh: the above shop
     (next his own land and that of the Hospital of S. John)
     and another next a tenᵗ of Henry Nadun: rent ½ᵈ, and
     6ᵈ to Leonius Dunning.   Witn. John Alvenechild.

  c The same Hugh to his uncle Thos. Potekin: the same two
     shops, the first described as betw. land of the Hospital
     of S. John and land of Thos. le Cutiler, the second as
     betw. land of Thos. le Cutiler and Will. le Lorimer: rent
     to Leonius Dunning 6ᵈ, and *gersuma* 6 marks.   Witn. Ric.
     fitz Laurence.

  d Thos. Potekin to John fitz Serlo de Upwenden: a rent of
     5ˢ out of the same shops.   Witn. Henry Nadon.

  e Indenture witnessing that the above grant is to continue

for 4 years, and that the said John has paid to the said
Thos. 16ˢ *ad urgens negotium suum*: if the said Thos. die
within the term of 4 years the rent to remain to John
for ever. Witn. Will. Elioth. Edw. I. 3.

f The same John grants to the Nuns (Pr. Agnes Burgeylun)
the above mentioned rent of 5ˢ for 4 years, the Nuns
for a like term paying to him a rent of 4ˢ 8ᵈ out of a shop
late held of him by Godfrey le Heymongere and 16ˢ 6ᵈ
gersuma. Will. Elihot, mayor.

220*a* Gilbert de Childerle to Will. Sweteghe: land in the
market betw. land of Symon de S. Botulph and land of
Rob. Sharp: rent to Margᵗ, widow of Reginald de Abintun
35ᵈ and a mallard: 4 marks *pre manibus.* Witn. Hervey
fitz Eustace.

b Agnes, widow of Will. de Colebrig, quitclaims the same to
Will. Sweteye. Witn. Hervey Parleben.

c Will. Sueteye to the Nuns: an annual rent of 8ˢ out of the
above mentioned land for the maintenance of a lamp in the
Nuns' choir, *ubicunque chorus earundem fuerit.* Witn.
John Ruffus.

221 Acquittance of the Nuns (Pr. Agnes) to Ric. Spycer for rent
of a tenᵗ with two solars in Sᵗ M. par. betw. a tenᵗ of
Corpus Chr. College W. and a tenᵗ of Ric. Busshee, E.,
ab. on a tenᵗ of Corpus Chr. College and on the Chese-
market, the rent of which, 8ˢ, was given to the Nuns
before the Statute (*i.e.* of Mortmain), the Nuns accepting
8ˢ in full discharge of all arrears. Nov. 12, Hen. VI. 11.

222 Walter Crochemun to Alex. Pecche, rector of Brandestone:
a mess. in Sᵗ M. par. betw. land of Margᵗ Pernes and land
of Hugh But and ab. on the highway, together with a
small plot adjoining: rent to Nuns 8ˢ, and 13½ marks
gersuma. John le Rus, mayor.

223 Ric. ad Portam to Nuns: a shop in the market betw. a shop
of John fitz Selid and a shop of Aca fitz Coleman: Nuns
to pay King's service 8ᵈ. Witn. Hervey fitz Eustace.

224 Nuns (Pr. Agnes Burgulun) to Reginald de Combirton:
land in Sᵗ M. par. given them by Thos. Potekin, clerk,

betw. land of same Reginald and land of Henry le Parche-
miner: rent to Marg^t, dau. of Thos. Wolword, 4^s 8^d, and
2^s *gersuma* to Nuns. Barth. Goggyng, mayor.

225 William, Prior, and the convent of S. Giles, Barnwell, to
Hugh, *selinarius*: a mess. in the street betw. S. Mary's
ch. and S. Michael's ch., betw. land of the Ely monks and
land of Barnwell Priory: rent 12^d. Witn. Mr Elyas.

Seal of Barnwell Priory: obverse, figure of S. Giles, legend
nearly defaced: reverse, figure of an ecclesiastic with legend
SECRETVM · WILL · PRIORIS · DE · BERWELL. This prior
was either William of Devon (1208—1213) or William of Bedford
(in 1213).

226 Ric. Martyn, Dr Will., vicar of All Saints' in Jewry, Simon
de Sleford and Dr Ric. Milde, chaplain, to Thos. Caldecote,
butcher, and wife Agnes: lease for their lives of a ten^t in
St M. par., in which they were enfeoffed by Will. de
Horewode, betw. a ten^t of John Gybon, senior, and a shop
of Hugh Stalle on one side, and the lane leading from
the highway to the Milk-market on the other: rent 40^s.
John London, mayor. Edw. III. 38.

227 Will. Rolf, vicar of All Saints', to John Bechampwell and
wife Marg^t: lease for their lives of a ten^t containing
two shops and a solar in St M. par.;betw. the churchyard
and the lane, and reaching from the church steps to a
ten^t belonging to a chantry of the ch.: rent 6^s. Ric.
Maisterman, mayor. Ric. II. 7.

228 The Nuns (Pr. Isabella) to Rob. Coker and his wife Marg^t:
lease for 99 years of a ten^t in St M. par., betw. a ten^t of
the lessees, S., and the highway called Cutler rowe, N.,
ab. E. on a ten^t belonging to a chantry of St M. ch. and
W. on a ten^t of Corpus Chr. Coll.: rent to the Nuns a
red rose, if demanded, the Nuns guaranteeing a quit-rent
to Corpus Chr. Coll. of 16^d. Rob. Coope, mayor. Dec.
10, 1468.

229 The Nuns (Pr. Joan Fulburn) to John Greene, peyntour,
and wife Cristiana: lease for 21 years of a ten^t in S^t M.
par. betw. the common entry leading to the churchyard,

E., and the almshouse late of Tho. Jakenet, W., and ab.
on the street, S., and on the churchyard, N.: rent 10ˢ.
June 17, Henry VII. 5.

Endorsed '1666. This is lease of the house that Mr Broughton
now has, being situate betwixt the Almshouse and the back gate of
S. Mary's churchyard.'

SAINT MICHAEL'S PARISH.

230a John fitz Geoff. Godard with assent of wife Eva to Nuns:
rent of 2ˢ out of land betw. land of Andr. de Middleton
and the river (ripa) and betw. land of Algar de Well and
land of John le [   ], and if he die childless the land
itself to Nuns. Witn. Thos. Tuilet.

b John fitz Will. de Trumpitune after suing the Nuns (Pr.
Milisentia) at London for the above mentioned land
confirms it to them for a sum of 20ˢ reserving to himself
a rent of 4ˢ. (The land is said to be at Keverelleshythe
in Sᵗ M. par.) Witn. John le Rus.

c Sayer de Trumpeton to his son Peter: the above rent of
4ˢ. (The land is said to be in Henneye.) Rob. Tuylet,
mayor &c. Edw. I. 22.

d Peter fitz Serle de Trumpytone releases to Pr. Christiana
de Braybrok and Nuns all arrears of above rent, retaining
however the rent itself. Edw. II. 5.

e Peter fitz Sayer de Trumpitone quitclaims to Nuns (Pr.
Cecilia) above rent of 4ˢ. Witn. Simon de Brunue.
Edw. II. 10.

f Nuns (Pr. Elena) to Will. de Lincoln: the above land
(described as in Henneye): rent 4ˢ. Witn. John But.
Edw. I. 21.

g Nuns (Pr. Dera) to Pet. de Middelton: the above land:
rent 10ˢ, and gersuma 10ˢ 8ᵈ: not to alienate to Jews.
Witn. Thom. Tuyllet.

231a Nuns (Pr. Dera) to Tho. de Depham, clerk: mess. in Sᵗ M.
par. lately held of them by Will. Pergamentarius, opp. a

mess. of Walter Crocheman, ab. E. on highway leading
from S. John's Hospital to Trumpitun gate: rent 3ˢ.
Rob. de S. Edmund's, *maior ballivus*.

b Nuns (Pr. Milesenta) to Pet. de Middelton : the same land
(described as at Flexhethe in Sᵗ M. par.): rent 6ˢ.   Witn.
Thom. Tuyllet.

c Mabilia, dau. of Sara, *lotrix*, wife of Edm. de Ringestede,
having claimed *extra iudicium* the above mess. granted
by the Nuns to Thos. de Depham, clerk, the latter
willing to indemnify the Nuns releases them from the
warranty given in their charter but only so far as relates
to the claim mentioned.   Witn. as in the last.

232 John de Crocstun to Nuns: land in Sᵗ M. par. extending
from the great street to the river (*filum aque*), being the
third part of the land betw. the lane and land of Walter
fitz Scolicia.   Witn. John Frost, *capellanus*.

233 Peter Macstan to Will. fitz Will. de Trumpiton: land in
Sᵗ M. par. betw. land of John de Welle, land of Rob.
Seman and the way to the common (*commune*), reaching
from the High Street to the river (*aqua*): rent 12ᵈ.
Witn. Ric. de Bernewell.

234 Nuns (Pr. Leticia) to Ralf fitz Henry: land in Sᵗ M. par.,
being two thirds of the land betw. the lane and land
of Walt. fitz Scolicia: rent 4ˢ, and 3 marks *gersuma*.
Witn. Hervey fitz Eustace.

235 Nuns (Pr. Leticia) to Ric. Shipwritte: land in Sᵗ M. par.
extending from the lane to land of Will. fitz Richard:
rent 2ˢ, and 4ˢ *gersuma*.   Witn. Thos. Tuilet.

236 The Master and Scholars of Sᵗ Michael's House covenant
to pay 1ˢ *per ann.* to Nuns out of some tenements, late
of John Ovinng, in Sᵗ M. par., ab. on the river, the Nuns
releasing to them the tenements themselves.   Witn.
Simon de Refham.   Edw. III. 5.

237 Will. de Nunancurt to John Crocheman: land in Sᵗ M.
par. held of Ely monastery, betw. land of S. Michael and
land of Maurice fitz Albric: rent 26ᵈ, and 10ˢ *gersuma*.
Witn. Fulk Crocheman.

238 Nuns (Pr. Cecilia) to Joh. de Ovynng, clerk : void place in
Henneye in St M. par. at Fflaxhythe : for term of 20
years, rent 2^s. Edw. II. 10.

S. CLEMENT'S PARISH.

239a Hugh fitz Absalon of Camb. by advice of Eustace, late
Bp of Ely, gives to the Almoner of S. Radegund of Camb.
the advowson of the church of St C. Witn. Bartholomew,
official of the Archdeacon of Ely, Fabianus, *capellanus*,
Robert, *capellanus* of St C. &c.

b Walter fitz Will. de S. Edmundo releases to the Nuns his
rights to the advowson, confirming the grants thereof
made by his ancestor Hugh fitz Absalon and his uncle
Walter. Witn. Philip de Stantune, Everarde de Trumpitune, &c.

c John, Bp of Ely, grants to the Nuns of St Rad. de Grenecroft the church of St C., saving a competent payment
for some priest to have the cure of souls. Witn.
Laurence, Prior of Barnwell, Bartholomew, official, &c.

> John de Fontibus, Bp of Ely, 1220—1225. Laurence de Stanes-
> feld, Prior of Barnwell, 1213—1251.

d Geoffrey, Bp of Ely, confirms the above charter. Witn.
Mr Will. de Bancis &c.

> Geoffrey de Burgh, Bp. of Ely, 1225—1229.

e The Prior (Roger) and convent of Ely confirm the grant of
Bp John (de Fontibus). Witn. Laurence, Prior of Barnwell, Bartholomew, *decanus*, &c.

> Roger de Brigham, Prior of Ely about 1215—1229.

240a Decree of Hugh de Stamford, Commissary General of the
Official of Ely, in a dispute betw. the Nuns and Sir
Geoffrey, vicar of St C., in the matter of a pension of five
marks due to them 'de bonis altaragii ecclesie predicte

secundum formam ordinacionis per felicis recordacionis
Hugonem quondam Episcopum Elyensem.'

For this matter, see p. 27.

   b A fragmentary charter, seemingly a confirmation to the
Nuns by John (Fordham), Bp of Ely, of the above
mentioned pension of 5 marks.

241 Eustace Oldcorn confirms to the Nuns (Pr. Custance) a
grant of Holdeburg, viz. an annual rent of 6^d out of
a tenement in St C. par., next land of Ric. Bulling.
Witn. Rob. fitz Anger le Rus.

242 The Nuns (Pr. Isabella de Sudbury), in consequence of the
representation of Adam de Walsoken, vicar of St C., to
the Archbishop of Canterbury in his metropolitical
visitation, assign to the vicars of St C. as a *mansum* a
house on the E. side of the church, next the churchyard.
July 11, 1402.

For this matter, see p. 28.

243 The Nuns (Pr. Elizabeth) present to the Bishop of Ely
Mr Joh. Barfot, nominated by them to the vicarage of
St C., vacant by the death of Joh. Damlett, late vicar,
reserving to themselves an annual pension of 5 marks.
1473.

244*a* Walter, the cook, for the health of the souls of himself and
his wife Agnes confirms in alms to the Nuns a grant
of 2^s made to them by Adam Wyriel out of land in
Bridge St., or in default thereof a similar rent from some
place in Camb. Witn. Hervey fitz Eustace.

   b Joh. fitz Bartholomew also confirms Adam Wyriel's grant.
Same witnesses.

245*a* Tho. Tuylet, clerk, to his *pueri*, Will. and Ele, and longest
liver of them : two mess. in Bridge St. in St C. par. betw.
a mess. of his father Will., S., and a mess. late of Koc, the
Jew, N., ab. on the street and on the lane towards
S. John's Hospital : rent 1^d to said Tho., to Barth.
Goggyng 2^s, to the Nuns 4^s, to Joh. Anured 4^s, to
S. John's Hosp., 4^s. Witn. Joh. But. Ed. I. 14. 1286.

b Bartholomew fitz John quitclaims to the Nuns the above
rent of 4ˢ out of a mess. lately held by Will. Prest of
Adam Weriel and next a mess. of Will. Toilet, the Nuns
paying to him a sum of 24ˢ. Witn. Joh. de Ry.

246 Johanna, dau. of Rob. de Schelford, widow, to Rob. le
Baker and his wife Johanna: a mess. in Sᵗ C. par., betw.
a mess. late of Walter de Horsethe and a mess. of Pet. le
Baker, reaching from Anngerys lane to land of Joh. de le
Seghalle: rent 10ˢ. Symon de Refham, mayor. Edw.
II. 4.

247 Alice, wid. of Alan Seghyn of Fen Ditton, quitclaims to Dˢ
Walter Poswyk, vicar of Sᵗ C., and Dˢ Henry Moryce,
chaplain of the same, her right of dowry in a mess. with
meadow adjoining it in Sᵗ C. par., late of Mʳ Rob.
Aunger, betw. a tenement of Ric. Laurence and a tenement of Cecilia de Berton, ab. on Aungerys lane and
a tenement of Reg. Bercar: the meadow betw. a meadow
of the Nuns and the *curia* of Ric. Laurence and ab.
on Grenecroft. Guy le Spycer, mayor. Ed. II. 5.

248 Alice le Rus and her children John, Margaret and Isabella,
lease for 10 years to Nich. le Redere and his wife
Katherine a dovehouse and curtilage with free access to
fetch water in the Nuns' lane, betw. a curtilage of the
Friars Minor and one of said Alice: rent 2ˢ. Edm.
Lytestere, mayor. Ed. III. 38.

Endorsed 'paroch. Sᵗⁱ Clementis.'

249*a* Rob. Peytevin, clerk, to Joh. Albon, clerk, a dovehouse
and void place in Sᵗ C. par. wh. he holds along with said
John and others by feoffment of Nich. Hethe. Hen. IV. 13.

b Joh. Albon, clerk, to Rob. Leeke and Dˢ Ric. Browne,
vicar of All Saints; the same dovehouse &c. Joh.
Gaynesford, mayor. Hen. V. 8.

c Ric. Browne, rector of Downham, to Ric. Cawdrey and
others: the above dovehouse &c. ab. on the river and
betw. lands of the Town of Cambridge. Ric. Wright,
mayor. Hen. VI. 24.

250a The Nuns (Pr. Margaret Clanile) to D⁸ Ric. Milde, *capellanus*, Joh. de Kelesseye, cooper, and Avisia his wife: a tenement in S¹ C. par., betw. a tenement of Joh. Dunton and one of S. Mary's chantry in S¹ C. church and ab. on the churchyard: lease for their lives: rent 7ˢ during Milde's life, afterwards 10ˢ. Will. Horwod, mayor. Edw. III. 47.

b The Nuns (Pr. Margaret Clanile) lease the same premises to Kelesseye and his wife for their lives and five years afterwards: rent 10ˢ. The lessees to maintain and repair the existing buildings, viz. a good hall on the N. side with a solar above it extending the whole length of the tenement to the churchyard, and under the solar three cellars, also a kitchen above the solar on the S. side of the tenement &c. Lessees also to build a new house of oak on the N.W. side of the tenement. Joh. Cotton, mayor. Edw. III. 51.

PARISH OF S. PETER JUXTA CASTRUM.

251 Roger fitz Ric. le Potter to Juliana, dau. of Walter Corde: a mess. formerly of his father, Ric., betw. land of Rob. Custance and land of Roger Russel in the par. of S¹ P. *ultra pontem*: hagable 1ᵈ, rent to Walter Corde, 2ˢ, and 5 silver marks *gersuma*. Witn. Hervey fitz Eustace.

252 The Nuns (Pr. Constance) to Rob. fitz Walter Wymund and his wife Marg.: land in S¹ P. par. *ultra pontem*, betw. a mess. of Jordan le Hattere and one of Roger Slipper, reaching from highway to land of Rob. de S. Edmundo: rent 12ᵈ. Roger de Wykes, mayor.

253 Joh. de Benyngton to Rob. le Long: void ground in S¹ P. par. *juxta castrum*, next Merton Hall lane, ab. on a tenement of Joan le Ploghwrygt and one of said Rob. Roger de Harleston, mayor. Ed. III. 31.

254a Maud Picot, wid. of Walter Bortone, to Will. Scherwynt and his wife Joan: four cottages in S¹ P. par. *ultra pontem* which she holds by feoffment of Ric. Yon, two of the cottages being betw. a tenement formerly of Rob. Seman and the lane leading to the King's ditch, the other two betw. a tenement of Tho. Wellis and the King's ditch. Joh. London, mayor. Ed. III. 38.

b The same to the same: reversion of the same four cottages, held by Symon de Kymbalton and his wife Ada for their lives: the two latter cottages described as ab. on the lane leading to the King's ditch and the Ree. Witn. and date as in the last.

The lane mentioned, known in the 15th cent. as Kymbalton's lane, ran between and parallel with the river and the S. wall of Magdalene College.

255 The Nuns lease to Ric. Stombill for 60 years a void place beyond the great bridge in St P. par. in a street called Fisher lane, betw. a tenement of Agnes Upwer and one of Joh. Wattys, ab. on the King's water and a tenement of Thos. Morys: rent 12^d. The tenants to erect thereon a new house. Joh. Gaynesford, mayor. Hen. IV. 10.

256 The Nuns lease to Marg., wife of Joh. Rankyn, for 40 years a tenement and stathe in Fysshcris lane in St P. par., betw. a tenement of Margerie Toogood and one of Simon Myer, late Nich. Preest: rent 4^s. The tenant to repair with reed the tenement and to make the stathe sufficiently according to other stathes adjoining. 1473. Ed. IV. 13.

257 The Nuns (Pr. Eliz. Walton) lease to Joh. Belton for 44 years two cottages in St P. par. *ultra magnum pontem* betw. a tenement of Joh. Morys, S., and one of Joh. Neell, N., ab. E. on the street and W. on a ditch of Corp. Chr. Coll.; rent 4^s. Joh. Wyghton, mayor. Ed. IV. 19.

258 The Nuns lease for 20 years to Will. Baker a garden in St P. par., betw. a tenement of Joh. Morys and one of Stephen Neell, ab. on the street and on the dyke reaching from the common bank (*ripa*): rent 3^s. Thos. Jacob, mayor. Hen. VI. 9.

259 Will. Salle of Fulburn quitclaims to Simon Rankyn a garden in St P. par. betw. a tenement of same Simon

and the common lane, ab. on Milne lane and on the river (*rivera*). Rob. Brigham, **mayor.** Hen. VI. 13.

PARISH OF S. GILES.

260 The Nuns (Pr. Leticia) to Will. Arnold and Will. Lomb: a mess. *ad castellum* betw. land of Joh. Aldred and **land** of Walter Papilun, **ab.** on the street opp. a mess. of Joh. Frost and on land of Henry fitz Norman: rent **2ˢ, and** **2ˢ** *gersuma.* Witn. John Frost &c.

In Hund. Rolls **II., p.** 362 **this messuage** is said to be in S. Giles' **parish.**

261 **Thos.** fitz Joh. de Cambridge, knight, grants **to the Nuns** and **to** his sister Eliz., for her use for the term of her life a **rent of** 13ˢ 4ᵈ out of a **tenement** in Sᵗ G. **par., called** Dunnyngistede. Philip Cayly, mayor. Ed. **III. 15.**

262 The Nuns **lease** to Tho. le Wryghte, his wife **and dau.,** for their lives, a void place in **Sᵗ** G. par., betw. a tenement of **Geoff.** Seman and one of Tho. Wolle, ab. on the street and on **a** tenement of Tho. de Cambridge: rent 2ˢ. Stephen Morice, mayor. Ed. III. 28.

263 The Nuns (Pr. Alice Pilet) lease **the** same premises for 30 **years to** Will. Salle of Cambridge: rent 2ˢ. Rich. II. 20.

264 **Rob.** Wodelarke, clerk, **to** John Aspelon and others: **a** tenement **in Sᵗ G.** par. extending from Cambrigge Brigge **to** land of Hugh Brook, citizen and clothier (*pannarius*) of London, towards E., **ab. on Brigge** street, **W.,** on **the** Hostel called Monkis place, **N.,** and on the river (*rivolus*) called **the** Ee, **S.,** wh. tenement **he held by** feoffment of Tho. Dekyn, deceased. **Oct.** 16. **Ed. IV. 12.**

Seal of Rob. Wodelarke.

Parish of All Saints juxta Castellum.

(The parish of All Saints next the Castle was united to
that of S. Giles by Simon Langham, Bishop of Ely,
in 1365.)

265a Baldwin fitz Baldwin Blancgernun to Walter Corde: a
rent of 2ˢ out of land held of him by the heirs of Will.
Blancgernun in A. S. par. *versus castellum*, next land of
Ketel, merchant: rent a pair of white gloves, value a half-
penny. Witn. Dˢ Maurice Ruffus.

b Walter Corde to the Nuns: the aforesaid rent of 2ˢ (the
premises being described as betw. land of Will. Braci and
land of Rob. Colt, ab. on the street and land of Anger
Ruffus): also a rent of 5ˢ out of land held by Hamo de
Colecestre, betw. land of Reg. Quantquilia and land of
Ric. Hopetune, reaching from the street to the river:
also a rent of 3ˢ out of land held by Will. de Furcis in S.
Clement's par., betw. land of Geoff. Gybon and land of
Hareflct, reaching from the street to the King's Ditch.
Witn. Hervey fitz Eustace.

266a Geoff. fitz Baldewin Blancgernun to Alex. fitz Hamo fitz
Theobald de Yselham: a mess. in A. S. par. *juxta
castellum*, ab. on the street between the Castle ditch and
land of Hervey fitz Eustace, on land of the same Hervey,
called Sale, on the Castle ditch and land of Thos. Lungis:
rent a pair of gloves, value a half-penny, and 18ˢ *gersuma*.
Witn. Ketel, merchant.

b Same Geoffrey to the Nuns: the above rent of a half-penny.

267 Alex. fitz Hamo de Yselham to Adam de Litlingetune,
clerk: land in A. S. par. *juxta castellum*, betw. land of
Godard Finch and land of Hen. Shepherd: rent 6ᵈ. Witn.
Rob. Saman.

268 Baldwin Blancgernun to the same Adam: a rent of 12ᵈ out
of land occupied by Will. Arnold: *gersuma* 7ˢ 6ᵈ. Witn.
Rob. Saman.

269 Adam de Litlingtun, *capellanus*, to the Nuns: all his lands
and rents in Cambridge. Witn. Richard, *decanus* of
Cambridge.

270 The Nuns (Pr. Custancia) to Elyas Hoppecrane: land
formerly held of them by Reginald Harecok at a rental
of 2ˢ 6ᵈ, in par. of A. S. *ad castellum*, between the street
and land of Eustace fitz Hervey, called Sale, the Castle
ditch, land of Ph. Baret and land of Thos. Long: rent 6ᵈ.
Witn. Walter Blancgernun.

271 Hugh le Tynour, fisherman, and wife Sarra to William,
merchant, and his wife Alice Blancgernun: land in par.
of A. S. *ad castellum*, betw. land of said Hugh and Sarra,
and land of said William, ab. on land of said Hugh
and on the street: rent ½ᵈ. Guy le Spenser, mayor.
Edw. I. 6.

272a Margery, wid. of Rob. Tuylet, to Ralf de Wendeye, vicar
of S. Clement's: land in A. S. par. *iuxta castrum*, betw.
a tenᵗ of David le Webster and a tenᵗ. of Walter de
Horsethe, ab. on the high street and the King's ditch.
Joh. Moryce, mayor. Edw. II. 8.

   b The above Ralf grants to the Nuns (Pr. Cecilia de Cressingham) the above-mentioned land for 60 years. Joh. Moryce,
mayor. 1315, Edw. II. 9.

273 Joh. de Toft to Joh. de Briceste, webster, and his wife
Alice, dau. of Joh. de Wachesham: a tenᵗ in A. S. par.
betw. a tenᵗ of Thos. de Cambridge and a tenᵗ formerly
of Ric. de Modebrok, ab. on the highway and the Hospice
of the Gild of the Blessed Virgin: rent 3ˢ. Ric. Tullyet,
mayor. Edw. III. 14.

BARNWELL PARISH.

274 The Nuns (Pr. Letitia) to Walter Cementarius fitz Henry
[   ] de Mordin: land in B. betw. land of Andrew
Molle and land of R [   ]: rent 6ᵈ. Witn. Magʳ
Martin de S. Radegund.

275 The Nuns (Pr. Leticia) to Robert fitz Will. de Nonacurt:
a croft formerly of Rich. Buche, betw. the lane and land
of Joh. de Sauxington: rent 20^d. Witn. Hervey fitz
Eustace.

276 Walter Sementarius fitz Hen. de Morden quitclaims to
the Nuns (Pr. Milesentia) a ten^t given by him to Roger
Carettarius in marriage with his sister Felicia of which
the fee belongs to the Nuns: also a rent of 6^d paid out
of the said ten^t by the said Roger. The said Nuns pay
4^s gersuma. Witn. Thos. Toilet.

277 John, the miller, and his wife Alice to Hugh Mayner: a
mess. at B. town-end next lands of S. Radegund and of
Rob. le Reder and next a mess. of the said Hugh:
gersuma 20^s. Witn. Hugh le Noreys.

278 Alice, dau. of Ric. ad caput ville de Bernewelle quitclaims
to Hugh Mayner a rent of 1½^d out of land at B. town-
end, betw. land of Isabel Page and the highway. Joh.
Martyn, mayor. Edw. I. 10. 1281.

279a Will. fitz Hugh le Noreys of Bernewelle to Adam de
Multun and wife Maud: a mess., &c. in B. betw. land of
Walter Cissor and land of Roger de Huntingfeld, reaching from the road to Grenecroft: rent 5^d and 5 marks
gersuma. Witn. Gilbert Bernard.

b Adam de Multun to Hugh Mayner and wife Claricia: the
above land: rent 5^d and 5½ marks gersuma. Witn.
Gilbert Bernard.

c Hugh and Claricia Mayner to their son John: the same
land: rent to his parents ¼^d and to Will. le Norreys 5^d.
Witn. Gilbert Bernard.

d John fitz John Mayner to Ric. fitz Rob. Attebroo: the same
land. Witn. Hugh, the smith.

280 John fitz John Mayner, clerk, to the above Ric.: land with
houses and grange thereon, betw. land of Ric. le Taylour
and a ten^t of said John, reaching from the highway to
land of said John, held of him by said Ric. Witn. Hugh,
the smith. Edw. II. 11.

281 The same John to the same Ric.: a rent of 1½^d out of a

mess. at Barnwell town-end towards Camb., betw. a mess. of Rob. Person and lands of Master Hen. de Trippelawe and of Geoff. Page, ab. on the highway. Witn. Hugh, the smith. Edw. II. 13.

282a Walter Mayner, chaplain, to John fitz John Mayner, his nephew: a mess. in B. betw. a mess. of Ric. Attebroo and a mess. of Simon de Stokton, ab. on the highway: also half an acre in B. croft betw. land of Hugh, the smith, and land of Ric. Attebroo, reaching from the said mess. to Grenecroft. Witn. Hugh, the smith. Edw. II. 14.

b The same John to the same Ric. and to Agnes de Mordyngton: the same mess. and half acre. The same witnesses and date.

283 Walter, son of Master Geoffrey, to Henry Milt: a mess. and croft in B. held of him by Rob., nephew of Wybert, betw. a mess. of said Henry and land of Barnwell Priory held by Rob. Gibet: rent 12^d, 2 capons, and 4^s *gersuma*. Witn. Roger Parleben.

284 Joh. de Fordham to Will. Paris and his wife Alice: a mess. &c. in B. betw. land formerly of Joh. Selyman and a mess. formerly of Joh. le Machon, ab. on highway and Grenecroft, being ½ an acre: rent a rose: to heirs of Rob. Cook a peppercorn: to heirs of Agnes le Hattere ½^d: to Leonius Dunning 5^d: to Will. le Nunnecurt 6^d: Paris and his wife further to give 3½ marks after death of Joh. de Fordham for the welfare of his soul, as he shall hereafter direct. Joh. But, mayor. 1278.

285a Margaret, wid. of Henry de Grantesete, quitclaims to Walter le Uscher a mess. in B. betw. land of Ric. Pede and land of Rob. Loverede, ab. on highway and a croft of said Rob. Witn. Simon de Stokton, mayor. Edw. I. 29.

b Walter le Uscher to Nic. le Barbour: the same mess. Simon de Stokton, mayor. Edw. I. 35.

c Nic. le Barbour to Adam de Clifford de fermeria de Bernewelle: the same mess. Simon de Refham, mayor. Edw. II. 4.

286 Simon Edyth de Stokton and Beatrix de Haselyngfeld to

Adam de la Fermerie de Bernewelle: a mess. in B. betw. a mess. of the said Adam and land of Silvester Carter: for 10 years: rent 3ˢ to Barnwell Priory. Witn. Alan le Wayte. Edw. II. 9.

287 Katherine, dau. of Simon de Stokton, to Adam de Clifford: a mess. in B. betw. a mess. of said Adam on either side, ab. on the highway and the Croft. Joh. Pylet, mayor. Ed. III. 3.

288 Margaret, wid. of Silvester de Bernewelle, quitclaims to Adam de Infirmaria de Bernewelle her right of dower in a plot iu B. sold to Adam by her husband. Witn. Hugh, the smith. Edw. II. 10.

289a Beatrix de Haselyngfeld to Joh. de Newton: a mess. in B. next the lane leading from the stone-cross to the river: also land in B. croft at the end of the same mess., betw. the same lane and land of Barnwell Priory, ab. on Grene-croft: for the life of said Beatrix: rent 12ˢ. Witn. Adam de Clifford. Edw. II. 16.

b John de Newton to Adam de Clifford: the above mess. granted him by Beatrix de Stokton. John Pilet, mayor. Edw. III. 4.

290 Adam de Clifford to his son Richard: a messuage, described as le Sperveres, in B. betw. a mess. of said Adam and a mess. of Silvester de Foulmer, ab. on highway and a croft of said Adam. John Pyttok, mayor. Edw. III. 8.

291 Thos de Elynhale, his wife Katherine and Beatrix de Hase-lyngfeld to Adam de Clifford: a mess. and croft in B., betw. Petes lane, land of Barnwell Priory and a tenᵗ of said Adam, formerly of John and Simon de Stokton, ab. on street and on Grenecroft. Ric. Tuyllet, mayor. Edw. III. 10.

292 Will. de Hynggeston and his wife Maud to Ric. Paule, pelliperius: two parts of a mess. in B. betw. a tenᵗ of Isabel Page and a tenᵗ of Joh. de Bokenham, which mess. was formerly held by Geoff. Page: also two por-tions of four acres, butted. [   ] Tuyllet, mayor. Edw. III. 20.

293 Stephen Moriz, Roger de Harleston, Ric. Martyn and Rob.
de Chaston to Alan Redheved and his wife Marg⁺: a
mess. &c. in B. between their own mess. and Silvestris
place, now held by Agnes de Grantesdene, ab. on highway: for term of two lives: rent 32ˢ. Witn. John Tele.
Edw. III. 33.

294 The Nuns (Pr. Margaret Clanyle) to Ric. Maystreman and
Sarra, his wife: a void place in B., betw. land of Barnwell
Priory and land of Joh. Cotes, ab. on the highway: rent
6ᵈ. Witn. Joh. London. Edw. III. 37.

295 Agnes de Grantesdene to Will. Tele, chaplain, Alan Redheved and Joh. Ryghisby: a void plot in B., betw. a tenᵗ
of said Alan and land of the Nuns, ab. on the highway
and Grenecroft: rent to chief lord 12ᵈ. Witn. Joh. Cotes.
Edw. III. 38.

296 The Nuns (Pr. Margaret Clanyle) to Alan Redheved and his
wife Margaret: a void plot in B., betw. a mess. of Will.
Tele, chaplain, and a void plot of said Alan, ab. on highway and the Nuns' croft: rent 6ˢ 8ᵈ. William Horwod,
mayor. Edw. III. 47.

297 Joh. Payn quitclaims to Alan Redheved the plot granted
to him by Agnes de Grantesdene. Edm. Lyster, mayor.
Ric. II. 4.

298a The Nuns (Pr. Alice) to Joh. Bruce, his wife Mariota and
son John for their lives: a mess. and croft in B. betw.
land of Joh. Blankpayn and a mess. of the Nuns, the
croft ab. on the same mess. and Grenecroft: rent 30ˢ.
Rob. Brigham, mayor. Ric. II. 22.

b Joh. Blankpayn to Joh. Bruys: the plot above-mentioned
held by Alan Redheved of the Nuns. Witn. Rob. Good-
rych. Hen. IV. 3.

299a Thos. Hamond, senior, to Ralf Bateman and Will. Lang-
forde, clerk: a tenᵗ in B. acquired by his marriage with
Rose, dau. of John Thriplowe. Witn. Will. Smyth, vicar
of Hynton. Hen. IV. 5.

b Thos. Hamond, junior, to Nich. Morys, Joh. Burgoyn, Ric.
Browne and Rob. Browne, clerks: a tenᵗ formerly of Joh.

Triplowe, betw. a ten^t of Barnwell Priory on either side
and ab. on the highway. Hen. V. 4.

300 Barnwell Priory (Pr. Will. Downe) acknowledges receipt
from Nuns (Pr. Agnes Seyntlow) of 40^s in full discharge of arrears due for two tenements in B. leased
by the Nuns to Alex. Westmorland and Joh. Bruce.
Hen. V. 3.

> Seal *ad causas* of Barnwell Priory.

301 The Nuns (Pr. Joan Chambryg) lease for 10 years to Joh.
Sokelyng and his wife, Margaret, a ten^t in B. in the par.
of the H. T., opposite the cross, betw. Pytys lane, E., and
a ten^t of the Nuns, W., ab. S. on the highway and on
another ten^t of the Nuns: also an acre of land diversely
situate in B. fields: rent 14^s. Ric. III. 1.

> ' Clay angles or Croft land. The first furlong is called Cadwell
> or Caldwell, and beginneth by the Lane side that leadeth from
> the town to Midsummer Green, or Green Crofts and by some books
> call'd Path or Pittes lane.' Old Book of Barnwell Field in Jesus
> Coll. Treasury.

CAMBRIDGE AND BARNWELL FIELDS.

302 The Nuns (Pr. Letitia) to Baldwin Blangernun: 2 acres
in Gretthawe: rent 8^d.

303 Maud, dau. of Hen. Kyrman, to Simon fitz Henry: ½ rood
in C. field. Witn. Adam fitz Eustace.

304 John fitz Ric. Pete to Simon de Stocton: lands in town
and fields of C. and B.: also the reversion of lands held
in dowry by his mother Isoda. Joh. Goldring, mayor.
Edw. I. 33.

305 Barnwell Priory (Pr. Laurence) undertakes to pay to the
Nuns a rent of 9^s, as an amicable composition for tithes
of a water mill, belonging in fee to Will. de Mortuomari
and situated in Cambridge. Witn. Mr Will. de Bancis,
Antony, dean of Cambridge, &c. March 20, 1230.

Laurenco of Stanesfield, 9th Prior of Barnwell, 1213—1251. The mill in question was that called Zouch's mill, which ceased to exist after 1353, when Newnham or Mortimer's mill was erected. Cooper, *Annals* I., p. 103.

306 Peter fitz Ric. de Berton to his bro. Giles: an acre in C. fields ab. on Huntingdon way. Witn. Barth. Goggyng. Edw. I. 20.

307 The same Peter to his sister Maud: 3 acres in C. fields, Witn. Joh. Bott, mayor.

308 Maud, widow of Will. Thele to Gilbert fitz Mich. Bernard and his wife Margaret: ½ acre in C. fields, ab. on Hadestoc weye and Litlemor: rent 1ᵈ. Witn. Joh. fitz Michael.

309 Cassandra, dau. of Warin Atkin, to Mich. Bernard: 1½ acre in C. field towards Trumpitone ford: rent 1½ᵈ. Witn. Symon de Agam.

310 Ric. fitz Bartholomew, *cissor*, to his uncle Thos. Potckin, clerk: 2 acres in C. fields next land of Thos. Dalles, of Prior of Barnwell, and Hinton wey. Witn. Will. Elyot.

311a Giles fitz Joh. de Berton to Walter de Possewy, vicar of S. Clement's: 7½ acres in C. crofts. Mich. Pylat, mayor.

  b Joh. Portehors grants the same 7½ acres to the Nuns (Pr. Elena). Witn. Joh. But.

312 Joan, dau. of Roger de Melreia, to her dau. Elice: homage of Thos. de Chesewic and ½ acre in Holm, ab. towards the Bridge. Witn. Will. le Puer.

313 Will. Martin, with consent of his son Robert, grants to his son Alan all his land in Holm, viz. 15 acres, and 11 acres in Holm which he holds of the Abbess of Chateriz: rent 32ᵈ. Witn. Alan de Sepeia.

314 Will. fitz Hen. Kankelya to Simon Godelote: an acre in Binnebroc in C. fields. Witn. Rob. de S. Edmundo.

315 Walter fitz Rob. Eadward to Joh. Goson and his wife Avice; a rent of ¾ᵈ out of land behind Hadestok Way. Joh. Martin, mayor.

316 Michael Parleben to Will. Sueteye and Hugh de Ragenhille: an acre in C. fields: rent 2ᵈ. Witn. Stacius fitz Hervey Dunning.

317 Robert, rector of All Saints' ch., to his bro. John: an acre
in Middelfurlong towards Howes, and ½ acre in the same
field next Wulwardesmere: rent 1½ᵈ to the vicar of All
Saints' for the soul of said Robert's mother. Witn.
Rob. Seman.

318 Same John to the Nuns: same 1½ acres: rent to celebrate
the anniversary of his mother, Margaret, to vicar of A. S.
as above. Witn. Hervey fitz Eustace.

319 Maud, widow of Simon Bagge, to Nuns: an acre in C. fields
next Trumpitun forde, which acre her bro. Robert gave to
her at the church door on the day of her betrothal. Witn.
Hervey fitz Eustace.

320 Warin Grim to Nuns: 2 acres in C. fields. Witn. Rob.
Seman.

321a Will. de Nonencurt confirms to the Nuns the bequest to
them by Will. Sueteye of the half part of 32½ acres in C.
fields. Witn. Nich. Childman.

  b The same Will. de Nonencurt confirms to the Nuns the 32½
acres above mentioned held of him by the same Will.
Sueteye and Hugh de Ragenhyll and assigned by the
former and the executors of the latter to the Nuns. Witn.
Nich. Childman.

322 Margaret, widow of Hen. Vivien, to the Nuns: 2½ acres in
C. fields: rent 3ᵈ. Witn. Rob. Seman.

323 Hen. fitz Goda of S. Radegund St. and his bro. Hugh to
Hugh and Will., brethren of S. Radegund; one selion in
C. field. Witn. Adam fitz Eustace.

324 Will. fitz Hugh de Trompiton to the Nuns: two crofts at
Howes. Witn. R., Prior of Bernewelle.

325 Hervey fitz Eustace to the Nuns: an acre in C. fields.
Witn. Rob. Seman.

326a Stephen fitz Alvene, with consent of his wife Maud, to the
Nuns: 5 acres 3 roods in scattered pieces in C. fields.
Witn. Hervey, alderman.

  b Hugh fitz Stephen fitz Alvene confirms to the Nuns his
father's grant of 5 acres 3 roods in C. fields. Witn.
Hervey, alderman.

c The Nuns (L. Prioress) to Maud, wife of Stephen fitz Alvenc and Hugh, her son : the 5 acres 3 roods given to them by said Stephen : rent 15^d. Witn. D' Hervey, alderman.

d Said Hugh quitclaims the same land to the Nuns. Witn. as above.

327 Margaret, widow of Ralf Person, grants to the Nuns, along with her dau. Sabina, 10 acres in C. fields. Witn. Hervey fitz Eustace.

328 Philip de Hochton to the Nuns in pursuance of a bequest of his mother Albreda : an acre in C. fields, called Binnebroc. Witn. Hervey fitz Eustace.

> Localities mentioned : Fossa iudicii, Rodolvesacro, Barnwell mill, Pishwell wey, Forde feld, Suinescroft.

329 Will. de S. Edmund with assent of his wife Alice and son Roger : an acre in C. fields. Witn. Hervey fitz Eustace.

330 Hervey fitz Eustace to the Nuns : 10 acres in various parts of C. fields. Witn. Rob. Seman.

> Seal of Hervey fitz Eustace. Localities mentioned : cheminum versus Bertun, pastura de Godgivesdole, cheminum de Cotes, Branderusche, cheminum de S. Neoto, and, on the other side of the town, Hokerenewell, Middelfurlong, Littlemor.

331 Nich. Saraut to Geoffrey fitz Ralf : 2 plots in C. fields : to be held ' ad sex vesturas plenas et integras inde percipiendas termino incipiente in festo Mychaelis proximo post primum passagium domini H., regis Anglie, filii J., regis, ciclo lune xv°.' Witn. D' Will. capell. ecclīe beate Marie.

332 The same Nich. Sarant to Orgar fitz Roger : 2½ acres at the Claipittes and 1½ acres ab. on Grenecroft, ' ubi homo suspensus fuit ' : to be held ' de Pascha cuius anni ciclus est quinque primum post obitum Hugonis de Chartuse episcopi Lincoln. usque ad novem annos.' Witn. Bernard Grim, Henry Frost &c.

> S. Hugh of Lincoln d. Nov. 16, 1200 : he took the vows of the Carthusian order in the monastery of the Grande Chartreuse.

333 The same Nich. Sarant to Ric. fitz Yvo: an acre in B.
fields: to be held 'quousque dictus R. perceperit inde
quatuor vesturas termino incipiente in festo scī Michaelis
ciclo lune xvij°, anno regni dm̄ H., regis, filii J., regis, xvj°.'
Witn. R. Saman.

334a Mich. le Rus fitz Joh. Michel to Joh. Bernard: 1 acre
3 roods in B. fields.   Rob. Tuyllet, mayor.

 b Joh. Bernard to Laurence Dixi and his wife Maud: the last
mentioned lands.   John Buth, mayor.

335 Mich. le Rus to Laurence Dixi and his wife Maud: a rood
in B. fields.   Joh. Dunning, mayor.

336 Laur. Dixi and his wife Maud to their son Richard and
daughters Roysia and Maud: 10 selions in C. and B.
fields.   Witn. Will. Tele.   Edw. I. 19.

> Localities: Middelfeld, Hynton wey, Hynton bridge.

337a Hugh fitz Apsolon to his cousin Aldusa: 6 acres in C. and
B. fields.   Witn. Baldwin Blancgernun.

> Localities: Binnebroc, via de heistrate, Bradmerefeld, Petites-
> halvaker, Estenhale, Netherexsotes.

 b The same Hugh to the Nuns: the same 6 acres.   Witn. Dʳ
Barthol., official.

338 Joh. le Meleward and his wife Alice to Hugh Mayner: half
a croft, formerly of Ivetta, wife of Ric. ad caput ville.
Witn. Geoff. de Burewelle.

339 Geoff. le Fittere to Joh. de Berton: 6 acres in C. fields: for
12 silver marks 'ad adquietandum me de Judaismo et
pro sustentacione mea tota vita mea.'   Witn. Adam fitz
Eustace.

> Localities: land of S. Radegund called Bothulveshak, road to
> Grenecroft.

340 Isabel, dau. of Alan de Theversham, to Hugh Mayner and
his wife Clarice: all her land in B. fields.   Witn. Gilbert
Bernard.   1277.

341a Gilbert Bernard to Hugh Mayner and his wife Clarice:
land in Barnwell.   Joh. Martyn, mayor.   Edw. I. 9.

b Clarice, widow of Hugh Mayner, quitclaims to her son John
all lands in wh. he was enfeoffed by said Hugh. Witn.
Ric. Peed.

342 Brother Olbertus, Prior of the Chapel of S. Edmund,
Cambridge, of the order of Simplingham, and of the
Convent there, to Joh. Mayner: ½ acre in Barnwell. Joh.
Goldring, mayor. Ed. I. 33.

343 John fitz John Mayner to Ric. fitz Rob. Attebroo: 1½ acres
in Barnwell, including the last mentioned. Eudo de
Helpringham, mayor. Edw. II. 12.

344*a* Henry le Gray bound in 40ˢ to Rob. le Longg to allow
said Rob. quiet possession of ½ acre in C. fields towards
Aldermanhyl. Witn. Will. Seeman. Edw. II. 9.

b The same Henry to the same Robert: ½ acre in C. fields.
Rob. Dunning, mayor. Edw. II. 10.

345 Agreement between the Master and Brethren of S. John's
Hospital and the Prioress (Elena) and Nuns. The
Hospital gives the Nuns 7 acres 1 rood lying in scattered
portions in B. fields in exchange for the same amount of
land in various parts of the Port Field. Joh. Dunnyng,
mayor. 1299. Edw. I. 27.

> Places named : in Barnwell Fields—the Windmill, Caldewelle
> next Grenecroft : in Port Field—Grantesete weye, Bertone weye,
> Dode dale, Eudeles weye, Musecroft.

346 Agreement between the Prior and Canons of S. Edmund's
Chapel, Cambridge, and the Prioress (Mabilia) and Nuns.
The Canons give the Nuns 4 acres, 3 roods, 16 perches
lying in 3 portions in B. fields in exchange for 3 acres,
2 roods, 13½ perches in 4 portions in Swynecroft. Joh.
Pylet, mayor. 1330. Edw. III. 4.

> One plot in Swynecroft ab. on the *curia* of the Chapel of S.
> Edmund.

347 Will. de Hynggeston to Ric. Paule, *pelliparius:* 4 selions
in B. fields. Ric. Tuyllet, mayor. Edw. III. 20.

348 Will. Lavenham to Ste. Moryce, Roger de Herlaston, Ric.
Martyn and Rob. de Chesterton : lands in C. and B. fields,

lately belonging to Joh. Purr. Witn. Will. Horwode. Edw. III. 33.

349 Joh. Stevenys to Geoff. Castre : 2 acres in small portions in C. and B. fields. Witn. John Blancpayn. Edw. III. 43.

Places named : Horspath, Grenedich, Blakacre, le Roser, Hynton weye.

350 The same to the same: 1 acre similarly divided. Joh. Moriz, mayor. Edw. III. 43.

Places named : Milk furlong, Clayhangels, Hynton weye.

351 Hugh le Smyth to Geoff. Castre : 2 acres in C. and B. fields, called Midelfield. Joh. Gybon, mayor. Edw. III. 45.

Places named : Pisshel weye, Cranedole.

352 Joh. Pilet to Mr Thos. Wormenhale, Adam Wyggomer, clerks, Will. Rolf, vicar of All Saints', and Hen. Baryngton of Ely : all his lands in the fields of Cambridge, Newenham, Chastreton, Watirbeche and Wycham. Joh. Gybon, mayor. Edw. III. 50.

353 Joh. Marchal, Will. Panfleon and Ralf de Watton to Joh. Payn of Swaffham, Rob. Beylham and Joh. Branforde : 12 acres in B. fields in wh. the former have been enfeoffed by Alice, widow of Simon Sleforde. John Gybon, mayor. Edw. III. 50.

354 Power of attorney from Adam Wyggemer, Will. Rolf, vicar of All Saints', and Hen. de Baryngton, chaplain, to Will. Andreu and others to deliver seisin to Joh. Gounsy and others of lands &c. in Camb. in which they are enfeoffed by Joh. Pilet. Ric. II. 6.

355 Rob. Beilham is bound in £10 to Rob. Brigham to give him peaceable possession of 4 roods in B. fields. Ric. II. 19.

356 Joh. Gounsy, in execution of the will of Joh. Pylet, to Thos. de Sopesfeld, Joh. Swynle, Joh. Burgoyne and Thos. Campes : all the lands of the said J. P. in Cambridge, Chesterton and Newenham. Witn. Nich. Morys. Hen. IV. 8.

357a Hugh Ploughwryght and Thos. Colleman, in execution of

the will of Joh. Marchal, directing them to sell his lands
in C. and B. fields and apply the proceeds to pious uses,
convey to Nich. Morys, Joh. Burgoyn, Joh. Bilney and
Simon Deye 14 acres in scattered portions. Joh. Gaynesford, mayor. Hen. IV. 9.

> Seventeen portions, containing 20 selions, in Bradmore Field
> and Middle Field : a long list of field and road names.

b The above Nic. Morys &c. with license grant to the Nuns
(Pr. Margery Harlyng) the said lands. Witn. and date
as in the last.

358 Joh. Wattys, Rob. Brigham and Isabel, widow of Rob.
Brigham, sen^r, in execution of the will of the said R. B.,
sen^r, to Joh. Sexteyn and Joh. Whaplode, butchers :
13 acres variously situate in C. and B. fields. Joh.
Gaynessford, mayor. Hen. IV. 13.

359 The Nuns (Pr. Agnes Sentelow) exchange $\frac{1}{2}$ acre in B.
fields for 20 years with Thos. Cotton. Joh. Bilney,
mayor. Hen. V. 3.

360 Will. Essex, baker, executor of the will of Joh. Prentys, to
Joh. Grenelane of Hadenham : $\frac{1}{2}$ acre in B. fields. Joh.
Bilney, mayor. Hen. V. 3.

361 The Nuns (Pr. Joan Cambryg) lease 2 selions for 20 years
to Joh. Hutham, cardmaker. Hen. VII. 1.

> A small and poorly executed seal, described in the deed as the
> common seal of the Nunnery : S. Radegund crowned, with both
> arms uplifted, standing between two palm branches.

MISCELLANEOUS GRANTS IN CAMBRIDGE AND BARNWELL.

362 Hervey fitz Eustace to the Nuns, with his sister Roda when
she has taken the religious habit in their house : various
small plots in C. and B. fields : 3 mess. in the par. of
S. John, held by Apsolon, son of the priest, ab. on the way
to the mill and the lane leading to S. John's church : a
mess. in the par. of S. Mary, held by Rob. Carpenter,

betw. Joh. fitz Elyas and Joh. fitz Selede: a mess. in the same par., held by Hosbert le Cambere, betw. Andr. de Winepol and Ernold, the plumber: a mess. outside Trumpington gates, held by the wife of Selede Pinberd, next Rob. Nadun: a mess. in the par. of S. Benedict, held by Hen. Bekke, betw. Apsolon, son of a priest, and Walter, son of Mr Geoffrey. Witn. Bartholomew, official of Ely.

363 Will. Pilate to Reg. fitz Reg. de Fordham, in marriage with his dau. Margaret: a mess. in the par. of S. Edward, betw. Geoff. Man and Emilius Pageles: 5 roods in Trumpington meadow: and ½ acre in C. fields. Witn. Ewerard de Trumpinton.

364 Joh. fitz Rob. Hubert of Cambridge to his father and mother, Robert and Sabina: land granted by Geva Key in the par. of All Saints' at the Castle: a ten' granted to him by Reginald de Alderheye beyond the bridge, next land of Rob. Saman in the lane leading to the King's Ditch: a ten' granted him by Margatt fitz Gilbert in the par. of S. Clement; a ten' in the same par. next land of Will. fitz Ivo: a rent of 6ᵈ from a ten' of Barth. le Noble in the par. of S. Mary, &c. Witn. Joh. Porthors.

365 Joh. Frost, *capellanus*, to Ric. fitz Laurence: a mess. in the par. of All Saints ad Castrum betw. land of Will. Kolvin, land late of Saman Holbing and land of Rob. Hubert: also 18 selions in C. fields: said Ric. to pay said John 10ᵈ every Sunday so long as he shall live and 5ˢ annually for *una roba*. Witn. Roger de Wykes. Hen. III. 47.

Places named in the fields: Wulwardesmere, Grethowell croft, Clayfeld, S. Neot's way, Cotes, Weyrode selion.

366 Final concord betw. Will. fitz Walter Sterne, plaintiff, and Rob. and Maud Sterne of Haselyngfeld, defendants: defendants to pay rent to plaintiff for 12 shops, 2 messuages, one solar and 23 acres, in all 61ˢ 2½ᵈ and eight capons. Edw. III., Angliae 25, Franciae 12.

367 Walter fitz Thos. le Mercer to Will. de Kyrkeby and his wife Alice: all his rents and tenements in and without Cambridge. Witn. Roger de Wykes.

368 Will. Blancgernun to Joh. de Waverun : lands and rents producing two marks *per annum* in the town and fields of Cambridge. Witn. Baldwin Blancgernun.

369 **Barnwell** Priory (Prior, Robert) to Hen. Mele : a *mansura* in Cambridge, held of them by Rob. Futigar, and another in Barnwell, held by Nicholas, with 3 acres adjoining the latter, which the Priory grants him in lieu of a *mansura* which said Hen. held of them in Pesecroft : rent for the whole 4ˢ so long as he remains a parishioner of Barnwell, if he reside elsewhere the rent of the house in Barnwell to be increased by 4ᵈ. Witn. Rob. de Bernewelle.

     Robert, 5th Prior of Barnwell, 1175—1208.

370 Warin Grim fitz Apsolon to the Nuns : all his rents in Cambridge, viz. 6ˢ from Peter Maxton *in stallis*, 12ˢ 4ᵈ from land opposite the last, lately of Stephen de Scaleriis, 4ˢ 6ᵈ from Rob. de S. Edmund in Miln St., 7ˢ from Thos. Wulward in the same street, 3ˢ from Geoff., the glover, in the market place, 2ˢ 6ᵈ from Bernard, the shepherd, towards Grenecroft, 6ˢ from the wife of Godfrey, the baker, 5ˢ from William, the carter, next the last, and 1ᵈ from Reginald Scherwynd next the churchyard of S. John. Witn. Rob. Seman.

     Endorsed 'de tenemento...in vico molendinorum, nunc infra clausum fratrum carmelit.'

371 Philip fitz Adam de Cestertune, with consent of his mother Albrida, gives to the Nuns with his sister Margaret a mess. held by Andrew, the carter, in Cambridge with 3 acres 1 rood in C. fields held by Teobald, bro. of Ascelin. Witn. Robert, Prior of Barnwell.

372 Thos. Potekin to the Nuns : a mess. in the par. of S. Mary, betw. Reg. de Cumberton and Henry, *percamentarius* : a shop in the market at the corner of Potters' Row, betw. a shop of Thos., cutler, and one of the Hospital of S. John : another shop betw. Thos., cutler, and Will. le Lorimer : 2 acres in C. fields, &c. Witn. Will. Elihot, mayor.

373 Will. le Gode to Stephen fitz Joh. Morize, Roger de Herlaston, Ric. Martyn and Rob. de Chesterton : a dovehouse
&c., a grange on the river bank in Cambridge, and a
mess. with 1 acre in Waterbeche. Stephen fitz Barthol.
Morize, mayor. Edw. III. 33.

374 Will. Paul to Nich. Gyloth of Fulborne : all his lands and
tenements in the town and fields of Cambridge and
Bernewelle. Joh. Gybonn, mayor. Edw. III. 44.

375 Katerine, widow of Tho. Dengayne of Ely, to the Nuns (Pr.
Margaret) and to Ric. Martyn of Cambridge : all her lands
&c., lately of Simon Stokton, in Cambridge town and
fields. Joh. Gybon, mayor. Edw. III. 46.

376 Nich. Ffraunceys of Fulburne to Joh. Payn and others :
2 mess. and 11½ acres in C. and B. fields. Joh. Blancpayn,
mayor. Edw. III. 49.

377 Roger de Herlaston to Dᵣ Will. Potton, rector of Harleton,
and others : all his lands &c. in Cambridge and Barnwell,
formerly of Joh. Purr. Ric. Maisterman, mayor. Ric.
II. 6.

378 Will. Bateman and others to the Nuns : 2 mess. in Barnwell,
next Pyttes Lane, one mess. in S. Radegund's par. and
3½ acres near Grenecroft. Ric. Maisterman, mayor. Ric.
II. 12.

379 Will. Rolf, of Ixnyng, chaplain, with license, to the Nuns :
2 mess. in Wales lane in H. T. parish : various tofts in
Baruwell, in S. Botolph's par. and S. Radegund's par. :
3 shops in S. Mary's parish, &c. Rob. Brygham, mayor.
Ric. II. 12.

380 Apsolon fitz Roger the presbyter, with consent of his wife
Maud, to the Nuns : various rents, viz. 12ᵈ from Simon
Bagge out of an acre in C. fields, 5ˢ out of a mess. in Miln
St. held by Brithnod Tanur, 2ˢ out of a mess. in the par.
of S. Botulph held by Ric. Kibelot, 20ᵈ out of land in
Miln St. held by Martin Wolward, 2ˢ out of land in the
par. of S. Benedict held by Andrew de Burgo, 20ᵈ from
land in S. Sepulchre's churchyard held by John, the
smith. Witn. Hervey fitz Eustace.

381 Simon Godelote and his wife Alienor to the Nuns: a mess.
in the par. of S. Andrew, betw. land of Chicksand convent
and land of Tho. de Taxtede: a shop in the market,
betw. Walter Corde and Hen. fitz Hugh: land in Miln St.
extending from the highway to the river (*filum aque*), &c.
Witn. Roger de Wykes.

382 The Nuns (Pr. Dera) lease the above premises to Alienor,
widow of Simon Godelote, for her life. Witn. Roger de
Wykes.

383 The Nuns (Pr. Letitia) to Hen. Devei: land given to them
by Mabilla, sister of Jonathan, betw. land of [   ]
Blangernun and land of Athelard le Thanur: rent 20^d
and a mark *gersuma*. Witn. Baldwin Blangernun, Sturmi,
'our brother' &c.

ACCOUNTS OF THE NUNNERY.

Compotus Domine Agnetis Banaster Thesaurisse ac Recep-
toris Denariorum Prioratus Sancte Radegundis
Cantebrigia ibidem a vigilia Sancti Michaelis Archangeli Anno
Regis Henrici Sexti XXVIII° usque ad vigiliam Sancti Michaelis
Archangeli extunc proxime sequentem Anno dicti Regis XXIX°
per unum annum integrum

Eadem domina respondet de liij⁵ iij⁴ ob. q. de arreragiis ultimi compoti sui anni proximo precedentis ut in pede ibidem de
Arreragia recordo apparet.

Summa liij⁵ iij⁴ ob. q.

Et de xxxij^li v⁵ x⁴ perceptis de redditu diversorum tenencium in
Cantebr., ut patet per Rentale hoc anno parcellatim super
Recepta dena- hunc compotum examinatum et tum hic oneratum hoc anno,
riorum de collec-
cione reddituum eo quod diversa tenementa ab antiquo devastata et ruinosa
in Cantebr. impresentibus reparata sunt et sic modo dimissa pro maiori-
bus summis per recognicionem Domine Priorisse super hunc compotum.

Et de iij⁵ iiij⁴ perceptis de Magistro Willelmo Spaldyng pro una
parcella prati iacente in croft vocato Nunnescroft sibi nuper dimissa per
Magistrum et confratres domus Sancti Johannis Evangeliste, Cantebr., ad
terminum annorum pro summa predicta per annum, que vero parcella
prati iam appropriata est domui sive Prioratui Sancte Radegundis,
Cantebr., per Dominum Regem Henricum VI^tum pro imperpetuum, ut pro
certo tenemento sub redditu xij⁵ per annum prefate domui Sancte Radegundis nuper pertinente et modo Collegio Domini Regis, Cantebr., appropriato per composicionem Domine Priorisse et Magistri dicti Collegii
Regalis pro redditu de xij⁵ predictis necnon pro certa summa eidem domui
Sancte Radegundis per prefatum Magistrum et socios Collegii Regis predicti pre manibus soluta, ut in compoto precedente plenius liquet.

Summa xxxij^li ix⁵ ij⁴.

Et de lxvj^s receptis de Rogero Hunte, firmario in West Wrottyng, sic
sibi dimisso per indenturam ad terminum xx^{ti} annorum, hoc

Firma in Patria

anno iiij^{to}.

Et de xl^s perceptis de Simone Thurgore, firmario terre dominicalis in
Abyngton, hoc anno.

Et de xl^s perceptis de Johanne Barnes, firmario terre dominicalis in
Shelford magna, hoc anno, ultra vj capones.

Et de xxij^s xj^d receptis de Johanne Pyte de Litlyngton et Roberto
Hawken de eadem, firmariis certe terre dominicalis ibidem sibi dimisse
per indenturam ad terminum xx^{ti} annorum, hoc anno iiij^{to}.

Et de [iiij^s ij^d] de firma certe terre in Coton sic dimisse Ricardo Waren
per indenturam.

Et de iiij^s receptis de Ricardo Hynton pro firma certe terre dominicalis
ibidem.

Et de iij^s viij^d receptis de Alicia Hynton pro firma certe terre dominicalis ibidem per annum.

Et de vij^s receptis de Thoma [Cole pro firma] certe terre dominicalis
ibidem per annum, ultra ij capones.

Et de ij^s receptis de Johanne Cole pro redditu assise ibidem, ultra ij
capones.

Et de v^s receptis de Edmundo Chapman de Whaddon per annum.

Et de xvj^d receptis de Johanne Burgoyn de Caxton per annum.

Et de xij^d receptis de Johanne Pichard de Trumpyngton per annum.

Et de vij^s vij^d ob. receptis de Sampson Aunger de Whitwell per annum.

Et de iij^s ij^d de certis tenencibus domine in Ely per annum, per
manus Vicarii Omnium Sanctorum, Cantebr.

Et de ij^s receptis de Thoma Perkyn, collectore redditus in Berden in
comitatu Essex, per annum.

Et de iiij^d receptis de redditu assise in Walden collecto per eundem
Thomam per annum.

Et de vij^s receptis de Thoma Perkyn de Stevyngton pro firma certe
terre ibidem per annum sibi dimisse per indenturam.

Et de xiij^s receptis de redditu assise Johannis Taylboys, domini de
Crawden, per annum.

Et de iij^d receptis de Roberto Skylman de Haselyngfeld per annum.

Et de ij^s iiij^d receptis de Priore de Bernwell pro certa terra in
Maddyngley vocata Maundysilver per annum.

Et de ij^d receptis de Johanne Clerk pro redditu assise in Walden per
annum.

Et de xx^d perceptis de Johanne Philipott de Trumpyngton pro firma
terre, hoc anno.

Et de xij^d receptis de Rectore de Fulbone pro certa terra ibidem per
annum.

Summa xij^{li} xiiij^s vij^d ob.

Et de v^e ij^d perceptis de profucuis nundinarum die Assumpcionis Beate Marie infra tempus compoti hoc anno.

Recepta forinseca cum profucuis nundinarum et repasti perhendinancium — Et de viij^{li} xiiij^s iiij^d perceptis de mensa sive repasto diversarum personarum generosarum, quarum nomina particulariter patent in libro computantis super hunc compotum ostenso et examinato.

Et de iij^s iiij^d perceptis de Magistro Willelmo Pyke de Aula Regia, Cantebr., ut de elemosina per ipsum huic domui data.

Summa ix^{li} ij^s x^d.

Et de xxiij^s vij^d perceptis de precio v quart. ij bus. frumenti venditi, ut extra.

Vendicio bladi et stauri — Et de li^s viij^d de precio xviij quart. ordei venditi, ut extra.

Et de viij^{li} ij^s ix^d de precio xlviij quart. v bus. brasii venditi, ut extra.

Et de xxj^d receptis de precio v porcellorum venditorum in foro hoc anno.

Et de xiiij^d de precio unius corrii taurini hoc anno venditi.

Et de v^s perceptis de precio pellium lanutarum hoc anno venditarum.

Et de xvj^s de precio xij bidentium sic venditorum Roberto Garlond hoc anno, pecia ad xvj^d.

Summa xiij^{li} xxiij^d.

Et de vj^{li} xiij^s iiij^d perceptis de firma garbarum decimalium cuiusdam porcionis in ecclesia Sancti Egidii, Cantebr., sic dimissa Johanni Hixon hoc anno.

Decime

Summa vj^{li} xiij^s iiij^d.

Et de lxvj^s viij^d receptis de quadam pensione per manus Vicarii Sancti Clementis, Cantebr., pro vestura monialium hoc anno.

Pensiones

Summa lxvj^s viij^d.

Summa totalis recepte cum Arreragiis lxxx^{li} xxij^d q.

E quibus computat in redditu resoluto Priori de Bernewell pro certa terra ibidem per annum vij^s.

Resoluciones redditus — Et solutum Maiori et Ballivis Cant. pro quadam consuetudine vocata le hagable per annum xiiij^s iiij^d ob. q.

Et solutum Thome Lovell de Chesterton pro tenemento ibidem per annum vj^s.

Et in redditu resoluto Johanni Radcliff, militi, pro certa terra ibidem et tenemento in Cant. vocato Mortymers per annum xv^s vj^d.

Et solutum Vicario Omnium Sanctorum, Cantebr., pro quadam [pensione sibi] concessa per annum xx^s.

Et solutum Collegio Corporis Christi per annum xvj^d.

Et in redditu resoluto Thome Cotton pro diversis terris in Cantebr. per annum iij^s vij^d.

Et solutum Rectori Ecclesie Sancti Benedicti per annum pro hospicio vocato le Booll iiij^d.

Et solutum Magistro domus Sancti Michaelis per annum iiij^d.

Summa lxviij^s v^d ob. q.

Et allocantur eidem pro uno tenemento in Precherche Strete nuper in tenura Rogeri Howprest pro x^s per annum et hoc anno

Decrementa redditus in manibus domine ob defectum conductionis, tamen contra annum futurum conceditur Johanni **Wattesson** pro xiij^s iiij^d per annum, x^s.

Et eidem pro j gardino nuper in tenura Johannis Chapman pro iij^s per annum et hoc anno ut pro prima medietate iacenti in manibus domine, xviij^d.

Et eidem pro certo tenemento per composicionem domine Priorisse et Conventus et Prepositi et sociorum Collegii Regalis Beate Marie et Sancti Nicholai, Cantebr., eidem collegio appropriato ut pro certa summa prefate domine Priorisse et Conventui pre manibus soluta, ut in compoto proximo precedenti **evidenter** apparet, xij^s.

Et eidem pro j tenemento nuper denovo edificato iacente in le Precherch Strete ad xj^s per annum, quod pro prima medietate huius anni stetit vacuum, v^s vj^d.

Et eidem pro j tenemento combusto nuper Johannis Ward in venella vocata Nunneslane ad vj^s viij^d per annum, quod pro primo quarterio huius anni stetit vacuum, xx^d.

Et eidem pro j tenemento in Walleslane nuper Johannis Walsheman pro vj^s viij^d per annum, qui quidem Johannes fugam fecit extra hanc villam infra primam medietatem huius anni nichil post se relinquens per quod distringi potuit preter vij^d inde levatos, et per ultimam medietatem huius anni dimittitur Philippo Jonesson pro iij^s, sic in decremento hoc anno iij^s j^d.

Et eidem pro j tenemento nuper in tenura Ricardi Pyghtesley quia excessive oneratur superius, ij^s iij^d.

Summa xxxvj^s.

Et in ij bus. sineris emptis pro vestibus lavandis, iiij^d.

Expense necessarie cum quindecima Et in xlj lb. candel emptis ad hospicium infra tempus compoti, iiij^s v^d.

Et in iij^bus lb. de le coton emptis pro candelis infra hospicium hoc anno faciendis per vices, ij^s.

Et solutum Thome Osbarne pro brasio integro hoc anno molendo, vj^s vij^d ob.

Et in spumato empto per totum annum, xxiij^d.

Et in j barello olei empto pro lampadibus ecclesie Sancte Radegundis, xiiij^d.

Et in candel empto erga festum Sancti Johannis Baptiste infra tempus compoti, ij^d.

Et in v ladels emptis ad coquinam, ij^d ob.

Et in slats emptis de Alex. Tebbe de Weston ad ustrinam pro brasio siccando, viij^s iiij^d.

Et solutum Thome Atkyn pro diversis laboribus indigentibus faciendis per xxxix dies, vj^s vij^d.

Et in pergameno et papiro cum encausto emptis tam per parcellas istius computantis de die in diem scribendo quam pro compoto anni revoluti, x^d.

Et solutum Johanni Cokk ad portandum stramen de orreo usque vaccariam, ustrinam et alia loca prout opus erat per vices, iiij^d.

Et in j le streynor (ij^d ob.) cum le bultell (vj^d) emptis hoc anno, viij^d ob.

Et in quadam muliere conducta ad filandum xxj^{lb} lane, xxij^d.

Et in Alicia Pavyer conducta ad idem opus in grosso continens xxxvj^{lb} fili lanei, vj^s.

Et solutum Petro Skynner adiuvanti cocum in coquina per vices, viij^d.

Et in una lagena cum iij pyntes olei emptis pro lana ungenda, xj^d.

Et in ij scutellis emptis, iij^d ob.

Et in furfure empto pro porcis assandis, vj^d.

Et in Johanne Mount conducto ad portandum stramen et alios labores indigentes faciendos per viij dies et di., xvij^d.

Et solutum Rogero Rede de Hynton pro le warpyng certi fili lanei, j^d ob.

Et in eodem conducto ad texandas lxxvij ulnas panni lanei pro liberatura famulorum, iij^s v^d.

Et solutum uxori Johannis Howdelowe pro le fullyng dicti panni, iiij^s v^d.

Et solutum cuidam le sherman pro tonsura eiusdem panni, xiiij^d ob.

Et in j cribro vocato a whete rydell, v^d, cum alio cribro vocato a melesyve, iij^d ob., et cum emendacione alius cribelli vocati an hersyve, j^d ob., necnon cum emendacione alius cribri, iij^d,—xiij^d ob.

Et solutum Johanni Everesdon pro bestiis usque mariscam de Wevelyngham fugandis, ij^d.

Et in iiij^{or} virgis cilicini emptis ad ustrinam, xiij^d.

Et in j le matte empto, ij^d.

Et solutum pro flebotomacione equorum carettinorum die Sancti Stephani, ij^d.

Et in j petra vocata a gryndstone empta de Johanne Chapman, bladsmyth, xvj^d.

Et in oleo empto ad ecclesiam Omnium Sanctorum, ij^s vij^d.

Et solutum Gerardo Wake pro ligatura unius libri vocati Sanctorum, vj^s viij^d.

Et solutum cuidam laborario pro fimo super terras arabiles spargendo, iiij^d.

Et in j sedlep empto, iij^d ob.

Et solutum Ricardo Cook pro scriptura ij par. indenturarum inter dominam et Johannem Styward pro j gardino sibi dimisso in Precherche Strete, ix^d.

Et in quadam olla terrea empta pro domo Refectorii pro cervisia imponenda, ij^d.

Et in Johanne Tommesson conducto ad **carucandum a festo Purificacionis Beato** Marie infra tempus compoti usque festum Sanctorum Philippi et Jacobi, **vij^s vj^d.**

Et in Thoma Kempe conducto ad idem opus per **xxxvj dies, capiente per** diem j^d ob., minus in toto ob., iiij^s v^d ob.

Et in Ricardo Sexteyn, slawterman, conducto pro bestiis ad coquinam mactandis, iiij^s ij^d.

Et in emendacione unius lavacri, ix^d, unius patelle **enee,** vj^d, cum ij patellis terreis emptis, j^d, ciphis **et** discis, vj^d, j duodena et dim. trencheres, iiij^d, j **loto** et j payle, vj^d, j fletyngbolle, j^d ob., j par. de les **bellowes, v^d** ob., excambio unius skymer, v^d, et excambio xxvj lb. stanni, **precio lb. j^d** ob., iij^s iiij^d—vj^s xj^d.

Et in castracione agnellorum et porcellorum hoc anno, x^d.

Et solutum Margarete Whyte pro pellibus lanutis lavandis, j^d.

Et solutum Johanni Clyfland pro tellura quinque acrarum **et j rodo** terre pro ordeo super seminando hoc anno, iiij^s ij^d.

Et in **scopis emptis** et similibus, j^d.

Et in Galfrido Sconyng et alio laborario conductis ad **faciendum unum** murum terrenum **pro pinnfald, simul cum emendacione alius muri infra** Prioratum, prout opus erat, per xxvj dies inter se **ad ij^d** per diem, iiij^s iiij^d.

Et in Simone Maydewell conducto ad **carucandum per vj dies tempore** seminacionis ordei, ix^d.

Et solutum Katerine Rolffe conducte **ad sarculandum in gardino per** iiij dies, iiij^d ob.

Et in **ij pipes emptis** de Johanne Heswell **pro kymlyns inde** fiendis, ij^s.

Et in Thoma Bottesham, cupario, facienti **de eisdem pipes vj kymlyns,** in grosso, ij^s iiij^d.

Et in **eodem** Thoma conducto ad **ligandum** cum circulis ligneis certa **vasa et** utensilia locis defectivis, vj^d ob.

Et in bidentibus lavandis, xiiij^d, **necnon** eisdem tondendis, **xiij^d,** et **lana** inde proveniente in vellera liganda,—iij^s j^d.

Et in Simone Maydewell per **vj dies, ix^d,** et Thoma Wynter per xij **dies,** xviij^d, laborantibus in prato et fodientibus argillam et aliis laboribus **indigentibus faciendis,** ij^s iij^d.

Et in iiij **ulnis vestis** linee emptis de Johanne Balle de Linea pro Refectorio, xij^d.

Et in viij ulnis **vestis** linee emptis pro **le Napr.,** ij^s vj^d.

Et in emendacione unius le Swep fontis ibidem, viij^d.

Et in emendacione quinque furcarum vocatarum Pyccheforkes, iiij^d.

Et solutum pro agistamento animalium depasturatorum in marisco de Wevelyngham, xix^d.

Et in j clat empt de Alicia Smalbon pro lana inde spargenda et verberanda, iij^d.

Et in cirpis hoc anno emptis per vices, ix^d.

Et in lij (*sic*) ulnis panni linei emptis de Johanne Ball de Linea pro mappis et manutergiis inde fiendis hoc anno, precio ulne ij^d, plus in toto ij^d—xj^s.

Et solutum ad pietanciam conventus, xviij^d die tricentali Johannis Broun nuper ballivi ibidem cum iiij^d pro cera et ij^d clerico pulsanti campanam, ij^s, in parte solucionis xxiij^s solvendorum forma sequenti, videlicet pro j bove, uno equo et aliis necessariis de predicto ballivo per dominam emptis ad utilitatem conventus, ultra quod dedit et procuravit conventui ; de quibus quidem xxiij^s domina habet solvere summo altari ecclesie Sancte Radegundis ad ornamentum eiusdem vij^s, et pro aliis xiiij^s annuatim die anniversarii dicti ballivi ij^s forma prerecitata per vij annos iam proxime futuros secundum ultimam dicti ballivi voluntatem, prout datum est intelligi auditori super hunc compotum.

Et solutum ad xv^{am} domini Regis ultime concessam, ij^s vj^d.

Summa vij^{li} vj^s vj^d ob.

Et in viij warp piscium vocatorum lyng emptis de Johanne Antyll apud nundinas Elienses infra tempus compoti, precio le warp viij^d,—v^s iiij^d, simul cum vj warp de codd, precio le warp vj^d ob., plus in toto j^d,—viij^s viij^d.

Empcio bladi et stauri

Et in j quart. ij bus. et dim. farine avene hoc anno ad coquinam emptis, precio bus. viij^d,—vij^s.

Et in xxxij pulcinis emptis ad staurum, ij^s viij^d.

Et in xiiij warp piscium vocatorum lyng emptis de predicto Johanne Antyll ad nundinas de Stiresbridge infra tempus compoti, precio le warp xj^d ob., minus in toto j^d,—xiij^s iiij^d.

Et in iiij^{or} bus. avenarum emptis ad seminandum, x^d.

Et in iiij^{or} quart. pisi emptis de Johanne Presote hoc anno, precio quart. ij^s viij^d,—xj^s.

Et in vj bus. viridis pisi emptis in foro pro potagio inde fiendo, iij^s.

Et in iiij^{or} bus. pisi emptis alia vice, xiiij^d.

Et in ij quart. de les tares emptis ad seminandum, v^s iiij^d.

Et in uno agnello empto de clerico Sancti Antonii, vj^d.

Et in semine vocato mustardseed empto, xij^d.

Et in ij bidentibus emptis de magistro Johanne Herrysson, capellano, xij^d et non plus hic in allocacione quia quoad residuum pardonatur conventui.

Et in viij unciis croci emptis ad staurum huius anni, vj^s xj^d.

Et in j lb. piperis, x^d ob.

Et in j equo empto ad nundinas Sancti Johannis Baptiste, ix^s vj^d.

Et in altero equo empto de Ricardo Baker de Bumsted, iiij^s.

Et in ij cades allec rubei, xv^s, j barell. et dim. allec albi, xiiij^s iij^d, ij cades do les sparlyng, ij^s viij^d, empt. apud Lincam hoc anno de Johanne Ball, xxxj^s xj^d.

Et in j quarterio fungaris vocati Wynterfyssh empto de eodem Johanne, v^s.

Et in ij quart. v bus. salis emptis ad nundinas Sancti Johannis Baptiste, precio bus. iiij ob.—vij^s x^d ob.

Et in j duodena caseorum empta de Willelmo Webbe de Balseham, precio casei iiij^d, plus in toto ij^d,—iiij^s ij^d.

Et in j bidente empto de Ricardo Sexteyn, vj^d.

Summa vj^{li} vj^s iij^d.

Et in les reynes emptis ad capistrum, v^d.

Custus carucarum et carettarum

Et in xvj par. tractuum, unde viij ad carucas, xvj^d, et viij ad carettas, ij^s j^d, emptis prout opus erat, iij^s v^d.

Et in emendacione duarum carucarum, xiiij^d.

Et in ij carucis denovo emptis de Michaele Bower de Fulborne, ij^s iij^d.

Et in xvij calcibus equinis emptis infra tempus compoti, xiiij^d.

Et in ccc clavis emptis pro ferrura equorum, viij^d.

Et in cartclowtnayll, v^d.

Et in iij^{bus} horsetrees, v^d.

Et in oxbowes, vj^d.

Et in cordula vocata whipcord empt., iij^d.

Et in j clave ordinata pro cerura equina, j^d.

Et in j horsecombe, ij^d.

Et in iij^{bus} pitcheforkes staves empt. ad nundinas Sancti Johannis Baptiste, ij^d.

Et in factura et emendacione coleres equinorum per unum hominem conductum per v dies, xxij^d.

Et in veste canabea empt. ad idem opus, ix^d.

Et in filo ad idem, iij^d.

Et in caretta axenda, vj^d.

Et in una ieruca empt. ad fugandos equos carettinos et carucarios, ij^d.

Et in j corda carettina empt. de Alicia Rooper, xvj^d.

Et in ij le Sheefs calibis empt., xviij^d.

Et solut. Waltero, ferrario, pro ferramento equorum carettinorum et carucariorum ac pro cubacione et acuacione puncture vomerum et culturarum per diversa anni tempora infra tempus compoti prout opus erat, xviij^s viij^d.

Et in uno correo equino dealbando, viij^d.

Summa xxxvj^s viij^d.

Et in stipendio Johannis Thressher conducto ad triturand. ccxxix quart. iij bus. ordei ad tascum, ut extra, capientis pro quolibet quarterio, ij^d, xxxviij^s iij^d.

Trituracio et Ventulacio

Et in eodem conducto ad triturand. lxxxj quart. vj bus. frumenti ad tascum, capiente pro quolibet quarterio iij^d—xx^s v^d q.

Et in eodem conducto ad triturand. vj bus. pisi ad tascum, ij^d.

Et in stipendio Johannis Mouut conducto ad portanda grana de orreo usque ventilabrum ad illa purganda per vices, x^d ob.

Summa lix^s viij^d ob. q.

Et in stipendio Henrici Denesson, carpentarii, conducti ad faciendum erigendum et preparandum in grosso in opere carpentrino Reparaciones duo tenementa sub uno tectu iacentia in venella vocata Nunneslane, in parte solucionis xxx^s cum finem fecerit operis predicti, xxiij^s iiij^d.

Et in Simone Maydewell conducto ad sarrandum maeremium operis predicti per iiij^{or} dies, xiiij^d.

Et in j carectata de les splentes empta ad tenementa predicta, iiij^s.

Et in splentes emptis alia vice, xxj^d.

Et in Johanne Cokke coadiuvante carpentarium predictum in opere predicto per x dies, xiiij^d.

Et in canabo cum clavis emptis pro ligatura murorum tenementorum predictorum, xvj^d.

Et in petra empta de Thoma Janes de Hynton ad supponendum gruncill tenementorum predictorum, vj^s viij^d.

Et in j fowder calcis adhuste empto ad idem opus, iij^s.

Et in vj carectatis luti emptis de Ricardo Poket de Bernewell ad opus predictum, xviij^d.

Et in Galfrido Sconyng et Willelmo Brann conductis ad supponendum gruncill tenementorum predictorum et ad daubandos muros eorundem in grosso, xvij^s iij^d.

Et in arundine empta de Johanne Bere, reder, ad tenementa predicta, ii^s iiij^d.

Et in D de les segh emptis ad idem opus, v^s.

Et in bordis emptis ad nundinas Sancti Johannis Baptiste pro ostio et fenestris domus predicte inde fiendis, ij^s x^d.

Et in xxij bunches virgarum emptis ad tenementa predicta, xxij^d.

Et in D clavis ad idem opus simul cum c clavis emptis postea, ii^s viij^d ob.

Et in Johanne Scot, tectore, conducto ad cooperiendum cum stramine duo tenementa predicta per xij dies, capiente per diem iiij^d, ad mensam domine, iiij^s.

Et in Thoma Clerk per viij dies et dim. et Nicholao Burnefygge per x dies tractantibus stramen et servientibus eidem coopertori, iij^s j^d.

Et in Katerina Rolff conducta ad idem opus per xij dies, ad j^d ob. per diem, xviij^d.

Et in Henrico Denesson, carpentario, conducto ad faciendum cum meremio domino j le Walshe (vj^d) infra tenementum in le Precherch Strete in grosso, simul cum factura unius muri vocati a pikewall (iiij^s), necnon pro factura gruncell alius muri vocati a pykewall tenementi predicti (ij^e iiij^d) et emendacione et erectione de les sparres ibidem, vij^s x^d.

Et in Johanne Freman conducto ad daubandum murum vocatum a pykewall et alios defectus tenementorum predictorum in grosso, iiij^s.

Et in iij^{bus} carectatis luti emptis ad opus predictum, ix^d.

Et in Johanne Richemond, Johanne Tommesson et Thoma Atkyn conductis ad daubandos et supponendos muros coquine tenementorum predictorum in grosso, ij^s viij^d ob.

Et in Johanne Wattesson pro le teryng dicte coquine in grosso, iij^s vj^d.

Et in splentes emptis ad muros coquine predicte cum canabo ad idem opus, xiij^d.

Et in xxiij bunches virgarum emptis ad tenementa et coquinam predictam, ij^s ix^d.

Et in MCC de les segh emptis de Ricardo Chandeller pro coopertura dictorum tenementorum et coquine predicte, precio centene xij^d, plus in toto ij^d,—xj^s x^d.

Et in Johanne Scot conducto ad cooperienda tenementa et coquinam predictam per xvij dies, capiente per diem iij^d ad mensam domine, iiij^s iij^d.

Et in Johanne Cokk tractante stramen ad idem opus per xvij dies, ij^s vj^d.

Et in gumphis et vertinellis (xiiij^d ob.), j lache (ij^d), j staple cum cerura (iiij^d) et cc clavis (viij^d) emptis ad tenementa et coquinam predictam, ij^s v^d ob.

Et in cc et dim. de les segh emptis pro coopertura domus proxime magnas portas exteriores, ij^s viij^d.

Et in iiij^{or} bunch virgarum emptis ad domum predictam, iiij^d.

Et in Johanne Scotte conducto ad tegendam domum predictam per xj dies ad iiij^d per diem et ad mensam domine, iij^s viij^d.

Et in Johanne Cokke conducto ad serviendum eidem per vj dies, xij^d.

Et in quodam alio laborario eidem tectori serviente per vij dies, xiiij^d.

Et in D de les segh emptis pro domu nuper combusta iacente in Nunneslane, v^s.

Et in iij^{bus} laborariis de Welle conductis ad emendandos et ad cooperiendos cum arundine certos defectus aule, coquine, et aliarum domorum indigentes per iiij^{or} dies, quolibet capiente per diem v^d ad mensam domine, iiij^s iiij^d.

Et in arundine empta ad emendandam domum Refectorii cum cariagio eiusdem, xxiij^d.

Et in eisdem laborariis conductis alia vice ad emendandos cum arundine predicta certos defectus domus Refectorii predicti et domus Granatorii per vij dies, inter se quolibet capiente per diem v^d, plus in toto j^d—iij^s.

Et in factura unius coopertoris pro le font ecclesie Sancte Radegundis, vj^d.

Et in bordis emptis de Edmundo Seyntlowe pro garner emendando, xij^d.

Et in Henrico Dennesson, carpentario, emendante dictum gerner cum bordis predictis per v dies, capiente per diem iiij^d ad mensam domine, una cum uno serviente suo ad idem opus conducto per tot dies ad iij^d per diem et ad mensam domine, ij^s xj^d.

Et in factura unius fenestre vitree cum vitro preparato domine in grosso, xij^d.

Et solutum Thome Lokyer pro iij^{bus} ceruris pro portis internis, ix^d.

Et in emendacione unius cerure cum clave empto ad eandem pro hostio coquine, iij^d ob.

Et in stramine empto pro tenemento in quo Thomas Brewer de Bernewell inhabitat, iiij^d.

Et in duobus ceruris emptis pro tenemento in quo Johannes Egate, tyler, inhabitat, vj^d.

Et in alia cerura empta pro tenemento in quo Johannes Tommesson inhabitat, iij^d.

Et in Johanne Cony emendante quemdam defectum ecclesie, ij^d.

Et in quodam plumbatorio conducto ad emendandam unam gutteram inter tenementum in quo Walterus Ferror inhabitat et tenementum Prioris de Bernewell et cum plumbo invento per ipsum Priorem, una cum emendacione unius defectus ecclesie Sancte Radegundis, xiiij^d.

Et in eodem plumbatorio conducto ad emendandam unam pipam plumbeam extendentem a fonte usque plumbum in domo pandoxatorii in grosso cum les sowder ipsius plumbatorii, viij^d.

Et in ccc clavis (xij^d) et c clavis (ij^d) emptis ad nundinas de Stiresbridge, xiiij^d.

Et in arundine empta de Thoma Manne de Welle, ut in precio iiij bus. brasii, xx^d.

Summa viij^{li} iij^s vij^d.

Et in butumine empto cum pyche hoc anno pro bidentibus signandis

[Custus Falde]   et ungendis, ij^s j^d.

Et in clatis emptis ad faldam, iij^s iij^d.

Et solutum pro remocione falde per diversas vices, iij^d.

Summa v^s vij^d.

Et solutum domine Priorisse et toto (*sic*) conventui pro vestura sua hoc

anno, in parte solucionis lxvj^s viij^d,—xliij^s viij^d et non

[Vestura Dominarum]   plus hoc anno in allocacione, quia Thomas Grey nuper

vicarius ibidem obiit ultimo anno elapso et residuum dicte summe executores testamenti dicti vicarii distribuerunt inter dominas in elemosina preter iij^s unde computans inferius allocat.

Summa xliij^s viij^d.

Et solutum magistro Nicholao Druell in plenam solucionem pro antiquo

[Debita Soluta]   debito, xxxiij^s iiij^d

Et Thome Cotton in plenam solucionem veteris debiti,

xxj^d.

Et domine Alicie Patryk nuper mortue in plenam solucionem omnium debitorum, iij^s iiij^d, ex legaciono Petri Erle, capellani, nuper defuncti.

Et domine Johanne Lancastre in parte solucionis vj^s viij^d sibi legatorum per predictum Petrum, iij^s iiij^d.

Et domine Agneti Swaffham, suppriorisse, in parte solucionis vj^s viij^d,— xx^d.

Et solutum magistro Ricardo Broun, nuper Rectori ecclesie de Dounham, pro vetere debito cum iij^s ij^d in manibus suis obstupatis pro redditu domine debito in Ely, et cum iiij^s in manibus suis obstupatis de redditu in Cantebrigia, vij^s ij^d.

Et solutum le dyer Sancti Ivonis pro antiquo debito, vj^s.

Et solutum Roberto Tyler de Reedwynter in plenam solucionem omnium debitorum pro tegulis ab eo emptis anno preterito, iiij^s.

Summa lx^s vij^d.

Et solutum Willelmo Rogger pro carne bovina, porcina, ovina et vitulina empta ad hospicium per manus Johanne Grauntyer, xxxiiij^s viij^d.

[Providencia Hospicii]

Et in pane, cervisia, carne bovina, porcina, ovina, vitulina, porcellina, gallina, pullina, ovis, butiro, et piscibus recensibus et marinis emptis per dictam ad hospicium infra tempus compoti, ut particulariter in uno libro papiri super hunc compotum examinato plenius patet, xj^{li} vij^s iiij^d ob.

Et in una vacca empta de Thoma Carrawey ad hospicium, vi^s viij^d.

Summa xiij^{li} viij^s viij^d ob.

Et datum iiij^{or} preconibus maioris Cantebr. pro eorum oblacione ad festum Nativitatis Domini infra tempus compoti, pro eorum serviciis domine Priorisse et conventui impensis et imposterum impendendis, ij^s ij^d.

[Dono; data]

Et in aliis donis (iij^s), cum iij^s iiij^d datis Thome Key (xx^d) et Johanne Granngyer (xx^d), et cum ij^s vj^d distributis inter pauperes die cene Domini, necnon cum les ernest penys (iiij^d) diversis personis datis que cum v^s ix^d certis tenentibus et servientibus domine ad diversa anni tempora per consideracionem domine Priorisse, ut parcellatim in papiro istius computantis annotatur, xiij^s xj^d.

Et in uno grue empto et dato Cancellario Universitatis ville Cantebr. pro bona amicitia sua in diversis materiis domine ad utilitatem conventus, xij^d.

Et datum ij^{bus} laborariis pro cariagio turbarum una vice, una cum iiij^d datis Johanni Nyxon ad tonsuram bidentium suorum et ij^d expenditis apud domum Johannis Ansty senioris et cum vj^d datis Ricardo Baker de Bernewell et Ricardo West, pandoxatori, pro tolneto colligendo et recipiendo tempore nundinarum ibidem, xiiij^d.

Summa xix^s iiij^d.

Et in viij paribus cirothecarum emptis pro diversis conductis in autumpno prout opus erat, xij^d.

Sumptus Aut-umpni.   Et in diversis laborariis conductis ad falcandas unandas
et erga carettas preparandas lxxxiiij^{er} acras ordei ad tascum,
capientibus pro qualibet xij^d,—iiij^{li} iiij^s.

Et in consimilibus laborariis conductis ad metendas ligandas et erga
carettas preparandas xxx acras et j rodam frumenti ad tascam, capientibus
pro qualibet acra ut supra, xxx^s iij^d.

Et in Thoma Atkyn conducto ad falcandas les tares in clauso vocato
Bartonescrofte per ij dies, viij^d.

Et in Thoma Heyreman (xx^d) per j diem, Johanne Trumpyngton
(viij^s iiij^d) per v dies conductis ad cariandum bladum cum carettis suis,
capiente per diem quolibet xx^d et mensam suam, x^s.

Et in Thoma Key conducto per totum tempus autumpni, ultra ij bus.
brasei, vj^s viij^d.

Et in Thoma Wynter conducto ad idem opus per idem tempus, x^s.

Et in Nicholao Burnefyge conducto ad idem opus per tempus predictum, ix^s.

Et in Johanne Knyght coadiuvante laborarios una vice ut in precio
unius paris sotularium, vij^d.

Summa vij^{li} xij^s ij^d.

Et solutum Edmundo Wyghton pro j brevi vocato Quod Dampnum
optinendo pro hospicio vocato le Facoun, iij^s j^d.

[Expense] forin-secc   Et solutum eidem pro transcriptura dicti brevis et pro
recordo placiti habendi, ij^s.

Et solutum Galfrido Fyssher pro feriagio per aquam piscium salsorum
(iiij^d) de Ely, unacum feriagio dimidii barelli olei vocati lnmmpe-oyle (ij^d)
de Linea et unius litere de Linea predicta domine misse, ac pro feriagio
allec de Linea usque magnum pontem, Cantebr., ij^s ij^d.

Et in expensis Thome Key pro feriagio usque Elien. (iiij^d) et ibidem
expectantis per^t ij dies pro piscibus salsis (v^d) et aliis expensis, simul cum
expensis apud Crawden (j^d) pro redditu ibidem levando, et apud Abyngton
et Wrottyng (iiij^d ob.) pro consimilibus, unacum expensis apud Litlyngton
(v^d) pro prato domine inter Thomam Campes et ipsam dominam sortendo
et in certum ponendo, xix^d ob.

Et in expensis Thome Key apud Cantebr. diversis vicibus pro redditu
levando et colligendo, v^d ob.

Et in expensis domine Priorisse pro tenencibus suis apud Cantebr.
supervidendis ad diversas vices, unacum colloquio habendo cum Johanne
Ansty, armigero, pro utilitate domus, xvij^d ob.

Summa x^s ix^d ob.

Et in v millibus cc terricidis hoc anno emptis cum iiij^d solutis pro
[Sumptus Foca-lium]   cariagio aliquarum earundem de aqua usque prioratum,
ix^s iiij^d.

Et in mcc de les segh emptis hoc anno, precio centene xx^d, minus in toto iiij^d,—xix^s viij^d.

Et in ccxxx fagottis emptis pro focalibus ibidem per diversas vices, precio centene [*erasure*] plus in toto j^d, xvij^s iiij^d.

Et in mcc terricidis hoc anno emptis de Almeris, turffeman, ut in precio vj bus. frumenti unde computans superius oneratur, iij^s vj^d.

Summa xlix^s x^d.

Et in salario fratris Roberti Palmer, confessoris dominarum, hoc anno ut in diversis annis precedentibus, vj^s viij^d.

[Stipendia] famulorum.   Et in salario magistri Johannis Herryson, capellani celebrantis missam pro dominabus per totum tempus computi, c^s.

Et solutum Johanni Peresson, capellano celebranti in ecclesia Sancti Andree Apostoli per vices, ij^s iiij^d.

Et in stipendio clerici ecclesie ibidem per annum, xiij^s iiij^d.

Et in stipendio Thome Key, colligentis redditus in Cant. et patria hoc anno, xiij^s iiij^d.

Et in stipendio Ricardi West, pistoris et pandoxatoris, hoc anno, xxvj^s viij^d.

Et in stipendio Johannis Everesdon, conducti ad carucandum per totum tempus compoti, xxvj^s viij^d.

Et in stipendium Johannis Wyllyamesson, bercarii ibidem, cum viij^d in precio unius paris caligarum hoc anno, xx^s viij^d.

Et in stipendio Roberti Page, carucarii, per idem tempus, xvj^s.

Et in stipendio Johannis Slibre, alterius carucarii, per annum, xiij^s iiij^d.

Et in stipendio Roberti Pykkell, bubulci, hoc anno, vj^s viij^d.

Et in stipendio Johannis Cokke, malster, hoc anno, xiij^s iiij^d.

Et in stipendio Johanne Granngyer, unius ancille domine, hoc anno, cum iij^s iiij^d in regardo sibi datis pro officio Purvis hoc anno, xiij^s iiij^d.

Et in stipendio Elianore Richemound, alterius ancille domine, cum xx^d in regardo sibi datis, viij^s iiij^d.

Et in stipendio Elizabeth Chaterys, alius ancille domine, ut in vestitu sua (*sic*) infra tempus compoti, iij^s j^d.

Et in stipendio Dionisie, yerdwomman, hoc anno ut in annis precedentibus, ix^s.

Et in stipendio Ricardi Porter, conducti a festo Sancte Trinitatis infra tempus compoti usque festum Michaelis ad omnes labores husbondrie, xiij^s iiij^d.

Et solutum pro liberatura Johanne Granngyer, pincernarie domine, vj^s viij^d.

Et solutum pro liberatura Johannis Slybre hoc anno, ij^s vj^d.

Summa xv^{li} xv^s iij^d.

Et in Thoma Atkyn et Johanne Tommesson, conductis ad falcandas ad
[Falcacio] stipuli tascum iiij^{or} acras et j rodam stipuli, capientibus pro qualibet acra viij^d—ij^s x^d.

Summa ij^s x^d.

Summa omnium allocacionum et solucionum lxxviij^{li} vj^s.   Et debet
xxxv^s x^d q.   De quibus allocantur ei, ut de certis denariis pendendis super
Thomam Key anno proxime precedenti ex mandato domine Priorisse,
iij^s.   Et eidem, de parte lxvj^s viij^d pro vestura dominarum hic allocantur
causa patente superius in titulo Vestura Dominarum, xxiij^s.   Et eidem pro
stipendio Roberti Page, unius carucarii ibidem, et anno ultimo elapso non
allocato, xvj^s.   Et sic excedit modo vj^s j^d ob. q.   Tamen postea oneratur
de lviij^s vij^d ob. q. receptis de domina Priorissa ut de parte xj^{li} xvj^s xj^d,
iuxta billam indenture inter dominam et ipsam computantem inde factam,
unde oneratur superius in titulo Vendicio bladi et stauri, et plus de
xiij^d ad complecionem integre summe de vendicione bladi, et hic oneratur
de lviij^s vij^d ob. q. predictis eo quod tum allocabatur isti computanti pro
trituracione bladi et solutum erat per dominam Priorissam et non per
istam computantem.   Et de xij^d de precio iiij^{or} caponum venditorum,
ut extra.   Et de xviij^s viij^d receptis de certis tenentibus pro veteribus
debitis unde in compoto precedenti nulla fit mencio.   Et modo debet
lxxij^s ij^d.

Unde super

Johannem Rychemound pro j tenemento, nuper Johannis Rychemound
ad iiij^s per annum, pro ultimo quarterio anni instantis   xij^d.

Ricardum Whetley de Bernewell pro parte unius tenementi iacentis in
Bernewell, pro hoc anno   v^s.

Henricum Symmesson pro ij tenementis scituatis in parochia Sancti
Botulphi ad iiij^s vj^d per annum, tam pro hoc anno quam pro anno proxime
precedenti   ix^s.

Willelmum Rogger pro j tenemento in stallagio, tam pro hoc anno quam
pro ij^{bus} annis proxime precedentibus, per annum xij^d, ultra xij^d inde
levatos   iij^s.

Eundem Willelmum pro j gardino in le Precherchestrete, pro consimili-
bus annis, per annum ij^s   vj^s.

Johannem Scot pro j gardino iuxta cimiterium ecclesie Sancti Edwardi,
pro tot annis, per annum xij^d, ultra iiij^d inde receptos annuatim   ij^s.

Johannem Barbor pro redditu exeunte de tenemento vocato le ffacoun
in Petycury, pro tot annis per annum xiiij^s vij^d   xliij^s ix^d.

Dominam Margaretam Huntyngdon pro uno tenemento vocato le Sword,
tam pro hoc anno quam pro anno proxime precedenti, per annum vj^s, ultra
xx^d inde levatos pro ij^{do} anno precedenti per manus Johannis Smyth,
webster   x^s iiij^d.

Magistrum Johannem Honythorne pro j gardino iuxta Bartonescroft,

tam pro hoc anno quam pro ij^{bus} annis proxime precedentibus, per annum
ij^s   vj^s.

Magistrum domus Sancti Johannis Evangeliste pro j tenemento in
parochia Sancti Edwardi, pro tot annis, per annum iiij^s vj^d   xiij^s vj^d.

Ricardum Busshee pro j tenemento ex opposito Beate **Marie,** pro tot
annis, per annum xij^d   iij^s.

Ricardum Wryght pro j tenemento nuper Johannis Essex, sadeler, pro
totidem annis, per annum xij^d   iij^s.

Predictum Magistrum domus Sancti Johannis Evangeliste pro j tenemento iuxta cimiterium ecclesie parochialis Sancti Sepulcri in vetero
Judaismo, pro tot annis, per annum xx^d   v^s.

Johannem Belton pro j tenemento iacente iuxta tenementum domine
Priorisse, pro tot annis, per annum vj^s viij^d   xx^s.

Magistrum Ricardum Pightesley pro j tenemento nuper Willelmi Burtones, pro tot annis, per annum ij^s   vj^s.

Magistrum et scolares Sancti Benedicti, Cant., pro j tenemento quondam Gybelotes, pro totidem annis, per annum ij^s ij^d   vj^s vj^d.

Thomam Lolleworth pro j tenemento in quo inhabitat, pro consimilibus
annis, per annum ij^s   vj^s.

Johannem Ncoll pro orto cum uno horreo nuper Hugonis Canesby, pro
tot annis, per annum xij^d   iij^s.

Johannem Leccham **pro** j tenemento in le Precherch Strete, pro ij^do
anno preterito   xx^d.

Robertum Mildenhale de Cant., ut de precio ij caponum venditorum
onerato superius, tam pro hoc anno quam pro anno proxime precedente,
per annum vj^d   xij^d.

Johannem Crofte pro j parlari prope Pylateslane, pro hoc anno et anno
precedente, per annum vj^d   xij^d.

Radulphum Attefeld pro j tenemento in parochia **Beate** Marie ad vj^s
per annum, pro tot annis detentos, parte ij^a inde levata   viij^s.

Predictum Magistrum Ricardum Pightesley pro j tenemento prope
Aulam Regiam, pro ultima medietate anni precedentis   xiij^d ob.

Stephanum Brasier pro j tenemento iacente in Nunneslane ad v^s per
annum, ultra iij^s ix^d inde levatos, pro anno proxime precedente   xv^d.

Johannem Webster pro j tenemento iacente in venella predicta ad
xij^s per annum, et per eundem Johannem detentos pro j termino anni
proxime precedentis (iij^s) et pro viij septimanis (ij^s)   v^s.

HENRY VI, 29—30, *i.e.* 1450—1451.

Compotus Domine Agnetis Banastre Thesaurisse ac Receptoris Denariorum Prioratus Sancte Radegundis a vigilia Sancti Michaelis Archangeli anno Regis Henrici Sexti xxix° usque ad vigiliam Sancti Michaelis Archangeli extunc [proxime sequentem]

Eadem computans respondet de lxxij⁵ ij⁴ de arreragiis ultimi compoti sui anni proxime precedentis, ut in pede ibidem de recordo apparet.

[Arreragia]

Summa lxxij⁵ ij⁴.

Et de xxxij^{li} v⁵ x⁴ perceptis de redditu diversorum tenencium in Cantebr., ut patet per Rentale hoc anno parcellatim super hunc compotum examinatum.

[Recepta denariorum de collecione reddituum in Cantebr.]

Et de iij⁵ iiij⁴ perceptis de Magistro Willelmo Spaldyng pro una parcella prati iacente in croft vocato Nunnescroft, sibi nuper dimissa per Magistrum et confratres domus Sancti Johannis Evangeliste [ad terminum] annorum pro summa predicta per annum, que vero parcella prati appropriata est domui sive Prioratui Sancte Radegundis, Cantebr., per dominum Regem Henricum vi^{tum} [pro imperpetuum], ut pro certo tenemento sub redditu xij⁵ per annum, prefate domui Sancte Radegundis nuper pertinente et modo Collegio Regali Beate Marie et Sancti Nicholai, Cantebr., [appropriato] per composicionem Domine Priorisse et Magistrum sive Prepositum predicti Collegii Regalis pro redditu de xij⁵ predictis per annum, necnon pro certa summa eidem [domui] Sancte Radegundis per prefatum Prepositum et socios collegii Regis predicti soluta, ut in compoto ij^{di} anni precedentis aperte et evidenter apparere poterit.

Et de [iij⁵ perceptis] de Johanne Shepperd pro uno tenemento nuper denovo edificato, iacente in vico vocato Nunneslane, unde in compoto precedente nulla fit mencio, ad vj⁵ per annum, [per ultimam (?)] medietatem anni infra tempus compoti prefato Johanni dimisso et non antea, tamen respondet anno futuro de vj⁵.

Et viij⁵ recipientur annis futuris de Johanne [pro] alio tenemento nuper noviter edificato iacente in vico prefato; nil hoc anno, quanquam dimissum est prefato tenenti per dominam contra tempus instantis compoti pro summa predicta [annis] futuris solvenda.

Summa xxxij^{li} xij⁵ ij⁴.

Et de lxvj⁵ viij⁴ receptis de Rogero Hunte, firmario in West Wrottyng, sic sibi dimisso per indenturam ad terminum xx^{ti} annorum, hoc anno quinto.

[Firme in Patria]

Et de xl⁸ perceptis de Simone Thurgore, firmario terre dominicalis in Abyngton, hoc anno.

Et de xl⁸ perceptis de Johanne Bernes, firmario terre dominicalis in Shelford magna, hoc anno, ultra vj capones.

Et de xxij⁸ xjᵈ receptis de Johanne Pyte de Litlyngton et Roberto Hawken de eadem, firmariis certe terre dominicalis ibidem sibi dimisse per indenturam ad terminum xxᵗⁱ annorum, hoc anno quinto.

Et de iiij⁸ ijᵈ receptis de firma certe terre in Coton sic dimisse Ricardo Waren per indenturam.

Et de iiij⁸ receptis de Ricardo Hynton pro firma certo terre dominicalis ibidem.

Et de iij⁸ viijᵈ receptis de Alicia Hynton pro firma certe terre dominicalis ibidem per annum.

Et de vij⁸ receptis de Thoma Cole pro firma certe terre dominicalis ibidem per annum, ultra ij capones.

Et de ij⁸ receptis de Johanne Cole pro redditu assise ibidem, ultra ij capones.

Et de v⁸ receptis de Edmundo Chapman de Whaddon per annum.

Et de xvjᵈ receptis de Johanne Burgoyn de Caxton per annum.

Et de [xijᵈ] receptis de [Johanne] Pycchard de Trumpington per annum.

Et de vij⁸ vijᵈ ob. receptis de Sampson Aunger de Whytwell per annum.

Et de [iij⁸ ijᵈ] receptis de [certis] tenencibus domine in Ely per annum, per manus Vicarii Omnium Sanctorum, Cantebr.

Et de ij⁸ receptis de Thoma Parkyn, collectore redditus in Beerden in comitatu Essex, per annum.

Et de iiijᵈ receptis de redditu assise in Walden collecto per eundem Thomam per annum.

Et de vij⁸ receptis de Thoma Perkyn de Stevyngton pro firma certe terre ibidem per annum sibi dimisse per indenturam.

Et de xiij⁸ receptis de redditu assise Johannis Taylboys, domini de Crawden, per annum.

Et de iijᵈ receptis de Roberto Skylman de Haselyngfeld per annum.

Et de ij⁸ iiijᵈ receptis de Priore de Bernewell pro certa terra in Maddyngley vocata Maundysilver per annum.

Et de ijᵈ receptis de Johanne Clerk pro redditu assise in Walden per annum.

Et de xxᵈ perceptis de Johanne Philypott de Trumpyngton pro firma terre, hoc anno.

Et de xijᵈ receptis de Rectore de Fulbone pro certa terra ibidem per annum.

Summa xijˡⁱ xiiij⁸ vijᵈ ob.

Et de vᵉ perceptis de profucuis et provenientibus nundinarum die
Assumpcionis Beate Marie infra tempus compoti.

Et de vjˡˡ ijˢ jᵈ receptis de mensa sive repasto diversarum personarum generosarum, quarum nomina particulariter in libro papiri computantis super hunc compotum
ostensum annotantur.

Recepta forin-seca cum profu-cuis nundinarum et repasti perhen-dinanclum

Et de xlixˢ jᵈ perceptis de domina Priorissa per billam indenture inter
dominam et ipsam computantem.

Summa viijˡˡ xvjˢ ijᵈ.

Et de vjˢ perceptis de precio j qrt. ij bus. frumenti venditi, ut extra,
unde in foro iiij bus., precii bus. viiiᵈ, Almeris Ffyddis ij bus.,
precio bus. viijᵈ, et Johanni Presot iiij bus., precii bus. vjᵈ.

Vendicio bladi et stauri

Et de xxixˢ viijᵈ perceptis de certis personis pro xij qrt.
v bus. ordei venditi ad diversa precia, vidlt. Johanni Presot ix qrt., precio
qrt. ijˢ iiijᵈ, (xxjˢ) Thome Key iij bus., precii   (xjᵈ), Ricardo Poket iiij
bus., precii   (xvjᵈ), et aliis certis personis in minutis parcellis ij qrt.
vj bus., precii qrt. ijˢ iiijᵈ (vjˢ vᵈ).

Et de vijˡˡ vˢ xᵈ perceptis de certis hominibus pro xlvij qrt. vj bus.
brasii venditi ad diversa precia, vidlt. Willelmo Bronn iiij bus., precii
(xxᵈ) Thome Key iiij bus., precii   (xxᵈ), Willelmo vocato Jacobo
Brewer xx qrt., precii qrt. iijˢ (lxˢ), Thome Coteler x qrt., precii qrt. iijˢ
iiijᵈ (xxxiijˢ iiijᵈ), Johanni Stephen iiij qrt., precii qrt. ijˢ viijᵈ (xˢ viijᵈ),
Ricardo Poket iij bus., precii   (xvᵈ), Johanni Clyyeloud iij bus., precii
(xvᵈ) et Johanni Thyrlowe de Hawkeston xij qrt., precii qrt. iijˢ (xxxvjˢ).

Et de xixᵈ perceptis de precio unius corrii bovis sic venditi in foro
infra tempus compoti.

Et de iiijˢ xjᵈ perceptis de precio xxviij pellium ovinarum lanutarum
et xvj pellecculis hoc anno venditis Johanni Wolleman de Cantebr.

Et de iiijˢ xᵈ perceptis de certis velleribus laneis hoc anno.

Et de viijˢ perceptis de Waltero Ferrario pro j qrt. iiij bus. frumenti
venditi Waltero Ferrario, bus. ad viijᵈ.

Summa ixˡˡ xixˢ xᵈ.

Et de vjˡˡ xiijˢ iiijᵈ perceptis de firma garbarum decimalium cuiusdam
porcionis in ecclesia Sancti Egidii, Cantebr., sic dimissa
Johanni Hyxon hoc anno.

Decime

Summa vjˡˡ xiijˢ iiijᵈ.

Et de lxvjˢ viijᵈ receptis de quadam pensione per manus Vicarii
Sancti Clementis pro vestura Monialium hoc anno.

Pensiones

Summa lxvjˢ viijᵈ.

Summa totalis recepte cum arreragiis lxxvijˡˡ xiiijˢ xjᵈ ob.

E quibus computat in reddito resoluto Priori de Bernewell pro certa
terra ibidem per annum, vijˢ.

Resoluciones reddituum

Et solutum Maiori et ballivis Cantebr. pro quadam
consuetudine vocata le hagable per annum, xiiijˢ iiijᵈ ob. q.

11—2

Et solutum Thome Lovell de Chesterton pro tenemento ibidem per annum, vj^s.

Et in redditu resoluto Johanni Radcliff, militi, pro certa terra ibidem et tenemento in Cantebr. vocato Mortymers per annum, xv^s vj^d.

Et solutum Vicario Omnium Sanctorum in Cantebr. pro quadam pensione sibi concessa per annum, xx^s.

Et solutum Collegio Corporis Christi per annum, xvj^d.

Et in redditu resoluto Thome Cotton pro diversis terris in Cantebr. per annum, iij^s vij^d.

Et solutum Rectori ecclesie Sancti Benedicti per annum pro hospicio vocato le Booll, iiij^d.

Et solutum Magistro domus Sancti Michaelis per annum, iiij^d.

Summa lxviij^s v^d ob. q.

Et allocantur eidem pro certo tenemento per composicionem domine Priorisse et Conventus et Prepositi et socios (sic) Collegii

Decrementa redditus

Regalis Beate Marie et Sancti Nicholai, Cantebr., eidem collegio appropriato, ut pro certa summa denariorum prefate domine Priorisse et Conventui soluta, ut in compoto ij^di anni proxime preteriti apparet, xij^s.

Et eidem pro j tenemento nuper in tenura Ricardi Pyghtesley excessive superius onerati, ij^s iiij^d.

Et eidem pro parcella unius gardini iuxta cimiterium ecclesie Sancti Edwardi onerata superius ad xij^d per annum et dimissa Johanni Scot pro hoc anno et diversis annis preteritis pro iiij^d per annum, tamen contra annum dimissa eidem Johanni pro viij^d, et ideo allocantur computanti cum viij^d pro anno instanti et ij^s pro iij^bus annis preteritis, unde ista eadem computans superonerata erat ij^s viij^d.

Et eidem pro parcella redditus debiti per Stephanum Brasyer propter paupertatem et inopiam eiusdem Stephani ex gracia domine Priorisse hac vice tantum, xv^d.

Et eidem pro parte unius tenementi nuper in tenura Johannis Webster pro xij^s per annum, unde levatur preter vij^s, eo quod predictus Johannes Webster noctanter devolavit nihil post se relinquens per quod distringi potuit, v^s.

Et eidem pro tenemento prope Aulam Regiam ad xiij^d ob. per annum, ultra ix^d inde levatos, iiij^d ob.

Et in decremento redditus Johannis Speed pro uno tenemento nuper in tenura Johannis Andrewe pro x^s per annum et modo dimisso prefato Johanni Speed pro viij^s per annum iuxta Rentale, ij^s.

Et in decremento redditus unius tenementi nuper in tenura Philippi Jonesson pro vj^s per annum et modo dimisso Thome Cordwaner pro v^s vj^d per annum, vj^d.

Summa xxvj^s ob.

Et in xiiij lb. candel emptis de Thoma Heyreman ad hospicium cum

Expense necessarie cum quindecima ij^d solutis Katerine Roolff ad adiuvandos factores candelarum infra hospicium ac cum ij^d solutis pro emendacione unius vasis vocati a payle, xviij^d.

Et in una situla vocata a boket empta de Thoma Bottesham cum ligacione eiusdem cum circulis ferreis domine, xiij^d.

Et solutum Philippo Perechyld pro emendacione fenestre vitree infra aulam, xvj^d.

Et in cinere empto, ij^d.

Et in spumatico empto, xj^d.

Et solutum Thome Osbarne pro brasio per totum tempus compoti molendo, vj^s viij^d.

Et solutum uxori Johannis Pavyer pro viij lb. lane ad tascam nendis et filandis, xvj^d.

Et solutum Margerie Gangefeyr pro consimili opere per vj dies, vj^d.

Et solutum Alicie Basse conducte ad preparandam lanam erga nentes ad filandum continentem xx lb. ad tascam, cum j lb. sic operata per Katerinam Rolff, xxij^d.

Et in Rogero Reed de Hynton conducto ad texandas lx ulnas vestis lanee, capiente pro qualibet ulna ob. q., minus in toto ij^d, cum iij^d pro le Warpyng eiusdem et cum ij^s vij^d solutis Willelmo Bank, fuller, pro opere et arte sua et spissitudine panni predicti, vj^s v^d ob.

Et solutum cuidam fabro de Bernewell pro factura unius securis, iiij^d.

Et in alia securi empta de Willelmo Brook de Saweston, vj^d.

Et in Johanne Trumpyngton per ij dies ad ij^d per diem cum alio laborario per v dies ad j^d per diem spargentibus fimum super terras arabiles domine, ix^d.

Et in una lagena dim. et j pynte olei emptis pro lana ungenda, ij^s j^d.

Et in emendacione iij cribellorum, iij^d.

Et in Thoma Atkyn, laborario, conducto ad diversos labores indigentes faciendos per diem, ut in parcellis super hunc compotum examinatis plenius apparet, vj^s viij^d.

Et solutum Waltero, ferrario, pro flebotomacione equorum domine die Sancti Stephani infra tempus compoti, ij^d.

Et solutum Johanni Thommesson, laborario, pro diversis laborariis (*sic*) oportunis per ipsum factis per x dies, xx^d.

Et in Johanne Presot conducto ad shidauda et succidenda ligna pro focalibus et ad loppandos arbores circa monasterium istud necnon ad faciendos alios labores prout opus erat per x dies ad ij^d per diem, unacum caruca sua et equis suis et famulo suo super terras domine tempore seminacionis ordei per alios x dies ad xij^d per diem, ac cum x^d sibi concessis pro punctura vomeris et culture sue per idem tempus, xiiij^s vj^d.

Et in Thoma Bottesham, cowper, emendanti certa utensilia lignea per vices, ij^s.

Et in furfure empto pro porcis assandis, vj^d.

Et in discis et siphis emptis, iiij^d.

Et in xiiij hames (sic) ferreis emptis pro carnibus per eosdem pendendis in coquina, viij^d.

Et in Galfrido Sconyng conducto ad faciendam quemdam (sic) sepem vivam inter nova tenementa iacentia in vico vocato Nunneslane per xiij dies, ij^a ij^d.

Et in Nicholao Toly conducto ad idem opus per x dies, xx^d.

Et in virgis emptis pro ligatura boum, j^d.

Et in una lagena olei empta pro lampadibus ad ecclesiam Omnium Sanctorum, xvj^d.

Et in scopis emptis, iij^d.

Et in papiro et encausto cum pergameno emptis pro compoto anni revoluti componendo et inscribendo, ix^d ob.

Et solutum Willelmo Dale pro emendacione plumbi extendentis de fonte usque domum pandoxatorii per diversas vices, iij^a iiij^d.

Et in D cirpis emptis pro diversis domibus sternendis et reficiendis infra tempus compoti, ij^a vj^d.

Et in castracione agnorum et porcellorum infra tempus predictum, x^d.

Et in Willelmo Broun et socio suo per ij dies conductis ad scindendas vites et illas erigendas, xij^d.

Et in clave vocata Spykyng empta ad idem opus, ij^d.

Et in j le Streynor empto, vj^d.

Et in ij skepp vocatis Skotell, iij^d.

Et in Ricardo Gardyner verberante fungaria per j diem, iij^d.

Et in ij duodenis cissoriorum emptis de Johanne Ball de Linea, viij^d.

Et in quadam pecia meremii vocata a mast empta apud Lynne predictam pro una scala inde fienda, iiij^s.

Et in v ulnis vestis cannabee empte ibidem pro fungaribus inde cubandis, xiij^d ob.

Et in j lagena et dimidio olei de Raap empta apud Lynn predictam, cum j^d precio unius olle terree pro eo oleo imponendo, xvj^d.

Et in una olla terrea vocata a Spensepott empta pro domo Refectorii, j^d ob.

Et in Thoma Kemp conducto ad carucandum per decem dies, x^d.

Et in Willelmo Malster laborante in Gardino et in aliis locis circa muros locis defectivis emendandos et in prato per xlvij dies et dimidium, capiente quolibet die ij^d ad mensam domine, vij^s xj^d.

Et in Johanne Celehay conducto ad evacuandam et ad purgandam latrinam pro conventu in grosso, ij^s.

Et in Johanne Speed per iiij^{or} dies laborante in Gardino et circa facturam unius sepis circa partem clausi dominarum per v dies, x^d.

Et in j vase vocato a Tubbe empto de domina Alicia Grannfeld, viij^d.

Et in emendacione ij furcarum vocatarum Pyccheforkes, ij^d.

Et in quodam extraneo laborante in prato per j diem et dimidium, iij^d.

Et in iiij^{or} instrumentis vocatis Weedhokys emptis, iiij^d.

Et in ligatura unius magni siphi vel disci vocati a Wasshyngboll, ij^d.

Et in ij paribus de les cardes emptis in foro, xix^d.

Et in j replegio prosecuto versus Johannem Pygot de Abyngton Myshell (*sic*) pro tenemento domine Priorisse, pro utilitate domine et conventus, ij^s iiij^d.

Et in Thoma Key ad emendanda rastra et scalam carettinam per iiij^{or} dies, viij^d.

Et in Thoma Goodwyn laborante in coquina circa cibaria preparanda in festo Assumpcionis Beate Marie infra tempus compoti, iij^d.

Et solutum Johanne (*sic*) Presot, Ricardo Philypps et Ricardo Baker de Bernewell pro colleccione theolani (*sic*) in Nundinis Assumpcionis Beate Marie predictis, vj^d.

Et in j le Scopet empto, ij^d.

Et solutum pro excambio vasorum de stanno ad Nundinas de Steresbridge, xj^d.

Et in quodam vase vocato a Cheerm empto apud Nundinas predictas pro butiro inde faciendo, x^d.

Et in veste linea empta de Johanne Ball de Linea pro mappis inde fiendis, iij^s ij^d.

Et in x lb. smigmatis emptis apud Nundinas predictas, x^d.

Et in pomis acerbis vocatis crabbes emptis pro salsagio vocato vergewes cum vinis domine mixtulando inde fiendo, viij^d.

Et in iij lb. piperis emptis apud Nundinas de Styresbridge, ij^s.

Et solutum pro agistamento animalium in marisco de Wevelyngham pasturatorum a festo Invencionis Sancte Crucis infra tempus compoti usque festum Michaelis extunc proxime sequens, iij^s vj^d.

Et solutum Willelmo Judde de Sancto Ivone pro veste lanea ordinata pro liberatura serviencium domine in colorem viridem et blodium fundenda et facienda, ix^s ix^d.

Et in discis et utensilibus de stanno emptis de domina Johanna Lancastre, iij^s vj^d.

Et in ij petris vocatis Saltstones emptis pro domo columbaria, vj^d ob.

Et solutum Henrico Denesson et servienti suo per iiij^{or} dies et dimidium facientibus j coopertorium pro plumbo infra Pandoxatorium scituato ac pro aliis laboribus indigentibus per mandatum domine Priorisse, iij^s.

Et in quadam cerrura (*sic*) cum clava (*sic*) ordinata pro portis vocatis feyregates, xij^d.

Et solutum ad pictanciam conventus die anniversarii Johannis Bronn defuncti, nuper ballivi ibidem, causa patente in compoto secundi anni precedentis, ij^s.

Et solutum domine Matilde Sudbury, sacriste ecclesie ibidem, ad ornamenta summi altaris, causa patente in compoto anni predicti, ij^s.

Et solutum Willelmo Horneby pro cariagio clx segh de le Grenocroft usque Pandoxatorium, xvj^d.

Et in Ricardo Sexteyn, slawterman, mactante bestias ad coquinam et illas ad commodum conventus preparandas, iiij^s ij^d.

Et solutum Johanni Richemond pro factura cuiusdam le Stokk infra tenementum in quo Johannes Blakney inhabitat, cum emendacione certi herpici et les Speers tenementi predicti, recognicione domine Priorisse, xij^d.

Et solutum pro quarta parte quindecime per clerum et civitatem regni Anglie domino Regi concesse, xv^d.

Et in farina aveno empta et liberata Johanni Wyllyamsson, bercario, v^d.

Summa vj^{li} xvj^s j^d ob.

Et in xxx fungaribus emptis apud Lynne per manus domine Johanne Lancastre ad staurum hospicii huius domus, v^s.

Empcio bladi et
stauri

Et in ij cades allecum rubrorum (x^a x^d) et j cado de Sparlyng (xiij^d ob.) emptis ibidem per manus predicte domine, xj^s xj^d ob.

Et in j quart. j bus. salis emptis de Thoma Peye ad Nundinas Nativitatis Sancti Johannis Baptiste, precio bus. v^d,—iiij^s ix^d.

Et in j quart. j. bus. et dimidio farine aveno hoc anno ad hospicium emptis per diversas vices, bus. ad viij^d,—vj^s iiij^d.

Et in j bus. pisi viridis empto de Alicia Smalbon ad potagium inde fiendum, vj^d.

Et in j quart. iij bus. pisi emptis ad seminandum et pro porcis assandis, precio bus. iij^d,—ij^s ix^d.

Et in j quart. iiij bus. de les Tares emptis, iij^s v^d.

Et in lviiij pulcinis emptis in foro diversis vicibus cum uno gallo (xvj^d) et iiij^{or} gallinis, xj pullis emptis de Katerina Rolff, vj^s.

Et in c clavis emptis ad staurum domus, xix^d.

Et in ij quart. vj bus. frumenti emptis in foro, precio quart. vj^s,—xvj^s vj^d.

Summa lix^s ix^d ob.

Et in quadam caruca empta de Michaele Bowyer de Fulbourne, x^d.

Custos caru-
carum et caret-
tarum

Et in cordula vocata Whipcord, j^d.

Et in emendacione ij carettarum vócatarum Dung-cartes, viij^d.

Et in les carstaves emptis de Rogero Hunte, ij^d ob.

Et in uno correo equino dealbando, ix^d.

Et in j ulna vestis linee empta pro emendacione coler' equinorum, iiij^d.

Et in filo empto ad idem opus, j^d.

Et in quodam de Haselyngfeld emendante hernes ad carettas et carucas pertinens per ij dies, vij^d.

Et solutum Alicie Rooper pro vij les Reynes et ij paribus tractuum, xij^d.

Et in Johanne Thommesson fugante et tenente carucam per vij septimanas, capiente pro qualibet septimana ix^d,—v^s iij^d.

Et in Ricardo Porter ad idem conducto per ij septimanas, xiiij^d.

Et solutum Waltero, ferrario, pro ferrura equorum, vomeribus et culturis punctandis et acuendis, ac pro les cartclowtes et aliis diversis ferramentis toto anno, x^s.

Summa xx^s xj^d ob.

Et in stipendio Johannis Clerk et socii sui triturantium xxxiiij quart.
Trituracio et
ventulacio vij bus. frumenti ad tascam, capientium pro quolibet quart. iij^d,—viij^s viij^d ob.

Et in stipendio Thome Atkyn per xxxvij dies, Willelmi Malster per xxv dies, et Johannis Caylly per xvj dies triturantium frumentum, quolibet capiente per diem ij^d ad mensam domine, xij^s ij^d.

Et in predicto Johanne Clerk et socio suo triturantibus cccxj quart. vj bus. ordei, capientibus pro quolibet quarterio ij^d,—lj^s xj^d ob.

Et solutum Willelmo Malster et Katerine Roolff pro granis portandis ventulandis et purgandis, xviij^d ob.

Et in Thoma Thressher conducto ad idem opus per vij dies et dimidium, xv^d.

Et solutum Johanni Stephen pro factura lxx quart. brasci et Johanni Presot pro factura decem quart. brasci, capientibus pro quolibet quarterio v^d ad tascum, xxxiij^s iiij^d.

Summa cviij^s xj^d ob.

Et in Thoma Atkyn daubante muros tenementi in quo Johannes
Reparaciones Fann de Bernewell inhabitat, necnon emendante certos defectus muri infra istud monasterium, xvij^d ob.

Et in Johanne Thommesson conducto ad idem opus super tenemento predicto ac super tenemento in quo Henricus Forstalff inhabitat et super stabulo in tenura Johannis Kason per xiij dies, ij^s ij^d.

Et in Johanne Watesson conducto ad simile opus pro muris tenementi in le Precherche Strete per iij dies, vj^d.

Et in Henrico Denesson et Johanne Algore, carpentariis, conductis ad gruncillandum et ad preparandum les Studdes et Sparres, necnon ad erigendum in opere carpentrino le Gable ends tenementi in quo Johannes Fanno inhabitat cum meremio domine per xij dies, utroque capiente per diem vj^d ad tascum, xij^s.

Et in meremio empto de Galfrido Hall ad opus predictum, xvj^d.

Et solutum prefato Henrico et servienti suo pro emendacione de le Poorche prope Aulam et pro erectione et cubacione de le Overwey magni orrei tempore autumpnali, necnon pro sarracione certorum les Legges ordinatorum pro fenestris Aule per vj dies, inter se, ij^s.

Et solutum prefato Henrico Denesson pro finali factura in opere carpentrino edificacionem (*sic*) duorum tenementorum sub uno tectu
iacentium in venella vocata Nunneslane secundum convencionem suam in
compoto anni proxime precedentis specificatam, vjˢ viijᵈ.

Et in canabo empto pro ligatura murorum tenementorum **domine** in
Bernewell locis indigentibus per vices, vijᵈ.

Et in lvj bunch virgarum emptarum **pro** les Spyttes et Byndwytthes **pro** emendacione tenementorum domine prout opus urgebat,
iiijˢ viijᵈ.

Et in xiij carettatis luti cariatis per Johannem **Poket ad reparacionem**
tenementorum domine, ijˢ ijᵈ.

Et in duobus les Sclatyours conductis ad emendandos certos defectus
claustri per iij dies, utroque capiente per diem vᵈ ad tascum, ijˢ vjᵈ.

Et in Johanne Egate conducto ad emendandum et punctandum cum
tegulis et Sclate portecum prope Aulam et claustrum necnon certos defectus
tenementorum domine in vico vocato Precherch Strete in quo (*sic*) Nicholas
Burnefyge inhabitat per xxᵗⁱ dies, **ad** iiijᵈ per diem **et** mensam suam,
minus in toto jᵈ, simul cum Nicholao Burnefyge (ixᵈ) **eidem** Johanni
serviente per iij dies, vijˢ iiijᵈ.

Et in **ccclx de les** Sclate emptis de Ricardo Pyghtesley ad **opus pre-**
dictum, iiijˢ.

Et in DCCLX **clavis** vocatis lathnayll (xvᵈ) cum iiijᵈ **solutis pro clavis**
ordinatis pro tenementis in le Precherch Strete, xixᵈ.

Et in ij fowder calcis vive emptis de Thoma Jamys de Hynton **pro**
tenementis et domibus predictis, vjˢ.

Et in ij carectatis petrarum cum cariagio earundem emptis **de** prefato
Thoma pro gruncill tenementi apud Bernewell in quo Johannes Fann
inhabitat subponendo, xvjᵈ.

Et in gumphis et vertinellis emptis de **Johanne** Smyth de Bernewell
pro tenementis predictis, viijᵈ.

Et in ccccxl de le Thak emptis de Johanne Bentley, precii xviijᵈ, et
ccc de Johanne Pacche, precii ijˢ iiijᵈ,—iijˢ ixᵈ.

Et in Willelmo Bronn et socio suo conductis ad emendandum murum
terrenum propter tenementum domine in Walleslane per j diem, iijᵈ.

Et in stipendio Johannis Egate emendantis unam gutter infra tenementum in quo inhabitat per j diem, iiijᵈ.

Et in ij bordis quercinis emptis ad Nundinas Nativitatis Sancti
Johannis Baptiste infra tempus compoti pro coopertura muri cuiusdam
tenementi **vasti nunc in** tenura Johannis Reedgrave, vjᵈ.

Et in iij bordis emptis de Thoma Brewer **de** Bernewell pro necessariis
inde faciendis, vjᵈ.

Et in M arundinum emptarum de quodam homine de Welle pro re-
paracione domorum, vidlt. aule, domus ordinate in brasium fundendum,
orrei et camere desuper portas exteriores huius monasterii, xiiijˢ.

Et in stipendio Johannis Cony de Welle predicta et servientis sui conductorum ad cooperiendum cum parcella arundinum predictarum domum tenementi in quo Thomas Brewer de Bernewell [inhabitat] locis defectivis per v dies, capientibus inter se vj^d per diem, ij^s vj^d.

Et in Johanne Lemman de Seynt Edmunds Bury conducto ad cooperiendum cum arundine predicta certos defectus aule et aliarum domorum huius monasterii prout opus indigebat per lx dies, capiente per diem iiij^d ad mensam domine, xx^s.

Et in uno laborario eidem serviente per totidem dies ad ij^d per diem, x^s.

Et in Roberto Kayle de Bottesham cooperiente cum stramine certos defectus tenementi in quo Johannes Stanlowe inhabitat et defectus stabuli in tenura Thome Careaway per iiij^{or} dies, xvj^d.

Et in uxore Nicholai Burnefyge per tot dies, xij^d.

Et in meremio empto ad Nundinas de Stiresbridge pro emendacione magni orrei, vidlt. vij cowple de les Sparres et iij aliis magnis peciis quercinis, vij^s.

Et in iiij^{or} ceruris pendulis emptis, vj^d.

Et in j cerura cum clave empta pro novo tenemento iacente in vico vocato Nunneslane in quo Johannes Shepperd inhabitat, iij^d.

Et in bordis emptis de domina Matilda Sudbury pro ostiis et fenestris novi tenementi in Nunneslane predicti, xij^d.

Et in Thoma Mylcham cooperiente cum stramine et solo quemdam murum terrenum inter tenementum Johannis Sex[teyn ?] et mansionem ipsius Thome Mylcham per con[vencionem ?] in grosso, iij^s.

Summa vj^{li} iij^s j^d ob.

Et in bitumine empto cum le Pycche hoc anno pro bidentibus signandis et ungendis, ij^s iiij^d.

Custus Falde

Et in iij^{bus} duodenis clatrorum emptis hoc anno, iiij^s viij^d.

Et in bidentibus hoc anno lavandis et tondendis, ij^s iij^d.

Summa ix^s iij^d.

Et solutum domine Priorisse et toto (*sic*) conventui pro vestura hoc anno, ut in annis precedentibus, lxvj^s viij^d.

Vestura dominarum

Summa lxvj^s viij^d.

Et solutum domine Johanne Lancastre in plenam solucionem debiti sui, ut ex legacione Petri Erle nuper defuncti, vij^s iiijd.

Debita soluta

Et solutum Thome James de Hynton pro calce ab eo empta annis preteritis in plenam solucionem, xx^d.

Et solutum Edmundo Wyghton in plenam solucionem debiti sui, vj^s viij^d.

Et solutum Willelmo Crook, capellano, pro antiquo debito in plenam solucionem, ix^s.

Et domine Agneti Swaffham, Suppriorisse, in partem solucionis v^s sibi debitorum, iij^s iiij^d.

Et solutum Johanni Pygott de Abyngton in **plenam** solucionem cuiusdam redditus resoluti pro diversis annis a retro existentis, xxiiij^s.

Et solutum Willelmo Stanclyff, fuller, pro veteribus debitis, ij^s ix^d.

Et solutum domine Johanne Lancastre in partem solucionis maioris summe, vj^s viij^d.

Summa lviij^s v^d.

Et solutum Willelmo Rogger et aliis in foro pro carnibus **bovinis,** porcinis, ovinis, vitulinis, porcellinis, gallinis, pulcinis, ovis,
Providencia Hospicii butiro et piscibus recencibus et marinis emptis per diem ad hospicium infra tempus compoti, una cum pane et cervisia, ultra quod furmentatum et pandoxatum est infra hospicium, ut parcellatim in quodam libro papiri super hunc compotum examinato aperte patet, xj^{li} xvj^s r^d ob.

Et in ij barellis cervisie vocato penyale emptis ad hospicium una **vice** infra tempus compoti, xviij^d.

Summa xj^{li} xviij^s xj^d ob.

Et datum iiij^{or} preconibus maioris ville Cantebr. pro eorum oblacione
Dono data erga festum Nativitatis Domini, ij^s iij^d.

Et datum aliis certis personis, vidlt. Thome Key (iiij^d), Johanne Graungyer (v^d) [   ] Brewer, Johanni Eversdon, (iiij^d), **Agneti Marche** (ij^d), Roberto Page (j^d), Johanni Knyght (j^d), Johanni Slybre (j^d), Dionisie, yerdwomman, (j^d), Emme Tayllor, nuper malstar, (j^d), Johanni Wyllyamesson, bercario, Ricardo Sexteyn (x^d), Avisie Basset (j^d), Emme Kyng, cum r^d datis certis pauperibus nuper in gwerris domini Regis laborantibus, iij^s xj^d.

Et datum Thome Burgoyn ut in precio v caponum emptorum in foro, xx^d ob.

Et in veste linea empta pro donis erga festum Nativitatis Domini, ij^s.

Et datum **custodi** ecclesie Omnium **Sanctorum ad** fabricam unius fenestre vitree, iiij^d.

Et datum Florencie Power et **sorori** sue (viij^d), uni **carucariorum** (ij^d), aliis certis personis (xvj^d) pro mandato domine **et** servienti Johannis Presot (iiij^d), ij^s vj^d.

Et datum et distributum inter pauperes die Cene, ij^s j^d.

Summa xiiij^s ix^d ob.

Et in **xij** paribus cirothecarum **emptis pro** diversis conductis in Autumpno, xviij^d.
Sumptus Autumpni Et in diversis laborariis conductis ad falcandas, unandas, ligandas, in mulliones colligendas et erga carettas preparandas lxv acras ordei, ad tascam, capientibus pro qualibet **acra** xij^d, ultra **xxvj acras falcatas per** conductos per diem, ut sequitur de nominibus unacum diebus, lxv^s.

Et in stipendio Johannis By de Haselyngfeld per ij dies (xij^d), Stephani **Shene de** Welle per ix dies (iiij^s vj^d) et Ricardi Whyte per j diem et dim.

(ix^d) conductis ad falcandum ordeum ad mensam domine, quolibet capiente per diem vj^d, vj^s iij^d.

Et in Johanne Tayllor conducto ad colligendum ordeum in garbas post falcacionem et super ligamina ponendum per ix dies, capiente per diem ij^d ob., et Thoma Key ad idem opus conducto, capiente per diem iij^d, ij^s x^d ob.

Et in certis laborariis conductis ad metendas, unandas, ligandas et erga carettas preparandas xxxiiij acras, ij rodas frumenti, ad tascum, capientibus pro qualibet acra xij^d, xxxiiij^s vij^d, ob.

Et in Ricardo Poket de Bernewell per iiij^{or} dies, Johanne Trumpyngton per iiij^{or} dies, utroque capiente per diem xx^d, et Johanne Stevenson de Bernewell per iiij^{or} dies ad xix^d per diem, cariantibus ordeum cum carettis suis, xix^s vj^d.

Et in stipendio Ricardi Whyte conducto ad carettas onerandas per ix^{em} dies, iij^s.

Et in Ricardo Philypp (xiij^s iiij^d) et Thoma Key (vj^s viij^d) conductis ad omnimoda opera autumpnalia facienda per totum tempus autumpni, xx^s.

Et in Willelmo Malstar per decem dies et servienti Thome Lemman per xvj dies conductis ad furcandas et levandas garbas ad carettas onerandas, utroque capiente per diem iij^d,—vj^s vj^d.

Et in Thoma Atkyn falcante j acram et dim. de le Bolymong ad tascum, xij^d.

Et in Roberto Walton falcante et erga carettas preparante j acram j rodam et dim. pisi ad tascum, xj^d.

Summa viij^{li} xvj^d.

Et solutum ut in regardo dato Johanni Gyrton pro bono consilio suo

Expense Forinsece domine impenso et in posterum impendendo in diversis materiis, et specialiter in quodam replegio prosecuto versus Johannem Pygot de Abyngton, xx^d.

Et in expensis apud Bernewell (ij^d ob.) super carpentarios operantes infra tenementum in quo Johannes Fanne inhabitat, per dominam Johannam Lancastre, unacum expensis Thome Key (xvij^d ob.) apud Abyngton, Litlyngton, Whaddon, Crawden, Bumpsted et Cantebrigiam in negotiis domine, et pro redditu levando, ac pro empcione meremii ad Nundinas de Stiresbridge, necnon pro feriagio unius barelli et dim. allec albi, ij cades allec rubri, ij cades de le Sparlyng, j qrt. fungaris et unius pecii meremii vocati a Maste ordinata pro quadam scala inde fienda (ij^s iiij^d), simul cum feriagio domine Johanne Lancastre, domine Margarete Metham, Thome Key et Elene Herward de Linea predicta usque Cantebr. cum companagio earundem (ij^s viij^d), viij^s.

Summa ix^s viij^d.

Et in vcc terricidis emptis de Johanne Fydde de Waterbech hoc anno, x^s iiij^d.

Sumptus Focalium Et in DCLX de les Segh emptis ad domum brasei et pistrinum, precio centene xviij^d,—viij^s iij^d.

Et in c los Segh emptis ad opus predictum, ij⁸.

Et in cc fagottis emptis de Willelmo Kannowe de Dullyngham, xvj⁸.

Summa xxxvj⁸ vij⁴.

Et in salario fratris Symonis Hemyngton, confessoris dominarum, hoc anno, ut frater Robertus Palmer defunctus percipere con-

Stipendia Fa-
mulorum   suevit, vj⁸ viij⁴.

Et in salario magistri Johannis Herryson celebrantis missam pro dominabus per totum annum, c⁸.

Et solutum Johanni Peresson, capellano celebranti in ecclesia Sancti Andree, apostoli, per vices, ij⁸ iiij⁴.

Et in stipendio clerici ecclesie ibidem per annum, xiij⁸ iiij⁴.

Et in stipendio Thome Key colligentis redditus in Cantebr. et patria, hoc anno ut in annis precedentibus, xiij⁸ iiij⁴.

Et in stipendio Johannis **Cademan**, pistoris et pandoxatoris, hoc anno, **xxvj⁸** viij⁴.

Et in stipendio Johannis Eversdon conducti ad **carucandum** hoc anno, xxvj⁸ viij⁴.

Et in stipendio **Johannis** Wyllyammesson, bercarii ibidem, hoc anno, **xxvj⁸** viij⁴.

Et in stipendio Roberti Page, carucarii, per tempus predictum, xvj⁸.

Et in stipendio Johannis Slybre, carucarii, per idem tempus, xiij⁸ iiij⁴.

Et in stipendio **Johannis Knyght,** alius carucarii, per supradictum tempus, **x⁸.**

Et in stipendio Roberti **Pykkell**, bubulci, hoc anno, cum vj⁴ sibi concessis in regardo, vij⁸ ij⁴.

Et in stipendio Emme Tayllor conducte ad **vertendum**, operandum et siccandum brasium hoc anno, vj⁸ viij⁴.

Et in stipendio Johanne Graunger, pincernarie **domine**, cum iij⁸ sibi **datis** in regardo **pro** officio Purvis domine, et cum vj⁸ viij⁴ pro toga **sua, xx⁸.**

Et in stipendio **Agnetis Marche** conducte ad omnimoda opera, **lactagii vaccarum,** facture **casei** et butiri et alia opera opportuna et necessaria facienda hoc anno, viij⁸.

Et in stipendio Elizabeth Chaterys, alius ancille domine, ut in vestitura **sua linea ac** lanea **ac** calciamentis, infra **tempus** compoti, ij⁸ viij⁴ ob.

Et in **stipendio** Dionisie, yerdewomman, per vices occupantis officia coci et **alia opera indigentia** hoc anno, vj⁸ viij⁴.

Summa xv^li vj⁸ ij⁴ ob.

Summa omnium allocacionum et solucionum, lxxij^li vj⁸ iiij⁴ q. Et debet cviij⁸ **vij⁴** q. ad quos oneratur de **xx⁸** receptis de executoribus Ricardi Busshe, nuper defuncti, pro redditu per ipsum retracto pro diversis **annis, antea non oneratis.** Summa debiti coniuncta, vj^li viij⁸ vij⁴ q. Et oneratur plus de vj⁴, precio ij caponum venditorum, ut extra. Et sic modo debet vj^li ix⁸ j⁴ q.

Unde super

Ricardum Wheetley de Bernewell propter redditum per ipsum debitum pro anno proxime precedente, vˢ.

Willelmum Rogger de Cant. pro j tenemento in stallagio, tam pro hoc anno quam pro iijᵇᵘˢ annis proxime precedentibus, per annum xijᵈ, ultra xijᵈ inde annuatim receptos, iiijˢ.

Eundem Willelmum pro j gardino in vico vocato le Precherch Strete pro consimilibus annis, per annum ijˢ,—viijˢ.

Johannem Barbor pro redditu exeunte de tenemento vocato le facoun in le Petykeuri pro tot annis xiiijˢ vijᵈ,—lviijˢ iiijᵈ.

Dominam Margaretam Huntyngdon pro j tenemento vocato le Sword, tam pro hoc anno quam pro ijᵇᵘˢ annis proxime precedentibus, per annum vjˢ, ultra xxᵈ inde levatos uno anno tantum, xvjˢ iiijᵈ.

Magistrum Johannem Honythorne pro uno gardino iuxta Bartonescroft, tam pro hoc anno quam pro tribus annis proxime precedentibus, per annum ijˢ,—viijˢ.

Magistrum Domus Sancti Johannis Evangeliste pro j tenemento in parochia Sancti Edwardi pro consimilibus annis, per annum iiijˢ viᵈ,—xviijˢ.

Ricardum Bushee pro j tenemento ex opposito ecclesie Beate Marie pro totidem annis, per annum xijᵈ,—iiijˢ.

Ricardum Wryght pro j tenemento nuper Johannis Essex, sadeler, pro tot annis, per annum xijᵈ,—iiijˢ.

Predictum Magistrum Domus Sancti Johannis Evangeliste pro j tenemento iuxta cimiterium ecclesie parochialis Sancti Sepulcri in veteri Judaismo pro consimilibus annis, per annum xxᵈ,—vjˢ viijᵈ.

Johannem Belton pro j tenemento iacente iuxta tenementum domine Priorisse pro tot annis, per annum vjˢ viijᵈ,—xxvjˢ viijᵈ.

Magistrum Ricardum Pyghtesley pro j tenemento nuper Willelmi Burtones pro tot annis, per annum ijˢ,—viijˢ.

Magistrum et Scolares Collegii Sancti Benedicti, Cantebr., pro j tenemento quondam Gybelottes, pro tot annis, per annum ijˢ ijᵈ,—viijˢ viijᵈ.

Thomam Lolleworth pro j tenemento in quo inhabitat pro tot annis, per annum ijˢ,—viijˢ.

Johannem Neell pro uno orto cum j orreo nuper Hugonis Canesby pro tot annis, per annum xijᵈ,—iiijˢ.

Johannem Leccham pro j tenemento in le Precherch Strete pro ultima medietate anni secundi preteriti, xxᵈ.

Robertum Mildenhale de Cantebr., ut de precio ij caponum tam pro hoc anno quam pro duobus annis proxime precedentibus, per annum vjᵈ,—xviijᵈ.

Johannem Croft pro uno parlar prope Pilateslane tam pro hoc anno quam pro ijᵇᵘˢ annis proxime precedentibus, per annum vjᵈ,—xviijᵈ.

Radulphum Attefeld pro uno tenemento in parochia Beate Marie, ultra ij⁸ inde levatos, per annum iiij⁸, et detentos pro consimilibus annis, xij⁸.

Et sic ista eadem computans habet in superplusagiis hoc anno lxxv⁸ ij^d ob. q.

EDWARD IV, 21—22, *i.e.* 1481—1482.

Compotus Domine Johanne Key, Receptoris Generalis
Domus Sancte Radegundis, Cant., et eiusdem loci
Conventus, a festo Pentecostes Anno Regis E. iiij^ti
xxj^mo usque in festum Annunciacionis Beate Marie Virginis extunc proxime sequentem (*sic*) Anno predicto Regis supradicti, ut per iij quarterios Anni

Cantebr. Moniale

Arreragia nulla quia primus annus dicte computantis.

Set respondet de lx⁸ iij^d percept. de redditibus assise diversorum tenencium domine infra villam Cant. per tempus compoti.

Redditus Assise

vj^li xiiij⁸ j^d de consimilibus redditibus assise diversorum tenencium hoc anno in patria, viz. pro termino Nativitatis Sancti Johannis Baptiste solut. ad terminos manerii usuales equaliter.

iiij^li recept. de Priore de Bernewell pro decimis Sancti Egidii, Cant.

xv^d recept. de aliis diversis personis per tempus compoti.

lxvij⁸ ob. percept. de consimilibus redditibus et firmis diversorum Collegiorum ac aliorum tenencium infra villam Cant., viz. pro termino Sancti Michaelis Archangeli per dictum tempus compoti.

iiij^li xj⁸ de redditibus assise infra villam Cant. predicte pro termino Sancti Michaelis predicti.

Et de c⁸ iij^d de redditibus assise diversorum tenencium, tam in patria quam alibi, solut. ad iiij^or anni terminos manerii usuales annuatim.

Summa xxvij^li viij⁸ ob.

Et respondet de xx⁸ recept. de Ricardo Woodcok pro communibus ij filiarum dicti Ricardi ut per [*blank*] septimanas iuxta per septimanam [*blank*].

Recepciones forinsece

Et de vj⁸ vj^d recept. pro communibus Johanne Tyler per tempus compoti.

xx⁸ in quodam regardo domine Priorisse et monialium ibidem per Rectorem de Over ex sua elimosina dato.

x⁸ in consimili regardo per W. Roger dato.

vj⁸ vj^d in quodam regardo per Johannem Smyth de Bury Sancti Edmundi dato.

Et de xᵃ de consimili dono Magistri Willelmi Dak per tempus compoti.

Summa lxxiijˢ ijᵈ.

Et ista idem (*sic*) computans respondet de xiiijˢ recept. de Thoma Ball

Vendicio Feni de Cant., ut in precio carectate feni sic per prefatam computantem per tempus compoti, ut extra, venditi.

Summa xiiijˢ.

Summa totalis recepte xxxjˡⁱ xvˢ viijᵈ ob.

E quibus iste idem (*sic*) computans allocatur de xvˢ et ij caponibus in redditu resoluto Mortymeres.

Resoluciones reddituum xiiijˢ iiijᵈ ob. in consimili redditu resoluto Maiori et ballivis ville Cant. pro le heygable.

vijˢ in redditu resoluto annuatim Priori de Bernewell.

vjˢ in consimili redditu resoluto Thome Lovell.

iijˢ vijˢ ob. pro redditu resoluto Thome Cotton.

iijˢ iiijᵈ solut. Priori Eliensi.

xijᵈ vice-comiti Cant.

xijᵈ solut. Johanni Skarlett.

iiijᵈ in consimili redditu resoluto Rectori Sancti Benedicti.

xvjᵈ solut. Collegio Corporis Xti, Cant.

iijᵈ solut. Waltero Trumpyton.

et de xijᵈ in redditu resoluto Thome Pygott.

Summa liiijˢ iijᵈ.

Et petit allocari ut pro diversis acatis recentibus, una cum stauro vivo

Custus Hospicii et mortuo, et ultra pisces salsos et duros ibidem per tempus compoti ad diversa precia empt. et in hospicio domine expend., ut per [*blank*] septimanas, quarum (*sic*) parcelle et summe eorundem in Jurnali hospicii predicti plenarie expressantur et sufficienter testantur (*sic*).

Summa vijˡⁱ xiiijˢ vjᵈ ob.

Et solut. inde vjˢ viijᵈ solut. (*sic*) Thome Brampton, armigero, ut in precio ij. quart. brasii de eo empt.

Empcio bladi et stauri iijˢ iiijᵈ, ut de precio unius quart. brasii empt. de Magistro Roberto Parys, armigero.

ijˢ Vicario de Abyngton ut de precio iiij bus. brasii de eo empt., una cum aliis de diversis personis ad hospicium domine empt., quarum parcelle, summe et nomina eorundem in Jurnali hospicii in parcellis expressantur et plenarie testantur, iiijˡⁱ vjᵈ.

et in iij vaccis cum eorum (*sic*) vitulis, una cum tractibus, cordis, cratibus, faldis et aliis necessariis ad husbondriam empt., ut in sepedicto Jurnali plene legitur, lxxiiijˢ viijᵈ.

Summa vijˡⁱ xvˢ ijᵈ.

Et computat in Thoma Payn, Willelmo Tomson, Michaele Savage et aliis

Custus Autumpni laboratoribus ibidem hoc anno per tempus compoti tempore autumpnali conductis ad falcandum, ligandum, metendum, cariandum et tassandum, tam infra moniale quam extra, prout in Jurnali huius hospicii particulariter in parcellis expressantur et nominatim nominantur.

Summa cix⁸ ijᵈ.

Et computat allocari, viz. in ij warp. de lyngflyssh, ij warpes piscium salsorum, ij bus. salis, ccxl clavis ferreis, papiro ac pergameno, una cum aliis necessariis ibidem per tempus compoti, ad nundinas de Sterebrege, et ad nundinas Sancte Etheldrede virginis ad hospicium domine empt. prout in sepedicto Jurnali hospicii in parcellis de recordo patet.

Expense Necessarie

Summa xlvj⁸ jᵈ.

Et computat solvisse xviijᵈ ut in precio unius caruce empt. de Willelmo Dey.

viij⁸ **solut.** pro ferramento equorum domine, una cum amendacione tocius apparatus ad husbondriam pertinentis et aliis necessariis per **dictum** tempus compoti ad husbondriam empt., prout in antedicto Jurnali hospicii **predicti** parcellatim expressantur et sufficienter testantur.

Custus carucarum et carectarum

Summa xvj⁸ xᵈ.

Et computat de **xxxj⁸** iiijᵈ solut. pro diversis reparacionibus ibidem per tempus compoti **infra** Ecclesiam factis et apposita.

Reparaciones domorum

xxix⁸ viijᵈ in consimilibus reparacionibus apud Bernewell factis et appositis.

et cum v⁸ xjᵈ in diversis reparacionibus **per tempus compoti** predicti intra villam Cant. factis, prout in **sepedicto Jurnali hospicii** predicti in parcellis plenarie expressantur.

Summa lxvj⁸ xjᵈ.

Et computat de v⁸ in parte stipendii magistri Upgayte, capellani; **xxᵈ** de parte stipendii domini Thome Kent, capellani; xx⁸ pro consimili stipendio magistri Malett, capellani; viij⁸ iiijᵈ pro stipendio magistri Roberti Burton, capellani; xx⁸ pro consimili stipendio magistri Pek; ix⁸ pro stipendio clerici et collectoris decimarum garbarum tempore autumpnali; iij⁸ ijᵈ pro parte stipendii Thome Baker; xv⁸ vjᵈ de consimili stipendio Georgii Geyr per tempus compoti; x⁸ pro stipendio pastoris; iij⁸ jᵈ pro stipendio Willi Plowman, conducti **ad** husbondriam; v⁸ ijᵈ pro stipendio pyncerne per tria quarteria; ij⁸ iijᵈ in stipendium coci; xx⁸ pro stipendio Vicarii Omnium Sanctorum; viijᵈ **pro parte** stipendii Johannis Wright; et cum xᵈ pro parte stipendii **Willelmi** Tomson; una cum aliis stipendiis et regardis per dominam datis, prout in Jurnali hospicii domus predicte plenarie expressantur et sufficienter **testantur.**

Stipendia Famulorum

Summa vijˡⁱ xv⁸ xjᵈ.

Et computat allocari de lx^s solut. Willelmo Pychard ut in precio
xj quart. ordei per tempus compoti empt.

Empcio ordei et aliorum grano- rum   xv^s de consimilibus denariis solut. Waltero Sergeaunt
ut in precio quinque quart. avenarum de eodem per dictum
tempus compoti empt.

vj^s x^d solut. Willelmo Barnard ut in precio ij quart. pisi.

xj^d ut in precio ij bus. vesse empt.

Summa iiij^li ij^s ix^d.

Summa omnium expensarum et liberatorum lvij^li v^s iiij^d ob. Et sic
ista eadem computans habet in superplusagiis xxv^li ix^s viij^d.

GLOSSARY TO THE NUNNERY ACCOUNTS.

[*Cath. Angl.* = *Catholicon Anglicum*, ed. Herrtage: *P. P.* = *Promptorium Parvulorum*, ed. Way : both in Camden Society's Publications.   N. E. D. = New English Dictionary.]

Acatum, a thing purchased (L. L. *ad-captatum*, Fr. *acheter*), **especially provisions**

Agistamentum, agistment, **the sum** paid for grazing **cattle in other** men's fields

Allec (allecs), herrings : *allec rubeum*, red herrings

Allocatio, a change in an account

Anniversarium, the anniversary **of a** deceased benefactor

Argilla, clay

Arreragia, arrears

Assare, to roast

Assise, Redditus, rent of land let for **a fixed sum of money**

Autumpnus, harvest

Avena (avenae), **oats**

Axare, to fit the **axle of a cart to** the **wheel**

Barellum, a barrel

Bercarius, a shepherd

Bladum, corn, L. L. *ab-latum*, Fr. *blé*

Blodius, blue (*Cath. Angl.*)

Bolymong, Harrison's *Description of England*, Bk. 1. ch. 18, ' mixed corn, **tares** and otes, which they call **bulmong** '

Brasium, malt

Breve, a writ

Bultell, **a** sieve, sieve-cloth

Bunches, bundles (of rods)

Busellus, a bushel

Butumen, either (1) clay used in making mud walls : ' Dawber or cleymann, *argillarius, bituminarius*' (P. P.) : cp. *teryng* : or (2) tar, used with *pycche* for marking sheep

Byndwytthes, osiers serving to 'bind' the plaster in a stud-wall

Cade, a barrel of herrings holding six great hundreds of **six score** each. (N. E. D.)

Calces equine, horse-shoes

Calibs, steel

Caligae, hose (P. P.)

Calx viva *or* adhusta, quicklime

Canabea vestis, canvas

Candel, wax &c., used for making into candles (*candelae*)

Canobum, hemp used to bind clay walls

Capistrum, a halter or headstall

Cardes, teasels used in combing wool

Carecta, caretta, a cart

Carectata, a cart-load

Cañagium, carriage by **land, opposed to** *feriagium*, carriage **by water**

Cariare, to carrry corn

Carstaves, i.e. cart-staves (for the spelling cp. *corsaddle* in Jamieson), cartshafts (N. E. D.) : Prof. Skeat in the **Glossary to his edition of the Tale of Gamelyn says ' Perhaps a staff to support the shafts of a cart.'**

Cartclowtes, clouts of iron for cart-wheels: 'A clowte of yrne, *crusta, crusta ferrea*' (*Cath. Angl.*)

Caruca, a plough

Cene Domine, Dies, Maundy Thursday

Cerura, i.q. *serrura*, a lock

Cheerm, a churn

Cilicinus pannus, hair cloth for the malt-kiln

Ciphus, i.q. *scyphus*, a cup or bowl

Cirothecae, reapers' gloves

Cirpi, i.q. *scirpi*, rushes

Cissorium, i.q. scissorium, a trencher (P. P.)

Clati, Clatri, i.e. *clathri*, hurdles used for sheep pens

Clavi, nails

Coleres equini, horse collars

Communae, commons, allowance of food

Companagium, any kind of food save bread : in the Accounts 1450-1 it appears to mean food taken by a company travelling together

Coopertorium, covering

Corrium, a hide

Crabbes, crab apples used in making verjuice

Cubare, Cubacio, to lay, laying: used of (1) the laying of the Overway of the Great Barn, (2) the laying of stockfish in layers upon canvas, (3) the 'laying' of sharp or pointed instruments, i.e. the repairing of them by placing fresh iron or steel on them. 'Pro le layng securium' &c. *Finchale Glossary*

Cultura, the coulter of a plough

Daubare, to daub, i.e. make walls of clay: *vide* 'Dawber' in P. P.

Dealbare, to whiten hides by drying and bleaching: leather so treated was called Whyteledr

Denarii, silver money

Devolare, 'to flit,' used of a fraudulent tenant

Dietam, per, from day to day

Dimittere, to let on lease

Domina, dame, the title given to a Nun and especially to the Prioress

Dominicalis, Terra, demesne land

Encaustum, ink

Excambium, exchange

Extra, ut, refers to the accounts of the Grange which were written on the reverse side of the Compotus roll

Facoun, le, the Falcon Inn in Petty Cury

Fagottum, a faggot

Falda, a sheepfold

Feriagium, carriage by water

Ferrarius, a blacksmith

Ferrura, smith's work

Feyregates, the gates admitting from Nunneslane to the fair held in the Churchyard

Firma, rent derived from land

Firmarius, a farmer

Flebotomacio, the blooding of horses, an annual ceremony on S. Stephen's day (Dec. 26)[1]

[1] Compare Tusser's Five Hundred Points of Good Husbandry (ed. Mavor, 1812), p. 62:

> Ere Christmas be passed let horse be let blood:
> For many a purpose it doth them much good.
> The day of *St Stephen* old fathers did use :
> If that do mislike thee some other day use.

For a fuller account of this ceremony see Barnabe Googe's translation of Kirchmaier's *Popular and Popish Superstitions and Customs* (1553) in the New Shaksp. Soc. Publications.

Fletyngbolle, a skimming bowl

Focalia, fuel (sedge, peat or faggots)

Fons, the Nunnery well

Fowder, a measure of lime, &c.

Fugare, to drive cattle or horses

Fundere, to steep (1) in dyeing, (2) in malting

Fungare, explained in Ducange as *doliolum, cadus.* In the Nuns' Accounts it means 'stockfish,' otherwise 'hard fish' or 'Wynterfyssh.' It was either cod or ling. It was kept in the Staurus in layers laid on canvas, and on account of its toughness required to be beaten before it was used ('verberante fungaria' in Accounts of 1450-1): it is said to have derived its name from the *stock* on which it was beaten. Comp. *Cath. Angl.* 'Stokfyche; *fungia*,' and Mr Herrtage's note thereon.

Garba decimalis, a tithe sheaf

Gardinum, a garden

Gersuma, a sum paid by a tenant on the entry of a lease : A. S. *gaersum*, treasure

Granatorium, the Garner, where corn was kept after thrashing

Grangia, a barn

Gruncill, 'in carpentry, the beam laid along the ground for the rest of the work to stand on.' *Architectural History*, Vol. III., glossary.

Gumphus, i.e. γομφός: the iron hook on which a hinge turns. 'A cruke of a dore, *gumphus*.' *Cath. Angl.*

Guttera, a gutter

Gwerra, war

Hagable, heygable, an annual payment (originally to the sheriff, later to the mayor and bailiffs) for each messuage occupied within the borough limits

Hames, qy ? for *hamis*, hooks

Hernes, harness

Herpicum, a harrow

Hersyve, a hair sieve

Horsetree, Prof. Skeat informs me that in the Eastern Counties this is the name of the swingle-tree, i.e. a bar behind a horse to which a field implement is attached by chains

Hospicium, (1) an inn : 'hospicio vocato le Booll,' the Bull Inn : (2) the chambers in the Nunnery used by guests and other lay persons

Hostium, i.q. ostium, a door

Ieruca, a goad. 'Gad, or gode, *gerusa, scutica*' (P. P.)

Indigentes labores, necessary work

Infra, generally = intra

Kymlyn, a shallow tub, or vat, used in brewing

Laborarius, a labourer

Lache, a latch

Lagena, a gallon

Lathnayll, nails used for fastening laths to studs

Lavacrum, a basin

Legges, window ledges (or perhaps bars), made of wood

Levare, to 'lift' rent, corn, &c.

Liberare, to give to a servant anything of the nature of food or clothing

Liberatura, clothing delivered to servants at stated periods, livery

Ligatura, fastening clasps on a book

Loppare, to lop trees

Lote, a wooden skimmer

Marisca, a marsh, fen

Mast, fir poles brought from Norway were generally called 'masts' : the place where they were kept was sometimes called the 'mast house' (*Durham Wills* &c. Surtees Soc. Publ.) : a mast purchased at Lynn to make a ladder

Maundy sylver, the name of one of the Nuns' estates at Madingley, the rent of which furnished the dole to the poor on Maundy Thursday. The sum so provided, 30^d, represented the thirty pieces of silver. For the monastic ceremony on the occasion see the *Rites of Durham* (Surtees Society), pp. 66, 67

Melesyve, a meal sieve

Mensam, ad, including ' table,' or provisions found by the employer

Meremium, Maeremium, timber used in building

Mulliones, mows of barley

Napry, includes tablecloths, napkins (*mappae*), towels (*manutergia*), &c.

Nundinae, a fair

Oblacio, Christmas gift to the waits

Obstupare, to stop, retain; used of money in hand and not brought to account

Onerare, to charge as a receipt

Overwey, a loft in the barn

Oxbowes, yokes for oxen: 'Oxbowe that gothe about his necke, *collier de beuf*' (Palsgrave)

Pandoxator, a brewer

Pandoxatorium, the Brew House

Parlare, i. q. *Parlura*, a parlour

Patria, the neighbourhood of Cambridge

Pellis lanuta, a fell, sheepskin with the wool on it

Ponyale, cheap ale sold at a penny a gallon. See Prof. Skeat on *Piers Plowman*, passus 5, l. 220

Perbendinantes, visitors to the Nunnery who paid for their board

Potrae, brought from Hinton, evidently clunch stone

Pietancia, a pittance, an augmentation of commons provided by benefactions

Pikewall, a gable: ' Pikewall or gabyl, *murus conalis, piramis vel piramidalis*' (P. P.)

Pincerna, Pincernaria, a female servant who controlled the Spense or Buttery

Pinnfald, a sheep-fold or pen

Pipa, a leaden pipe

Pipe, a cask or tub

Pisces duri, stockfish, opposed to salted fish

Pistrinum, the Bake House

Plumbum, a copper (anciently called a 'lead') used in the Brew House

Potagium, soup

Pre manibus, a sum in ready money, opposed to a reserved rent; see *gersuma*

Precones, the town waits

Profucua, profits

Pulcinus, a chicken

Punctare, to point with tiles or slate, i.e. to fill up holes in masonry

Punctura vomeris, the point of the share

Purvis, a servant who acted as purveyor, *provisor*

Quindecima, a subsidy of one fifteenth

Raap, rape, from which oil is extracted

Redditus, a rent: *redditus resolutus*, a quit rent

Reder, one who deals in reeds (used for walls and roofs)

Regardum, a reward, gift

Rentale, a rent book

Replegium, a writ of replevin

Salsagium, pickle (verjuice)

Saltstones, food for pigeons: see the *Arch. Hist.* Vol. III. p. 593

Sanctorum, i.e. Legenda Sanctorum

Sarculare, to weed

Sarrare, to saw wood

Sclat, slate, distinguished from *tegulae*, tiles. In the Accounts of 1450-1 360 sclates are recorded to have been bought from Ric. Pyghtesley,

the possessor of Tyled Hostel, which
was bought by Henry VI. and transferred to King's Hall in 1449. The
Hostel was roofed with *tiles* (see the
quotation from Dr Caius in *Arch.
Hist.* II. p. 426)

Scopae, a besom

Scopet, a scoop or shovel

Scutella, Skotell, a hollow basket,
A. S. *scutel*; *scutella* is a diminutive of Lat. *scutra*

Sedlep, a basket carried on the arm
in sowing: the word is still in use
in Essex

Segh, sedge. Straw, sedge and reed
were the usual materials for thatch-
ing: see Harrison's *Descr. of England,*
Bk. II. ch. 12

Sheaf, a certain quantity of steel:
'thirtie gads to the sheffe and twelve
sheffes to the burden.' **Harrison's**
Descr. of England, Bk. III. **ch. 11**

Sherman, a clothier

Shidare, to cut wood into billets: cp.
Talshide in *Arch. Hist.,* glossary

Sinis, i.q. cinis, ash-lye used in
washing

Siphus, i.q. *Ciphus* (scyphus), a cup

Slats, slates on which barley was dried
in the kiln

Smigma, soap

Sortendo, i.e. *sortiendo,* 'sorting' lands,
defining the intermixed lands of
different owners

Sotulares, shoes

Sowder, solder

Sparling, smelts; Fr. *esperlan*: but
the word is Teutonic, = spare ling

Sparres, Speers, timber used for rafters:
'sparre of a roofe, *tignum*' (P. P.)

Spensepott, an earthen vessel used
in the Spense or Buttery

Spissitudo Panni, thickening of cloth
in the process of fulling

Splentes, small pieces of wood laid
horizontally in a stud wall

Spumatum, Spumaticum, yeast

Spykyng, a kind of bolt, called 'spyk-
ynge nayll' in P. P.

Spyttes, rods used in a stud wall.

Stallagium, the market place occupied
by stalls

Stannum, pewter

Staple, a loop of iron in a wall for
fastening chains

Staurus, (1) articles kept in stock,
(2) the Storehouse

Stokk, the hearth stock, a large log on
which the fire was piled

Streynor, a strainer

Studdes, the upright posts in a wall
of plaster and timber

Swep, i.q. *Swipe,* a crane for drawing
water out of a well

Tascus, Tasca, a definite amount of
work set for a labourer to do (Lat.
taxare); *ad tascum,* piecework

Tellura, apparently means the marling
of soil

Terricidium, a peat turf

Teryng, either tarring a wall, covering it with *butumen* (q. v.), P. P.,
'terryng': or covering it with earth,
P. P., 'teryng, or hylle wythe erthe.'

Thak, thatch

Theolanum, Tolnetum, tolls of the fair

Tractus, traces

Tricentalis dies, the last day of a
trental, or month's mind, period of
commemorating the dead.

Trituracio, thrashing of corn

Turba, a turf, which was delivered as
a rent in kind to the lord of the
manor at Abington. Accounts 1604
-5, "To Bonde for carrying a torv
to Abington" &c.

Ustrina, the malt-kiln

Vaccaria, the Cow House

Ventilabrum, a winnowing fan

Ventilacio, winnowing

Vergewes, verjuice

Vertinelli, hinges
Vessa, vetch, *vicia*
Virgae, wattles used in stud walls
Voluntas Ultima, last will, testament

Walshe, qy ?
Warp, parcels of four dried fish.
Warpyng, weaving

Weedhokys, weeding hooks
Wheterydell, a riddle to separate grain from chaff
Wynterfyssh, stockfish

Yerdwomman, a woman who attends to the farm-yard : cp. *yardman* in Halliwell's Dictionary

INDEX TO THE CHARTERS.

I. Personal Names.

(This list does not contain the names of witnesses.)

II. Localities.

CAMBRIDGE: PRINTED BY J. AND C. F. CLAY, AT THE UNIVERSITY PRESS.

www.ingramcontent.com/pod-product-compliance
Lightning Source LLC
Chambersburg PA
CBHW030826270326
41928CB00007B/916